POST 86

Fiesta

IDENTIFICATION
AND
VALUE
GUIDE

RICHARD RACHETER

db
COLLECTOR BOOKS
A Division of Schroeder Publishing Co., Inc.

The current values of this book should be used only as a guide. They are not intended to set prices, which vary from one section of the country to another. Auction prices as well as dealer prices vary and are affected by condition as well as demand. Neither the author nor the publisher assumes responsibility for any losses that might be incurred as a result of consulting this guide.

On the cover:

All photographs by the author unless otherwise noted. Photograph processing was completed by KC Deacon II of Wolf Camera, Tyrone Square, St. Petersburg, Florida.

Pyramid candleholder (persimmon), MegaChina Mystique coffee server (sea mist green). Tripod bowl (persimmon), Looney Tunes Bugs Bunny sauceboat (periwinkle blue), Napkin ring (white), Round serving tray (persimmon), 6" plate (rose). AD cup/saucer (turquoise), Mini disc pitcher (persimmon), Goblet (chartreuse), MegaChina Moonshine carafe (persimmon), Bud vase (yellow), 9" platter (apricot), 10" plate (juniper), Tumbler (persimmon), Round candleholder (periwinkle blue), Millennium candleholder (pearl gray), Plate (cobalt).

Cover design by Beth Summers
Book design by Joyce Cherry

Searching for a Publisher?

We are always looking for knowledgeable people considered to be experts within their fields. If you feel there is a real need for a book on your collectible subject and have a large comprehensive collection, contact Collector Books.

Collector Books
P. O. Box 3009
Paducah, KY 42002-3009

www.collectorbooks.com

Copyright © 2001 by Richard Racheter

Contents

Dedication

This book is dedicated with thanks to Ted and Laurie Holms, the former for his guidance on the computer; the latter for her delightful optimism which makes gray days shimmer with sunlight!

In Remembrance

Jonathan O. Parry
(1948 – 2000)

Jonathan Parry was the fifth in the line of Art Directors at Homer Laughlin China. When appointed to that prestigious post in 1983, Jonathan became the psychological and philosophical successor of Frederick Rhead. Rhead was named the first Art Director in 1927 and within less than a decade was grappling with the greatest dinnerware line ever produced in America — Fiesta. So in 1986, just three years after he assumed his position, Jonathan was confronted with the challenging re-introduction and redesign of the Rhead signature shape — and this challenge was superbly met: Post86 Fiesta was born and now stands as the perfect memorial to the creative genius of a man who left us physically Friday, April 28, 2000, but who will remain with us spiritually and emotionally for a long time to come.

Personally, I never met Jonathan, but we spoke often on the telephone, and he — with patience and care — answered my many questions regarding all manner of Homer Laughlin subjects. Questions sent through the mail were always solved in detail. I still marvel at his consideration and tolerance.

As the twenty-first century rolls on, Jonathan Parry will be sorely missed at the Homer Laughlin Company; his act will be almost impossible to follow. How can Post86 Fiesta continue without his artistic guidance?

Thank you, Jonathan, for so ably completing the full circle first contemplated in 1936 by Frederick Rhead.

Acknowledgments

During the researching and writing of this book, I have grown more cautious, perhaps even fearful of the Fiesta marketplace. Some people who were kind and helpful at one time have turned away — perhaps for the better, perhaps not! But what I have lost in numbers I have gained in quality!

Jonathan Parry was always kind and helpful. Poor Jonathan, constantly besieged by all manner of inquisitive Homer Laughlin researchers, always insisted (and rightly so) that all Fiesta, both old and new, was basically produced for the retail trade, not collectors. He will be missed.

Joe Solito, one of the three owners of MegaChina, has suffered my many questions with a gracious manner and has kindly sent me not only information about his products but also some actual examples. Thanks, Joe!

John Iams — how can this resident of East Liverpool be thanked enough. Quick, astute, and above all extremely knowledgeable regarding all facts of Post86 Fiesta and its history past and present. He also has quite an eye for the future! His assistance cannot be measured.

Steve Sfakis provided some insightful ideas.

Thanks also to Mark Gonzalez.

I wish to commend both Lisa C. Stroup, my editor, and Amy Hopper, assistant editor, for their encouragement and help. Also thanks to Beth Summers for a magnificent cover design, and book designer Joyce Cherry. All these people at Collector Books expended considerable effort to make this book not only possible but quite physically splendid.

Finally, this book never could have been completed without the guidance and sharp advice of H. William Ohman, a partner and friend for over 40 years.

Billy was just one of the boys.
He played with considerable noise.
But one of his wishes
Was to collect dishes.
So Billy abandoned his toys.

Introduction

The Time has come, the Walrus said,
To talk of many things;
Of shoes — and ships — and sealing wax —
Of cabbages — and kings —

Can we possibly talk together and say something new about Fiesta? Has not this colorful dinnerware been "talked to death?" Can readers be regaled with new insights worthy of their time and effort? Yes, we the readers and the author can have a conversation worthy of the time, the effort, and the price of this book!

Fiesta books have existed for years. They come in many varieties — from the charming friendliness of Bob and Sharon Huxford all the way to recent research ridden tomes spouting facts, figures, and in-depth commentary concerning mold books and jigger points. Other books are filled with such overwhelming, minute information that, point by point, the reader wonders if all this knowledge is worth remembering. Some books are technical; some are overflowing with a verbose subjectivity. However, there is room for all approaches. You, the reader, make the choice! One or all of the available books lie strewn like cabbages or carrots just waiting to be picked up, read, and digested!

This book will be filled with verbosity — I talk of many things. All manner of information interests me — and this book is also washed with subjectivity. Facts are presented firmly and correctly. Yet the interpretation of these facts is, must be, subjective. I write what I feel, and if the individual reader does not feel the same along with me, I am most sorry, but that's it! Readers are encouraged to disagree with any opinion because it is tiresome to go round-and-round caught in the tangled web of a continually circling mutual admiration society. Thus it is a mark of self-confident intelligence to disagree! There can be no room here for

hypocrisy, snobbery, or alienation. What is stated in these pages about Fiesta is stated with honesty — at least honest as it is personally seen. My tongue is often in my cheek, but no harm is meant to any individual, or to any association: an eye for an eye is not part of my plan!

Everyone has his own individual ideas about new Fiesta. Even the powerful arbiters of taste and home — in this case the earth mother Martha Stewart — have opinions on the Post86 line. "The new Fiesta is insipid," Stewart remarked in an Associated Press article dated April 15, 1997. She most certainly could not have been discussing vibrant persimmon! She continues: "Why do you need lilac? It is not a primary color. There is no need to water down the original!" Wonder what primary color when watered down produces lilac? Such is the opinion of the famous queen of complicated television cookery! A friend of mine suggested SHE be watered down!

However, it must be admitted Ms. Stewart has class! During her television cooking show, *From Martha's Kitchen*, I never grow tired of trying to "peek" into the glass-fronted cupboards behind her head to catch a glimpse of Post86 Fiesta. Have any readers seen that plump sea mist green teapot? Maybe this lady tres distingue should be watered down with a vintage champagne — a Dom Perignon perhaps?

But now it must be determined just what to call this colorful reissued dinnerware? In 1986, it was certainly "new Fiesta." But is it technically still "new" some 15 years later? "New," in the world of American dinnerware, ages rapidly. "Contemporary Fiesta" is better, but the word "contemporary" — to me — always implies a comparison with another form or being. For example: Queen Elizabeth I of England was a contemporary with King Philip II of Spain. Or Homer Laughlin Harlequin line was a contemporary of vintage Fiesta. An alternative definition (the third in my Webster's) is "modern" or "current." Well, these could fit the reissued Fiesta, but what is "current" is based upon time, and the term "modern" quite surely lies in the eye of the beholder. Many mid-century modern dinnerware collectors view Fiesta as trapped in the Art Deco form and slightly old-fashioned. Indeed Fiesta could be considered "un-cool" when compared with the biomorphic stretched elegance of Eva Zeisel's Hallcraft lines, or the pulled shapes of Ben Seibel's Roseville Raymor!

So, even if the reader does not agree, in this book it is Post86 Fiesta all the way!

So why a book on a line of dinnerware still available in Bloomingdale's, Macy's, Dillard's, and Burdine's — among other places. Some powerful pundits in the world of vintage Fiesta do not believe Post86 is collectible at all! It is merely to be accumulated. This opinion is infuriating for here lies another type of snobbery — as if some vintage Fiesta collectors can pronounce what is or what is not collectible! This is snobbish balderdash! This book is about a true and established "collectible" enjoyed for its own beauty and colorful charm. It is a collectible whose devotees rise from all people — even those who dote on the vintage lines of Fiesta, Harlequin, and Riviera are invited to participate.

In an attempt to glean information about the place occupied by Fiesta in the world of collecting, I sent an acquaintance, Dr. Eric Stevens, several sections of this book when they were in the draft stages. Dr. Stevens, a pathologist of a very discerning nature, e-mailed the following comment. "The whole Post86 collecting scene is very strange as you describe it. It seems odd for collectors and a company to have such an immediate relationship. (Iroquoise and Roseville can't respond to my collecting interests, or try to manipulate me!)" Without really realizing the fact, this is exactly what makes the collecting of new Fiesta both so exciting and so inherently disconcerting.

Yes, it must be admitted one can pick up the telephone or travel to the local large mall and purchase *some* pieces of reissued Fiesta! But as years pass and the marketing philosophy of the Homer Laughlin Company changes and becomes slightly more devious, it becomes less and less easy to simply accumulate Post86 Fiesta! Look at the November 1999 "scandal" of the chartreuse sugar caddy! The company seemed to have stipulated the sugar caddy in chartreuse would be available to all collectors through the retail outlet. Now a "stipulation" cannot really be considered a "promise," but when only 300 chartreuse sugar caddies were made, announced, and sold immediately at a sale in November 1999, many collectors, who had placed telephone orders for the piece, felt betrayed and angered. The situation was aggravated when some of these desired pieces were — within hours — placed on the Internet's premier auction house, eBay!

It is thrilling and frustrating to write about a line of dinnerware still in production — still undergoing changes and additions. Vintage Fiesta is static! It is beautifully but generally motionless. Naturally there are surprises, new revelations to be sure, but these revelations really only affect the most advanced of vintage collectors — those with the interest or the money to acquire and participate.

Post86 Fiesta presents a vastly different proposal! Imagine then the dizzy whirl greeting the researcher who studies this line! Post86 is alive. It kicks and jostles, beckons and eludes, teases and angers! Ever exploding changes burst settled ideas — in fact, nothing is settled about Post86; researching has become a matter of complex ferreting.

Part of the problem is the Homer Laughlin Company apparently has embarked on a new philosophic approach regarding collectors. Manipulation is a harsh word, but perhaps, at the present time, it suits the manner in which the company views the collector. The aim and the approach have changed! A few years ago, say in 1995, Homer Laughlin China was known as a producer of restaurant china without a very strong focus on retail marketing. Remember that newspaper article posted on the wall of the Homer Laughlin China Retail Outlet? The article gave the impression that the new Fiesta line was seen (by the company?) as a vehicle to produce the cash required to improve equipment so that a pure white china ware could be produced for future lines of restaurant dinnerware (For further information, see *Fiesta Collector's Quarterly*, Winter 1996, issue 17, p. 4.)

Today the merry-go-round is playing a different tune! Post86 Fiesta has become a more than major line with hours and hours and hours of managerial strategy expended upon all manner of ways to entice and, to some extent, exploit those very collectors whom the company continually insists are not important factors in its marketing schemes.

During 1999, as the countdown to the end of the second millennium loomed joyously and forbiddingly, the Homer Laughlin Company embarked, as far as Post86 Fiesta was concerned, on a period of great creativity. One after another, new items have tumbled forth, gushing from the art department in joyous spurts! Not only was an entire series of Millennium pieces devised for collectors, including Millennium candleholders (expensive at $39.00 a pair), but the general run of regular items has been expanded! The pizza tray, for example, in October and November 1999, created unusual collector excitement. What about the new 8" vase? Its appearance renders the high prices paid by wealthy collectors for the early 1985 – 1986 prototypes a waste — unless it will not be glazed in white, rose, or cobalt blue! There are goblets (announced to be made in two sizes), a large oval vegetable bowl, spoon rests, flowerpots, and further rumors of a divided bowl! And what of those covers for the mixing bowls — seen by a few, but never offered to the public!

Now certainly, the frenzy Homer Laughlin China generated for the Post86 Fiesta collector has calmed. But just months ago — oh, what a Fiesta feeding frenzy it was!

All this "end of the millennium" activity, all this pulsating artistic activity culminated, as everyone remembers, with the announcement (November 1999) of a new color — juniper. Homer Laughlin China has learned well the lesson regarding the profitability of limited edition glazes, and juniper was available for only two years. But admittedly, the decision to limit the production time of this new green color was also motivated by creativity. With a solid base of regular colors maintaining a sense of customer equilibrium, these limited and exclusive glazes can represent flights of fancy and periods of excitement that propel collectors (and other customers) into those frenzies of buying.

Then in October 2000 another surprise! Cinnabar! As John Iams, one of my advisors, said: "Wow! Take the purple out of raspberry and add a touch of brown and you have cinnabar." The excitement continues!

Writing this book on Post86 Fiesta has been washed with problems, filled with frustrations, and marked by the alienation of a California someone who had been considered a friend. With help, the problems did prove surmountable, the frustrations cause me to grapple and learn, and the loss of a supposed friendship made me wiser and more cautious. So now, with all this said, let my talking cease and your reading begin!

Color and Post86 Fiesta

What is Fiesta but COLOR? The shapes are refreshingly simple, highly individual, and almost compulsively attractive. Eye-catching in 1936, new Fiesta dinnerware remains so today: heavily secure, masculinely dependable, sturdily well-set on the table, but having a rather feminine color palette — yet what is Fiesta but color?

When I was a child, imaginative and solitary, my overactive mind would categorize continually! For example, I used to assign a sex to Arabic numbers — without a clue to the reason. The numbers 2 and 8 and 12 were unabashedly feminine, surrounded, as these three were, by swarms of little male 1's, 7's, and 9's! Silly perhaps, but fascinating to recall!

Colors are assigned sexual roles. But here the reasons are more easily understood as our Western society determines which sex should prefer which colors. Unquestionably, pink and rose are feminine hues, violet and lavender also. Blue, inherited from the all-knowing sky, and red, gleaned from the terrors of war, became colors equated with maleness! Fascinating how the human mind continually assigns roles!

Until the snappy advent of turquoise, Post86 Fiesta was predominately pastel, pale, and frankly feminine!

Before going further in a discussion of color and how it works in our world, a few easy terms will allow a preciseness and clarity to our understanding. (Based on information taken from Augustine Hope's *The Color Compendium*. Van Nostrand Reinhold, c. 1990.)

In order to describe the general character or nature of any Fiesta color, the careful collector resorts to three major terms: (1) hue, (2) intensity, and (3) tone.

HUE: This term is often considered a synonym of the word "color," but it also refers to the attribute of a given color by which it is distinguished from other colors. Thus crimson, vermilion, and pink — while different colors — are similar in hue! Ditto sea mist green, chartreuse, and juniper. Black, white, and the gray lack hue; they are neutral or basically colorless.

INTENSITY: Also referred to as "saturation," this term is a reference to any particular color's purity or brightness or density. Maximum saturation or intensity means a color that is bright, strong, clean, and not dulled or muted by the addition of black or another color.

TONE: Also known as "value," refers to the lightness or darkness of a color. When a color has a neutral white added, it is lightened and becomes a "tint." When a color has the neutral black combined with it — in whatever amount — it is darkened or becomes a "shade." Thus pink is a tint of red, and maroon might be considered a shade of red.

With these terms one can become reasonably proficient in color language. But beware of some natural crossover within these definitions. For example, while pink is a tint of red, it also can be highly saturated. Add a drop of blue to a bright pink and its saturation (intensity) level drops and it becomes muted, less intense!

While we are discussing color, a few other expressions need defining.

9

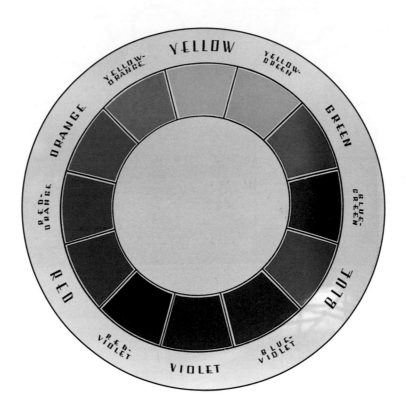

Color Wheel

Primary colors: Red, blue, yellow. Colors that are not formed by any mixture of other colors. These stand alone, and when mixed together in equal amounts add up to black. These three colors, when mixed in various combinations and proportions, give rise to all other colors.

Secondary colors: Purple, green, orange. Obtained by the mixing — generally in equal amounts — of two primary colors.

Tertiary colors: These are hues formed by the mixing of a primary color with its adjacent secondary color. A mixture of blue and green gives rise to turquoise. When the proportions are altered slightly, i.e., more green than blue, the color becomes teal. Most of these tertiary colors do not have individual names.

Complementary colors: The colors that lie directly across the color wheel (circle) from each other are said to be "complementary," and they relieve each other's intensity. These paired complementaries give rise to a number of the western world's holiday colors, i.e., red and green for Christmas, purple and yellow for Easter. This complementary relationship works also for tints and shades; Post86 Fiesta's rose (remember, really a pink) is a complementary of sea mist green. And, under some circumstances, a shade can be complementary to a tint — for example, this works when lilac is placed on the table with the highly whitened yellow!

As we view the 18 colors having to date appeared on Post86, they can be fairly easily separated into hues.

rose, apricot, persimmon, cinnabar

cobalt, turquoise (to some collectors), periwinkle blue, sapphire

turquoise (when viewed as teal), sea mist green, chartreuse, juniper

white, black, pearl gray

lilac, raspberry; yellow stands alone.

And during the early years, the Post86 palette tended to be pastel tinted rather than vibrantly shaded, and the use of vintage Fiesta's color terminology is somewhat unfortunate — especially for those collectors new to the line.

Rose, cobalt, yellow, turquoise, and chartreuse were all transferred without qualms from old to new. If one gets sloppy in terminology (pearl gray reduced to plain gray), then there is size. However, only two — chartreuse and (pearl) gray (well, perhaps turquoise might make three) — can be confused with the vintage colors. Gray (introduced in mid-1999) is the most problematic, even to collectors with some years experience.

Rose, apricot, periwinkle blue, persimmon, lilac, raspberry, and juniper draw their names from a botanical background. The rare sunflower yellow belongs here also.

Periwinkle blue, sea mist green, and pearl gray make use of descriptive double names.

Turquoise, sapphire, and pearl gray are named after jewels.

Some detail is necessary if the collector is to be fully conversant about these 18 colors and their places in the scheme of Post86 Fiesta. All these glazes are lead free, although this assurance did not appear in the mark until 1992.

Color Dates

white: 1986 –

black: 1986 – 1997

rose: 1986 –

apricot: 1986 – 1997

cobalt: 1986 –

yellow: 1888 –

turquoise: 1988 –

periwinkle blue: 1989 –

sea mist green: 1991 –

lilac (first limited color):
    1993 – 1995

raspberry (*): 1997

persimmon: 1995 –

sapphire (second   limited
    color): 1997

chartreuse (third   limited
    color): 1997 – 1999

pearl gray: 1999 –

juniper: (fourth limited
    color): 2000 – 2001

sunflower yellow (*): 2000

cinnabar: 2001 –

* Raspberry was limited officially to 500 presentation bowls, of which only 15 were available for public sale. The sunflower yellow glaze appeared only on one Millie III vase and dinner plate. There were auctioned June 10, 2000, for the benefit of the HLCCA. The Homer Laughlin Company might very well revive sunflower yellow for use in the future.

(derived from the Old English *with*, c. 899): By their numbers ye shall know them! White is the first of the first, the premier color of the line. Not to be translated as the most important color, merely the first one to have been chosen. But, after my preceding discussion, how many readers have caught my mistake? White is not a color at all! It is, along with the blacks and the grays, achromatic, which simply means it has no particular hue.

WHITE (F-100)

A pure white pigment reflects all the color wavelengths. But, pure white is notoriously difficult to produce, and since the human eye is extremely sensitive to the slightest change in white's purity, there are thousands of tints of whites

Post86 white is very cool — it is a blue white. Like blue milk, it has all the cream and butterfat removed.

White was chosen first because it goes with everything. Just as the extra eligible bachelor fits in at any dinner party, so this cool white mingles most beautifully with all the other colors. Place a white cup upon a rose or persimmon saucer, and this cup reflects, slightly but perceptively, the color of the saucer. Mingle yellow and white, dress the table with orangey linen, and bathe in candlelight, and the white glows warmly. Arrange white place settings on a black tablecloth and illuminate with cool electric light, and the plates become as stark as chalk.

White is versatile, and yet, if the host forgets its reflective qualities, the use of this "non-color" can be tricky.

BLACK (F-101)

(derived from the Old English *blaec*, c. 700): Virtually discontinued December 1997. Here is the Yang to white's Yin. The dark Satan to balance the snowy Angel Gabriel. Just as white reflects all the color wavelengths, Post86 black absorbs them — swallows them and becomes the second achromatic "color." Considered shades of mystery, blacks also move from warm to chilled — they can be touched with reds or cooled with blues. If the artist or the curious mixes the three primaries together — red, blue, yellow — the results will be a black.

Black Post86 Fiesta always had a number of problems. It was never a big seller, but the hollowware was much more popular than the place settings. This sounds as if black was purchased in the form of carafes, large bowls — accent pieces. Black also caused trouble in the kilns: it "fumed." Which simply means the fumes arising from black glazes can distort the other colors being fired at the same time. Black Post86 is, like white, high reflective, a mirror: it is glassy and sharp. Due to this reflective quality, black easily displays all its imperfections and scratches. It is a hard glaze to keep in mint condition.

There were rumors about black being discontinued for years, and in December 1997, it was announced that black would be a special order glaze produced a few times each year dependent upon large orders from commercial customers. In late 1999, new Fiesta hollowware was no longer officially being glazed in black!

Jonathan Parry has spoken of the desire of Homer Laughlin China to discontinue completely the black glaze, but there are hotel customers who keep coming back for the color. "We haven't been able to make it go away," he concludes (Terri Polick, "Pick Your Color," *The Dish*, Vol. 2, No. 2).

Joel Wilson, the Fiesta guru who directs the Fiesta Collectors Club and publishes the group's celebrated quarterly, expresses extremely positive opinions regarding black. He decrees that in the years to come, black will be the most collectible of all the Post86 colors. Despite the inherent problems, black is the single most unique color in all American dinnerware, and once the public becomes removed from it — in space and in availability — its uniqueness will become widely appreciated.

(derived from the Latin *rosa*, originally from the Greek *rhodon*): This is NOT the rose that by any other name would smell as sweet. This color is not really rose — it is purely PINK!

ROSE (F-103)

Remember the movie "Funny Face" where the editor (played by Kay Thompson) of a fashion magazine declares to the world THINK PINK? Pink, as a fashion color, comes and goes, and it is a difficult color. Pink, in all its varied presentations, is merely a tint made by adding white to red; pink can be very soft and delicate or sharp and strident. Post86 rose has been changed over the years. This change is subtle but obvious. The original color was somewhat soft, and with the passage of time it has brightened, and to my eyes, become very slightly tinged with light blue. There are two pink teapots in my collection. One was purchased early in 1987, the second just recently. The lids are not color interchangeable. Unfortunately, the camera cannot capture this difference, but the eye can.

This rose can never be mistaken for the much grayer and softened vintage rose, and rose did not really come into its true popularity until periwinkle blue came onto the new Fiesta scene. These two joined forces for the American "country kitchen" look.

APRICOT (F-104)

(derived from the Arabic word *al-bar-quq*), apricot has the dubious distinction of being the first Post86 glaze to be discontinued. It is much less orange than a true apricot, but is a warm sandy tint with slight "peachy" overtones that bespeak the American Southwest.

Apricot was introduced in 1986, because the rage for the colors of Arizona and New Mexico was just beginning. Very popular (according to the Homer Laughlin China Art Department) for many years, apricot ceased in December 1997 because persimmon was considered a brighter version of the same color. Apricot is very similar to the warm tan used on some of the 1939 World's Fair potter's plates. But, like the different versions of the Post86 pink, it is hard to assess without careful comparison.

(derived from the German *Kobald* — a goblin. These goblins resided in German silver mines and left a worthless silvery metallic element in exchange for true silver): The last of the five original 1986 colors, cobalt, like rose, was named after a vintage color. But, also like rose, this glaze could never be mistaken for the older version.

COBALT (BLUE) (F-105)

Cobalt is dark, deeply saturated, nearly black in certain lighting. Everyone seems to like cobalt and this shade has always been very popular in the American Midwest. It might be considered a substitute for the stark black. Cobalt is reminiscent of desert night moonlit skies where the deep blue flutters at the fringes of the eye. It is the color of the moon-goddess Artemis, hunting with her celestial dogs in the deep night sky. There is something romantic about cobalt. Erte, the great Deco designer, dressed many of his elongated female figurines in dark, dark blue sprinkled with silver stars. Cobalt does not mix kindly with white or not at all with black, and for some reason it is cheapened next to the very pinky rose. It is a stellar dinner companion for apricot — especially if the wise host uses the cobalt for accent.

In mid-1999, collectors began to notice a change in the cobalt glaze. After 13 years of being inky, opaque, and thick, the glaze was becoming more transparent, and as a result, richer. Since black is now virtually discontinued, rumors were flying among the Post86 cognoscenti: cobalt was doomed to be discontinued! These rumors were crushed by Dave Conley, the Homer Laughlin marketing chief: cobalt would not be retired. It was now the most popular color in the Post86 palette.

Please note that the word "blue" was in parentheses after the name "cobalt." Even though the company does not add "blue" to the name, this is technically necessary.

The term "cobalt" refers to a metallic compound that is combined with other compounds to produce a range of colors. Besides cobalt blue, there is cobalt ultramarine, cobalt turquoise, the yellowish cobalt green, and cobalt violet. Cobalt yellow, a mixture of cobalt and potassium nitrate, is bright and transparent — an artists' and glazers' favorite.

But does any astute reader see a gap in these original five colors, white, black, rose, apricot, and cobalt blue? Where is F-102? According to Jonathan Parry, past Homer Laughlin China Art Director, F-102 was the original number for gray. Gray was to be one of the

original colors, but was withdrawn just before the introduction in 1986. Mr. Parry states that the 1999 pearl gray is not the same as the original gray. With F-102 unassigned, the number is believed to have been given to white Fiesta with yellow and blue bands. This was supplied for a short period to Chili's, but that restaurant chain no longer purchases the line.

In 1988, two new colors were introduced.

YELLOW (F-106)

(derived from the Old English *geolu*): A very whitened and softened pastel yellow. Yellow is one of the three primaries and is the most reflective and luminous of the three.

Because it is the "color of the sun," yellow has always been a sacred color among ancient peoples, and some of this reflective awe continues. Yellow is also a color that must remain pure: add a touch of black or blue and its purity and "sun-like" qualities fade into greenness. During the first months of its introduction, yellow stood alone; it really did not mingle well with

any of the existing colors except cobalt blue, and it seemed to be the color for the kitchen lunch or the informal ladies' afternoon tea — if, upon reflection, ladies still take tea in the afternoon.

In late 1999, when mentioning cobalt as the most popular of all the glazes, Mr. Conley announced that yellow was the second consumer favorite!

(derived from the Old French *turqueise* which meant simply Turkish stone — the semiprecious stone found in the Turkish dominions): The fourth color to have the same name as a vintage glaze exploded on the scene in late 1988.

Here was a revolutionary change — a new approach. This color, a very bright deep teal blue, sparked up the Post86 Fiesta palette: it sang. However, this turquoise was the first new color that, under certain circumstances, might be mistaken for its vintage namesake. Not, of course, when the two were compared side by side, to but separated, there might be questions among novice collectors.

The original turquoise was the color of an Arizona sky, a true blue, so blue that the American Southwest Indians thought the stone had fallen from the heavens. The 1988 turquoise was infused with more green: it was almost a teal. This color blended perfectly with all the existing glazes, except perhaps cobalt. It mingled in stunning combinations with apricot. Turquoise's deep penetrating richness enlivened all dinner tables, but like black and cobalt, it accomplishes its purpose more dramatically when used as accent.

Attempting to be logical, the first seven colors are linked together. They make a very nice unit, and end on the very striking note: turquoise.

From now on, colors are added one at a time. Remember, the power and meaning of color lie in the province of the intuition and the emotions. Even though color itself is an exact science, its interpretation is archetypal. Color becomes a primordial way to convey human hopes and fears. No one can really interpret color without resorting to archetypal emotive feelings. Green both refers to new spring growth (the hope of agricultural man) and the horrors of mold, decay, and putrefaction. Red belongs to blood, fire, and war, and also to Santa Claus and St. Valentine's Day. Yellow is linked both with warmth and sunshine, and cowardice (a yellow streak). Man's feelings for color rise directly from his psyche, and are perhaps the result of actions and events having been set in the brain before man actually became man.

PERIWINKLE BLUE (F-108)

(derived from the Old English *perivince*): While Post86 cobalt is technically a blue, its darkness pushes it to the fringe of the color, unlike vintage cobalt which is immediately recognized as being a "true blue!" However, in 1989, Homer Laughlin attached a descriptive to a color: a blue that is the color of periwinkles! In nature, the periwinkle flower possesses more sparkle; the Post86 version is very grayed, very muted.

Blue is the color chosen by people who tend to be withdrawn and quiet, and the softness of this blue reinforces these introverted tendencies. Periwinkle blue is a "country blue," developed rather obviously as a foil for the pinkness of rose: a very happy marriage that was celebrated in thousands of quasi-colonial kitchens throughout America, kitchens replete with plump geese marching on cabinetry and appearing on cookware, and heart-shaped cut-outs everywhere. Despite constant rumors regarding its discontinuance, this gentle blue remains.

(derived from the Old English *grene*): This descriptive color cropped up in 1991! Homer Laughlin China's Art Department and Administration were continuing the emphasis on the pale and the pastel.

SEA MIST GREEN (F-109)

A friend insists that this green reminds him of pistachio. When, as a young boy addicted to knitted sleeveless sweaters, my mother made one for me she called sea foam green. This color, at least in my memory, is very close to that favored sweater. With pleasure and amazement, it was noted that in the Betty Crocker catalog, this color was labeled seafoam! This term is more appropriate as it duplicates to quite a degree the color of the briny foam sun-dancing between weedy dark rocks.

Sea mist green extends somewhat the interest in the American Southwest color palette. Unlike blue, the greens can be extracted from many natural materials — buckthorn berries, ragweed flowers, iris petals. Thus early or primitive man makes use of much green in clothing, pottery, and weaving. As a color, sea mist green was rejuvenated in the year 2000. It became a perfect foil for the dark shimmering juniper.

The numbers F-110, 111, and 112 were assigned to Holiday Fiesta, a green and a red line of flatware produced only for the Christmas table.

LILAC (F-113)

In 1993, a new color and a new concept swept from Newell, West Virginia, taking Post86 Fiesta collectors and acquirers and accumulators by surprise! The color was lilac (F-113) (derived from the Persian *lilak*), and the concept was the introduction of the first limited color.

In the words of Jonathan Parry: "Lilac was the beginning of the neon '90s colors because the market was going to brighter colors, and I always make intelligent color choices." In 1993, many people did not think Mr. Parry's choice was so wise because lilac is indeed a complete reversal of any color that came before! Lilac is domineering, psychedelic, overpowering. A table set with lilac might be considered chic and trendy, but it certainly limited the food to be served. Almost all foods look appetizing on a white or a black plate. When using lilac, one must choose food for its adaptability with the color. The cook had to consider with care what was to be launched on a lilac luncheon plate!

One either adored lilac or abhorred it: there was little in-between. Many rejected it — to their profound sorrow once it was discontinued in 1995. As the years pass, lilac has become the most desirable, one of the most coveted colors in modern American dinnerware. Prices for the most collectible pieces are phenomenal. Lilac was indeed a wise color choice.

But would lilac prices be so outrageous now, if were not the concept of a limited color also involved? Every Post86 piece available in 1993 – 1995 was glazed in lilac. After 1995, no more lilac would be produced. For two years every piece of new Fiesta was available in this outrageous color, then wham, enough, finito, goodbye and God bless!

Supposedly, however, there exist over 100 gallons of the lilac glaze, sequestered somewhere in the plant. All of a sudden will we see a brief lilac resurgence?

The following pieces are known to exist in lilac, but are considered unofficial or "rogue." While not seemingly as sensitive about these as the rogue items in sapphire, the Homer Laughlin Company is still angered over any unofficial piece in private hands:

> Carafe
> Colonial teapot (Fiesta Mate)
> Hostess tray
> Serving tray

A color dictionary will inform the reader that lilac is a pale purple color named after the blossoms of the hardy shrub (*Syringa vulgaris*) belonging to the olive family. It is slightly more intense than lavender, but less

reddened than violet. There is a great deal of red in this lilac and for all its assumed brightness, there is considerable softness residing underneath. But lilac did have many problems. Due to its richness and depth of saturation, the glaze was not consistent. There were fading, paleness, color globs, and mistakes. It was a temperamentally difficult color to produce. Any potential purchaser has to examine carefully the lilac piece to be bought. There is much that can be incorrect! Glaze skips are common and noticeable while inadequate glaze coverages are notorious. Pieces too blue or too red are undesirable.

One of the interesting asides regarding the purple color family is that most of the names refer to flowers or fruits: i.e., plum, eggplant, grape, damson, violet, heliotrope, hyacinth, fuchsia, dahlia, orchid, pansy, mulberry, and so on.

Lilac ceased in 1995. Immediately afterward, another striking color was added to the Fiesta family: persimmon.

PERSIMMON (F-114)

(derived from the American Indian Algonquin *pasimenan*, coined by Captain John Smith in 1612): This bright color continued marching up the path away from pastels.

Persimmon is a rich orangey red that sparkled on the table and was introduced as the '90s answer to vintage Fiesta red — blending very excitingly with black and turquoise. The rise of persimmon caused the discontinuation of apricot. Persimmon could be considered a stand-in for vintage red: it was richly saturated, intense, and moderately deep, but unlike the other colors, persimmon was also transparent.

Transparent and opaque are two more terms valuable to the colorist and the collector. Transparency allows, obviously, what is below the glaze to show through. Post86 white and black are opaque — details are covered. But look at persimmon! Note how the rings, lines, or any curling details are clearly evident, often as paler lines. A transparent glaze flows off the ridges, as cold air floats down from the surrounding hills into the valleys, leaving them lighter.

As a color, it is stunning with cobalt blue — almost breathtakingly so! Sapphire and persimmon also climb dramatic heights together. Or turquoise (a Southwest combination), and to a lesser extent, pearl gray. A friend speaks of persimmon and pearl gray as reminding him of a military uniform. Sea mist green combines well for a holiday table.

Persimmon is friendly, adaptable, and a marvelous party mixer! Also, this hue seems to unify an otherwise conglomerate of colors. Tuck six or so smaller persimmon items (tripod bowl, pyramid candleholder, mini disc pitcher, tumbler, shakers) in among larger pieces of disparate colors (sea mist green coffee server, black large disc pitcher, plates of juniper, apricot, sapphire, cobalt platters), and the grouping solidifies as a unit. Possibly because of this brilliance, the eye is captured and runs quickly from persimmon piece to persimmon piece!

The white plate with a red Fiesta logo has garnered the number F-115.

Sapphire is vibrantly bright, intense, and glamorous. This color could be called a shimmering vintage Fiesta cobalt — put them side by side and see!

SAPPHIRE (F-116)

Sapphire, as did lilac, has glazing problems. Some pieces (I own a medium vase like this) look "peppered." Not only is it the second limited color, sapphire's claim to Post86 distinction is the extremely short time it was produced. Bloomingdale's came to the Homer Laughlin Company with the glaze color, the number of pieces, and the firing days already chosen. So for only 180 days in 1997, the sapphire glaze was used on the following items:

1 – 5. Place setting consisting of 10" plate, 7" plate, tea cup, tea saucer, 7" straight-sided bowl
6. Disc pitcher
7. Disc pitcher with 60th Anniversary Logo
8. Medium vase
9. Clock
10. Clock with 60th Anniversary Logo
11. Tumbler
12. Tumbler with 60th Anniversary Logo
13. Straight-sided vegetable bowl
14. Medium platter
15. Jumbo cup
16. Jumbo saucer
17. Chili bowl
18. Handled serving tray
19. Handled serving tray with FCOA logo

Fred Mutchler contributed the following list of unofficial or "rogue" sapphire pieces. The company is quite disturbed about their existence in private collections. There have been accusations of stolen property, police involvement, and official harassment. But Homer Laughlin China can hardly be blamed for this action — it is a very awkward situation to have collectors paying extremely inflated prices for sapphire pieces that legally were never made:

Stacking fruit bowl	Pepper shaker (6 holes)
Butterdish	Salt shaker (7 holes)
Pyramid candleholder	Relish/utility tray
Round candleholder	Hostess tray
Mug	Bud vase

Mr. Mutchler mentions one sighting of the presentation bowl in sapphire.

This is the official list, but there are rumored to be others. These rogue pieces have been surreptitiously sequestered in the collections of the wealthy and the ambitious, and have been labeled as stolen pieces by Homer Laughlin China.

RASPBERRY

When the kiln workers rolled out the trolley containing the 500 millionth piece of Fiesta, the Homer Laughlin Company celebrated; the date was December 5, 1997. The date and event were commemorated by the introduction of a new piece, at first named the celebration bowl, and soon known more prosaically as the presentation bowl. Its designer was Mr. Parry.

A new and most glamorous glaze graced the first 500 of these bowls: raspberry, another dip into the world of botany. The glaze is deeply saturated and highly translucent which simply means there is a fine contrast between the encircling rings and the rest of the bowl. The Art Deco designs on the bottom are also outlined to perfection. While not exactly the color of the red raspberry that hangs in tempting clusters in gardens and fields during the months of summer, the glaze is exceptionally beautiful. So tempting, in fact, there are rumors that the medium vase was glazed for a few of the top HLC management.

Yet very, very few will experience the joy of owning a piece of Post86 in raspberry. Of the 500 bowls, only 15 were made available to the public through a series of well-organized auctions. All proceeds went to charities chosen by HLC management. The other 485 raspberry celebration bowls went to the officials of the company and Post86 retailers and distributors. It cannot be predicted if any of these bowls will ever reach the secondary market.

Thus the color raspberry will be the rarest and most prized.

The company insisted upon some theatrically inspired events surrounding the disposal of the shards of Post86 pieces glazed in raspberry. These bits and pieces were smashed into tiny, tiny fragments and buried in a secret disposal site. Were the men who performed this duty HLC employees sworn to secrecy and well-searched for any stolen bits of raspberry glazed shards? Or were they day laborers — men who wisely had no knowledge of or interest in Fiesta. Men brought to do the deed, and then whisked away in silence? Who knows? (See section on presentation bowls for more information.)

We are, of course, talking about high camp theater!

Raspberry remains as a glaze, perhaps to cover other pieces in the future or perhaps not! Again, who knows?

CHARTREUSE (F-117)

(derived from *La Grande chartreuse*, the chief monastery of the Carthusian monks who there produce a greenish liqueur) arrived on the Post86 stage in 1997, just as sapphire was retired.

This became the third limited color, doomed for oblivion on December 31, 1999. Once again the name reverts to a former vintage color, but this chartreuse is much brighter: "sassy" and "yellowed." At this time, Homer Laughlin China decided to "spread the wealth" and created a series of exclusive items. This simply meant that at the beginning, certain items in chartreuse could be purchased only at a single retailer, for example, the chartreuse pie baker was available solely through the Betty Crocker catalog. But as dealers and collectors rushed about in a "chartreuse-madness" and purchased items in multiples, the "extras" were immediately offered on the secondary market. Almost all the regular items became available in chartreuse, with the napkin rings, AD cups and saucers, and finally, the sugar caddy supposedly so glazed under pressure from the collector/consumer.

As is mentioned later in this book in a discussion under Fiesta Mates, the chartreuse AD cup and saucer were exclusive to the retail outlet in Newell, West Virginia, and were sold with no problem. The Homer Laughlin Company decided to play games with the chartreuse sugar caddy. After announcing that it would be available for general purchase through the

We are currently paying 6.125% mortgage

11-8-0#   no point 30 yr. fixed 6.375
      no point 15 yr. " 5.875

Class # MSL Thurs afternoon X 3.40
$ 2000 March 28

bowl = 250 400's
CFH - Charles F. Haviland; porcelain mfg in 1800's
Bakelite by Tony Grasso
19.95 Art George by Michael _____ Schiffer Pub.
150.00 Lamps of the 19th Century - Schiffer Pub.
025.00 Frederick Garden & Steuben Glass
159.99 Lalique by Jessica Hodge - Thunder Bay Press

Worcester 1894 - 1916 (never been reproduced)
milk glass tops - even with a small clock
collar & cuff box $850. (without clock would
be double)
Coralene Vases made latter part of 19th Century
A type of satin glass   1800's

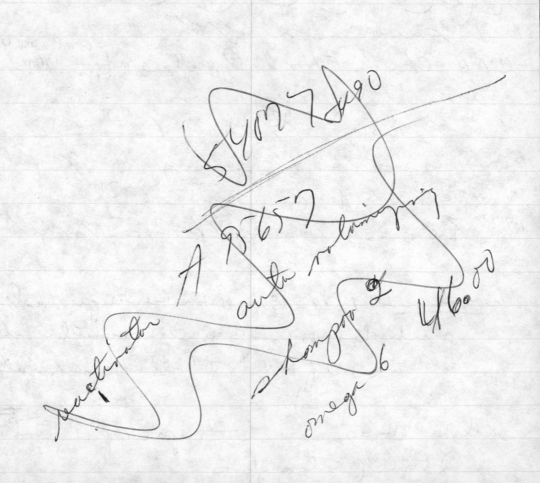

outlet, a quick last moment decision limited the numbers to 300, available only to a select few who happened to be at the warehouse sale in early November 1999. This manipulation caused hopes to fade for the production of the promised napkin rings, but orders placed in September were finally honored in late November. It is thought that the napkin ring was the last piece to be glazed in chartreuse.

This new chartreuse is easily mistaken for the vintage color by beginning collectors. It is wise to have examples of both chartreuses in hand before making a final decision. Strangely, some particular items are easier to confuse: the sauceboat is one, the disc pitcher another. But this confusion might lie only in my eyes; others wiser and more clever will have no trouble! Also, the company has wisely thought to place a raised "H" on the underside of Post86 pieces easily confused with the vintage, i.e., both candleholders and the sauceboat, among others.

Like persimmon, chartreuse mingles very well, excitingly well, with cobalt blue, sapphire, turquoise, and when used to accompany a myriad of chrome, glass, or black lacquer, it becomes sleek, sophisticated trendy Deco camp!

PEARL GRAY (F-118)

Since chartreuse disappeared at the end of the second millennium, Homer Laughlin's marketing personnel decided to introduce a new regular color in mid-1999. Thus about May, pearl gray arrived, somewhat dully, upon the scene.

This is the third neutral color, and, as such, can mix with any other color. In fact, the softness and slight shimmer of pearl gray have proven more malleable than the starker white and the now discontinued black. But this glaze does have a problem: it is the one Post86 glaze almost identical with the vintage gray. Even the experienced collector will have to study the pearl gray Post86 sauceboat and plates; they are barely distinguishable from the vintage gray! Again the "H" appears as it does in chartreuse, and with pearl gray the identifying letter is absolutely necessary!

At first pearl gray was thought dim and drab yet within a year or 18 months — by 2001 — its merits as a mixer became appreciated.

Jonathan Parry wanted a gray to appear among the original colors, but the company administrators thought that three neutrals was pushing the acceptance of the reissued line into a corner. Who knows which side made the correct decision. As a regular color, pearl gray is a marvelous mixer and maintains a solid but soft background for the other glazes.

JUNIPER (F-119)

(derived from the Latin *juniperus*): The new millennium introduced a new color — a mingling, according to some observers, of sapphire and chartreuse. I have heard it labeled "peacock colored." Then those fortunate people with access to the inner sections of the Homer Laughlin Company made it known juniper was similar to Harlequin's spruce glaze, but richer, deeper, and more densely saturated.

Again, we are confronted with a limited color, the fourth (becoming quite normal?), and juniper will disappear at the end of 2001.

Although slated to become available as a brief exclusive (three months was the time often mentioned) early in January 2000, it began to be seen by December 15, 1999, in scattered Bloomingdale's locations. The choice was limited: 5-piece place setting, round serving bowl, 13" platter, and the mug. At the same time, these same items could be bought through the Homer Laughlin China retail outlet in Newell, West Virginia.

When received and handled, the newest color was quite startling. In poor light it seemed berry blue, almost a dull sapphire, but when placed in bright light, juniper exploded. It indeed has the qualities of iridescence with a shimmering intermingling of blues and greens. The glaze glows from within, and it becomes the antithesis of the pale surface colors apricot and yellow, and the neutral to white and pearl gray. Like turquoise, juniper could be considered possessing ambiguity: neither green nor blue, it fuses these two hues into the richness of watered silk.

Many people did not immediately appreciate juniper. With which existing Post86 glaze would it combine? The general consensus was juniper was a perfect match with pearl gray, but who can really decide! This is a glaze that requires an ongoing, well-aged relationship before all the intricacies of its beauty can be assessed and appreciated. As the year 2000 progressed, other juniper pieces were introduced and welcomed by collectors. Unfortunately, HLC has continued the same exclusivity with juniper as with chartreuse. This means scurrying among the collectors to find certain pieces.

SUNFLOWER YELLOW

While raspberry is considered the rarest of all Post86 glazes, this appellation truly belongs as of early 2001 to sunflower yellow. This bright sparkling yellow — much brighter actually than Harlequin yellow — appeared mid 2000 on only two pieces: the Millie III vase and the dinner plate. Both were donated by HLC to the Homer Laughlin China Collectors Association (HLCCA) to be auctioned for the club's benefit.

Strawser, who conducted the auction, advertised as follows: "Over 1,000 pieces of vintage Fiesta to be auctioned off, including a vintage maroon Fiesta vase, and an exciting Post86 Millennium III vase. This Millennium III vase is glazed in the color sunflower yellow. This color has not yet been put into production. This is the only vase of this color which will be sold. In addition to this piece, a dinner plate in this color will be auctioned off at the banquet to be held on June 10, 2000."

The interesting sentence in this quote is, "This color has not yet been put into production," and implies that sometime in the future, sunshine yellow will be used on other pieces of Post86. The announcement also assures any prospective bidder that there will never be more than one Millie III vase in this really very startling color. Thus collectors can await the regular appearance of sunflower yellow.

CINNABAR (F-102)

Early in May 2000, rumors of a possible new glaze began to waft very gently to my ears. Some new ideas were beginning to come together in the decision-making offices at Homer Laughlin. Actually there were two possibilities: a color tentatively titled "blueberry blue," and a second close to vintage Fiesta's red-orange.

During the first weeks of July, further news was being passed along. The idea of a blue was fading, and the reddish color was becoming troublesome. Pieces glazed with the experimental color did not come true in the kiln — there were too many different shades. Also some gossip about sea mist green arrived: it was not doing well and could be discontinued. This rumor was accepted with great caution because this soft green and the new juniper were meshing quite well, and one of the owners announced juniper was their most popular color. What is one to believe?

Finally, with the suddenness of a cobra's strike, in late September, Dave Conley posted a query on his favorite message board: "What is cinnabar?" Immediately one of the important contributors to this information sharing Internet site asked:

1. Will it be a limited production time run or a permanent color?
2. Will it be limited to a specific retailer?
3. Will there be cinnabar exclusives?
4. Will there be cinnabar napkin rings?
5. Will all the items be produced in cinnabar?
6. When can we expect to see a sample?
7. When can we expect to be able to buy some?
8. With the addition of this color are you discontinuing any other color?

These questions are interesting in themselves, for by the time this is read, all answers will probably be known.

This must be the red/orange glaze that was giving trouble in the kiln. Trouble, but obviously, now not as troublesome.

In trouble to be troubl'd
Is to have your trouble doubl'd.

(Daniel Defoe,
The Further Adventures of Robinson Crusoe)

We must certainly hope that the new glaze cinnabar (a sure match for the Harlequin maroon!) will not cause undue double trouble to the kiln masters, chemists, and the fine workers in the Art Department.

Looking at my list of items available in this new regular glaze (no limited run this time), we can see it presently is slated to bathe the most popular items: tumbler, bouillon, napkin rings, AD cup/saucer set, sugar caddy, round candleholder, bud vase, medium vase, 2-cup teapot, and tripod bowl. Doubtless, this list

could change as production fury betrays weaknesses not yet known. The two items most obviously missing are the pyramid candleholder and the troublesome goblet.

For some reason, the number for cinnabar is F- 102: the number, if my information is correct, to have been used for the original gray. So HLC has done a loop here and filled the gap. This might be sequentially confusing since juniper is F-19.

Whatever happened to blueberry blue?

This is a listing of pieces to be available in the new regular color cinnabar. Please note the absence of the pyramid candleholder, the hostess bowl, and the goblet.

Item	Description	Item	Description
0098	Jumbo Bowl 18 oz.		
0149	Jumbo Cup 18 oz.	0475	Miniature Disc Pitcher 5 oz.
0293	Jumbo Saucer 6¾"	0478	AD Cup and Saucer
0409	Oval Serving Bowl 7½"	0479	Sugar Caddy 3½" x 2⅜"
0421	Small Mixing Bowl 7½ " 44 oz.	0482	Large Mixing Bowl 9½" 70 oz.
0422	Medium Bowl 8½" 60 oz.	0484	Pitcher Large Disc 67¼ oz.
0424	Pedestal Mug 6"	0485	Pitcher Small Disc 28 oz.
0446	Tumbler 6½ oz.	0486	Sauceboat 10½"
0448	60 oz. Handled Carafe	0487	Deep Dish Pie Baker 10¼"
0450	Bowl 6¾ oz.	0488	Candleholder Round 3⅝"
0451	Rim Soup 9"	0490	Vase Bud 6"
0452	Cup 7¾"	0491	Vase Medium Fiesta 9⅝"
0453	Mug 10¼"	0492	Cream Individual 7 oz.
0455	2-Quart Serving Bowl	0493	Covered Coffee 38 oz.
0456	Oval Platter 6" x 9⅝"	0494	Butter Covered 36 oz.
0457	Oval Platter 8" x 11⅝"	0495	Covered Casserole 70 oz.
0458	Oval Platter 10" x 13⅝"	0496	Teapot Covered 36 oz.
0459	Fruit 6¼ oz.	0497	Salt & Pepper Set
0460	Bowl Small 14 oz.	0498	Sugar Ind. Covered Large 9 oz.
0461	Bowl Medium 19 oz.	0499	Relish/Utility Tray 9½"
0462	Pasta Bowl 12" 23 oz.	0505	15" Pizza Tray
0463	Plate B&B 6⅛"	0753	Hostess Tray
0464	Plate Salad 7¼"	0756	Rangetop Salt & Pepper Set
0465	Plate Luncheon 9"	0760	Welled Snack Plate 10½"
0466	Plate Dinner 10½"	0764	2-Cup Teapot
0467	Plate Chop 11¾"	0765	Pedestal Bowl
0468	Round Serving Tray 12"	0766	Tripod Bowl
0469	Napkin Rings, 4 pc. set	0821	Sugar/Cream Tray Set
0470	Saucer 5⅞"	0830	Place Setting 5 Pc.
0471	Bowl Large 1-qt.	0831	Place Setting 4 Pc.
0472	Bowl Stack Cereal 8½"	0837	3 Pc. Mixing Bowl Set

The Colors of Fiesta

THE GREENS (8):
Vintage: (Light) green
Chartreuse
(Forest) green
(Medium) green
Ironstone: Turf green
Post86: Sea mist green
Chartreuse
Juniper

THE REDS (8):
Vintage: (Fiesta) red
Rose
Ironstone: Mango red (exactly the same as Fiesta red)
Post86: Rose (pink)
Apricot (pale orange?)
Persimmon
Cinnabar

THE BLUES (6):
Vintage: Cobalt
Turquoise

Post86: Cobalt
Turquoise (teal?)
Periwinkle blue
Sapphire

THE YELLOWS (4):
Vintage: Yellow
Ironstone: Antique gold
Post86: Yellow
Sunflower yellow

THE PURPLES (2):
Post86: Lilac
Raspberry

THE NEUTRALS (5):
Vintage: Ivory
Gray
Post86: White
Black
Pearl gray

Someone up there likes green! Wassily Kandinsky (1866 – 1944), the very influential Russian avant-garde painter, speaks of green as "representing the social middle class, self-satisfied, immovable, narrow — absolute green is the most restful color, lacking any undertone of joy, grief, or passion. On exhausted men this restfulness has a beneficial effect, but after a time it becomes tedious."

Rudolf Steiner, (1961 – 1925) German colorist, philosopher, educator, states: "green represents the lifeless image of the living. . . ."

The Chrysler Corporation reports that during times of economic growth, green becomes the favorite automobile color.

Deryck Healey, author of the fascinating book *Living With Color*, comments: "greens are a matter of life and death — from the vital gleam of lush foliage to the murk of mould and decay. Green is nature's number one color. . . ."

Pliny the Elder (23 – 79,) famed Roman naturalist, observes that "emerald delights the eye without fatiguing it."

All theaters throughout the ages have offered the backstage sanctuary known as the green room.

And traffic lights in modern China are reversed: red means go, and green means stop!

So when the reader thinks of greenbacks, green-horns, green thumbs, and the innumerable uses of the color green, Fiesta must be acknowledged as playing its professional part!

This discussion has been couched in bare outline and deceptively simple. Always desirous of learning more about the technicalities of color, when employed as a librarian at a small independent design college, I once spoke to a professor who was also a friend. She taught a color theory class, and since I was entitled to take one free class each quarter, I questioned her. Liz D'Ambrosio was a brilliant colorist, and could look at any hue and tell almost exactly its color components. She dazzled us with her knowledge.

"You are, of course, welcome to take my class," Liz spoke gently, " but I feel you will be disappointed. The students here really do not want to learn about color science — all they want to do is play with finger paints and come away with A's and B's. If I tried to teach them what they should know about color, they would complain, and I would be in trouble. Students here are paying customers, and they are always right!"

I did not take Ms. D'Ambrosio's color theory class. Perhaps I should have, despite her warning. However, this anecdote relates a lot about the seriousness of color science, and considerably about the state of education at this small college.

Post86 Fiesta Color Palettes

February 29, 1986 to 1988 — Five Original Colors

white (F-100)
black (F-101)
rose (F-103)
apricot (F-104)
cobalt blue (F-105)

Early 1988 — Six Colors

white
black
rose
apricot
cobalt blue
yellow

Late 1988 to 1989 — Seven Colors

white
black
rose
apricot
cobalt blue
yellow
turquoise (F-107)

1989 to 1991 — Eight Colors

white
black
rose
apricot
cobalt blue
yellow
turquoise
periwinkle blue (F-108)

1991 to 1993 — Nine Colors

white
black
rose
apricot
cobalt blue
yellow
turquoise
periwinkle blue
sea mist green (F-109)

1993 to 1995 — Ten Colors

white
black
rose
apricot
cobalt blue
yellow
turquoise
periwinkle blue
sea mist green
lilac (F-113) (first limited color)

1995 to 1997 — Ten Colors

white
black
rose
apricot
cobalt blue
yellow
turquoise
periwinkle blue
sea mist green
persimmon (F-114)

Early 1997 — Eleven Colors

white
black
rose
apricot
cobalt blue
yellow
turquoise
periwinkle blue
sea mist green
persimmon
sapphire (F-116) (second limited color, 180 production days)

Late 1997 — Eleven Colors

white
black
rose
apricot
cobalt blue
yellow
turquoise
periwinkle blue
sea mist green
persimmon
chartreuse (F-117) (third limited color)

1998 to Mid-year 1999 — Nine Colors

white
rose
cobalt blue
yellow
turquoise
periwinkle blue
sea mist green
persimmon
chartreuse

Mid-year 1999 to December 1999 — Ten Colors

white
rose
cobalt blue
yellow
turquoise
periwinkle blue
sea mist green
persimmon
chartreuse
pearl gray (F-118)

2000 — Ten colors

**white
rose
cobalt blue
yellow
turquoise
periwinkle blue
sea mist green
persimmon
pearl gray
juniper (F-119) (fourth
limited color)**

2001 — Eleven colors
(No photo available)

**white
rose
cobalt blue
yellow
turquoise
periwinkle blue
sea mist green
persimmon
pearl gray
juniper
cinnabar**

Form and Function

"Form versus function" is an adage to be considered seriously. There should not be any antagonism between the two terms; the "versus" does not intimate the necessity of a battle. It should not give rise to a potential wrestling bout between two opposing forces. The adage is of great value and should be of considerable concern to all serious designers. Some of these concerns are blatantly obvious, almost amusingly so: a room must have a door or entrance (form) into it in order that the space be functional! But while a room must have an entrance, it need not have windows to function — unless of course, the architect has decided the window is the mode for entering!

Unmarked square oriental cup.

The function of the teacup (form) is to hold liquid, and the teacup form must allow easy, convenient access to the mouth. Yet, a teacup does not need a handle. In fact, the cultures of the East tend to disdain this appendage. Most teacups with handles were meant for export from East to West. Yet, it is best that a teacup be round to be functional! A good number of very beautiful teacups have been viewed that are square, with the handle placed directly on one of the angles. Lovely to look at indeed. The form is delightful, but the teacup does not function. Lovely to look at, but impossible to drink from — an interesting form, but almost non-functional.

In the Western world, the proper function of a teacup (to hold liquid and to transfer this liquid to the mouth) demands some type of handle. Unfortunately many English teacups — of the bone china variety — have delicately conceived handles obviously meant to be grasped by ladies. Readers surely have seen a man try to manage the female oriented handle? Usually he grapples the teacup by the side, and shatters "all to hell" any semblance of delicacy!

Now, if the constructed form deliberately limits the function of any given object, then problems arise. Yet these problems might have been deemed necessary by the conceiver of the design. This concept is allowable. One of the best examples of this philosophy is the Germanic drinking horn: it was meant solely for male use. The form does not allow the horn to be returned to the table without being completely drained: it cannot stand on the table, it must lie on its side! So the horn is meant for quaffing by a man. Women are served their ale or foaming beer in goblets meant for delicate sipping! Another shade of sexism!

What I am trying to explain is that sometimes a form is deliberately designed to be nonfunctional. If the designer knows what is being done, and has a positive (to him) legitimate reason for doing so, then the form is acceptable. If the designer makes a mistake or creates a design for negative reasons, then the form is really unacceptable. This sounds complicated, but if the reader uses common sense, my premise becomes clear.

Remember those joke glasses with the tiny holes near the rim that causes the unknowing drinker to "dribble?" This form is acceptable because the designer wants the dribble! If the edge of the glass was ornately curved and delicately serrated and the liquid spilled by mistake, the form would not be acceptable!

Those wide open saucer-like champagne glasses with the hollow stems are another example of an absolutely unacceptable form for the function of drinking champagne or sparkling burgundy, if that is your forte. The stem is terribly difficult to clean and the bubbles dissipate. The correct form is the tall tulip glass.

The basic function of a shoe is to allow a man or woman to walk securely and with comfort. Very often fashion works against function by encouraging and accepting shoes designed in such a form as to make walking a travesty, e.g., stiletto heels!

We could continue, but the point has been made.

So we come to an important decision. What is more important — the form or the function? Are we invoking the indefinable opinion of what comes first, the chicken or the egg? Or are we listening to the unanswerable Abbot and Costello routine "Who's on first?"

No, to all three questions. For here, or so I believe, the function must come first — the function must be determined before the form is even a glimmer in the eye! Or a whistle on puckered lips! Is it possible to design a beautiful and elegant form and then say, "What is this for?" Or perhaps, in this case, the function of the beautiful form is simply to be beautiful! Here we are stepping away from "functional art" into the ethereal level of "pure art," and this is too lofty an exercise for this Fiestaware book.

What we are discussing here is whether the function (holding tea) is accomplished in the most beautiful manner possible. Function versus form! Some items fulfill their function so simply, so purely, that this purity becomes a source of beauty in itself.

No one would quibble, in my estimation, with the statement that the Fiesta teacup, both vintage and Post86, is a perfectly designed form for the function of drinking tea. Perhaps the newer version of the teacup is a little more positively designed because the "C" handle is easier to grasp than the older circle handle. And it must be accepted that the "stick" handle of the AD cup, while visually very attractive and unusually charming, is a poorly designed form.

Function and form must be evenly matched — balancing delicately on the teeter-totter of correct design. What is beautiful and acceptable in form changes quite radically from one generation to another. The lush form of Lillie Langtry — known as "the Jersey Lily" in the late Victorian period when feminine "plumpness" was the vogue — enhanced her function immensely. As the world slips into the third millennium, dear Miss Langtry would hardly attract the attention of today's sophisticated male! The function has remained the same, but society has demanded a change in the form!

So to return to dinnerware. The primary acknowledged function of a Post86 Fiesta teacup is to hold hot liquid, and to convey this hot liquid to the mouth in the easiest, most convenient manner possible. If this is done purely and simply, the harmony between form and function gives rise to noticeable inherent beauty. The perfect marriage leads to perfect beauty.

Now, naturally, form can, as pure artistic beauty, exist without function, and the latter can exist without form. If a man wishes to drink beer, he has the option to drink it straight from the can — function is accomplished, but the form is absent! On second thought, the form of a flip-top can for Bud-Light is perfect for what it does — and who, especially with today's lessening social mores, can say drinking a can of brew on the farmhouse porch lacks form?

Another excellent example of how function can affect form can be seen by comparing the vintage Fiesta carafe with the Post86 Fiesta one. The vintage example was perfectly designed, footed and stoppered for the home table. It was designed for occasional use and under highly restrained surroundings.

This vintage carafe would crumble and be crushed and carried away in pieces in the rough and tumble surroundings of even the most elegant restaurant. The stopper became a useless and an irritating burden, the throat was too narrow to admit ice, and the foot allowed for table unsteadiness. Thus literally the carafe's function changed, and the form had to follow suit! I remember questioning Jonathan Parry about the absence of the stopper in the Post86 verson. Many collectors were annoyed! But Mr. Parry was aware of the carafe's new function, and the change in form was both wise and necessary.

Thus a good designer of dinnerware inquires first — what is the function of each piece of dinnerware to be designed? Where will it be used, and how will it be used? With these functional parameters firmly in mind, the designer begins to draw. At this point, the merely adequate designer is separated from the good designer, who is also in turn divided from those geniuses who conceive fantastically beautiful dinnerware wherein form is perfected and welded to function. And these ceramic geniuses are a rare breed indeed!

When a line of dinnerware continues to exist for many years, there will logically be some change in the

Vintage and Post86 carafes.

function of the entire line, or in certain parts of the line.

When Mr. Parry contemplated the redesign of Fiesta, he, again wisely, closely copied the vintage line. After a very brief flirtation with some use of the Ironstone shape, he settled for (1) judicious copies and (2) careful modifications. The medium vase, the pyramid and round candleholders, and the sauceboat, among others, fit into the category of judicious copies. The teapot, the coffee server, the casserole, the sugar belong to the second group, careful modifications.

There was only one new item in the 1986 Fiesta line — the bouillon cup. This item first appeared in the mold book on March 26, 1986. If this entry is correct and no one in Homer Laughlin China's Art Department forgot to list an earlier "bouillon" entry, then this can only mean it was not among the pieces first displayed to industry representatives on February 29, 1986. So can it be imagined that some restaurant mogul suggested the design and inclusion of the bouillon cup? This piece has been described as "basically a handless teacup needed by the restaurant trade and loved by collectors." Truth indeed!

The two platters on the 1986 list are technically modifications. The smaller (9½") had been introduced in Fiesta Ironstone, while the larger (11½") is exactly the same shape as the vintage platter only ½" smaller.

In 1988 (or thereabouts) an entirely new form entered the Fiesta family — the butterdish. Never had a butterdish been included in the vintage line, and this has long been considered a mystery. The Post86 example was designed precisely for the function of holding a quarter-pound of butter or margarine. The old Jade butterdish shape would not have accomplished the task as well because, as we all know, butter is most often in quarter-pound sticks. And like Miss Lillie Langtry, the rounded butterdishes of the early twentieth century simply would not do! The butterdish form had adapted.

As the 1990s progressed, the observant collector began to note a new thrust in the philosophic aim of Post86. While still acknowledging, or protesting, that the contemporary line was primarily geared for commercial consumers, the company was adding pieces having strong appeal to retail customers. When asked whether the welled snack plate was an attempt to reissue the 1950s TV plate, Mr. Parry replied negatively. Since informal home entertaining was on the rise, three fairly recently designed plates added to the hostess's battery of dinnerware: round serving tray, snack plate with well, and the larger hostess tray. Then very recently (October 1999) a fourth "entertaining" piece was made available: the huge pizza tray and in early 2000 came a fifth, the hostess bowl. Formal dining was being replaced by buffets and barbecues, and Mr. Parry was designing forms to fit new functions.

Here again functions are noted and absorbed, and the forms are designed to follow. Would it not be jolly to anticipate the changes in American lifestyles and try to predict new pieces of Post86 Fiesta? A large lidded mustard jar! An oblong dish divided into three or four compartments for olives, pickles, relishes! Pepper grinder! Let not lack of imagination hold you back!

So function continues to lead the way, and a good form to fit the function is still, like a good man, hard to find!

Comparison of Available Vintage and Post86 Fiesta Pieces

What is available today only in vintage Fiesta? What is appearing in the line-up of Post86 Fiesta? What pieces are common to both? These are three exciting questions because they deal with decision-making at the highest levels of the Homer Laughlin Company, and they deal also with changes in American society and in our dining habits.

And the way Americans dine has changed indeed since the days when Fiesta first exploded onto the scene!

Today I wonder, do Americans dine? Doubt it! Or at least they rarely do on ordinary days. When I was quite young — say up until the age of seven or eight — my supper was served in the kitchen around 6 o'clock. My parents had their meal two hours later at the large round table in the dining room. During the war years, when my father was an aircraft designer at Bendix, I graduated to the dining room where the table was always set in a relatively formal manner. Even if he were absent, my father's place had its setting. We often used Harlequin (no, I am not making this up) for regular meals — with knife, forks, spoons, in correct place. There was (and here my memory is stretching) often a soup, then the main course, perhaps a salad, and then dessert.

The remnants of one course were completely removed before the next, and the table was essentially bare for dessert — even if it was only Jell-O whipped to a foamy froth!

No elbows on the table. No talking with food in the mouth. No disagreeable subjects discussed. No feeding the dogs. No using the fingers, except with "finger" food.

None of these rules were oppressive to me nor to any of the children I knew. The reason we ate after 6 o'clock was simply to allow me to listen to "Jack Armstrong" (that perennial All-American Boy) at 5:30 and then "Sky King" at 5:45. In the winter, dark had fallen, the drapes pulled shut against the black cold, and supper time was a calm period, a shared time. Not that it was always calm around the table. It was also a time of parental pronouncements, and since I was an only child, all pronouncements were aimed squarely at me!

One could always hear and listen. One could always talk and be heard.

Could this peaceful semi-formality at the supper or dinner table be termed "the June Cleaver syndrome?" At my grandfather's house (where a maid often served) it was peaceful, but much less pleasant for me.

"A child is meant to be seen, but not heard!" Or, "We eat with genteel sufficiency!" were my grandfather's pronouncements harking back to sterner Victorian times. My mother's parents were German, and the sense of gemütlichkeit around their table depended upon my mouth remaining shut! Did this bother me? I doubt it, because a child can learn more — much more — by listening! Through listening to adult conversations, I was aware of many things that would have shocked my elders.

What does this have to do with dinnerware, my reader mumbles! Well, how and when we approach the dinner table, what and how we eat, how we act and react, what we hear and what we say — all this bears greatly on the pieces of china that are on or are not on the table before us. Or even if there is a table at all!

There are a number of Post86 collectors who want to see certain Fiesta items returned to the fold. The one vintage item most often requested is the AD coffee server. Will it ever return? Will the Post86 AD cup and saucer ever be reunited with this signature piece? This is to be doubted. The stick-handle would cause, I believe, immense problems in the kiln. But even if the stick-handle sailed through the intense firing unharmed, who really drinks after dinner coffee now?

A Homer Laughlin shape of the turn of the twentieth century was named American Beauty. The pieces were indeed startlingly beautiful, gracefully ornate, and numbered 96 individual pieces. So ornate are the curlicues, the knobs, and the fretwork, one cleans a piece carefully with a soft toothbrush. All this beauty and delicacy have banned American Beauty from our table. Gone is the grace, and gone is much of the charm of living.

Even in the late 1930s, Frederick Rhead miscalculated when he designed a covered bowl concerned only with the serving of onion soup!

And egg cups? In the year 2000, who regularly eats a soft-boiled egg for breakfast?

And marmalades and mustards? What woman (or man) removes marmalade from its glass jar and places it into a special container all its own? Or who has the time to fill the tiny mustard jar? Now cream soups held on much longer — they fought a good fight down until the mid-1960s, but now the double handled cream soup bowl has disappeared (forever?) just as the smaller, slightly taller double-handled bouillon cup gave up the ghost sometime soon after World War I.

The large footed salad bowl? Where would one store such a large piece, just to bring out for a Christmas punch once a year! And relish trays with compartments so hard to clean! And syrups — what is wrong with syrup squeezed directly from its plastic bottle? And compartment plates? They are still unnecessary superannuated items from the 1930s!

However, there are several vintage items that cause wonderment about why they were not translated to the Post86 line.

The ashtray? Even with all the negative feeling directed toward to smoking today, the ashtray still has its role to play in restaurants.

And the ice pitcher! This piece could be practically occupied today, and, while not as graceful as the carafe, it would, perhaps do the job in a much better fashion. But of the 22 vintage Fiesta pieces not making the 1986 transition, not thought necessary to the world of 2000, only two or three have the slight possibility of,

in the future, being belatedly chosen to cross over!

Studying the list of shared pieces can be rewarding. These are, obviously, the items thought absolutely vital to the Post86 line — decisions made at the highest managerial and artistic levels at Homer Laughlin. Look at the illustrated page sent out to wholesalers, jobbers, and important Homer Laughlin China customers perhaps as early as late 1985 (pg. 47). This page consists of actual photographs of those vintage pieces — translated, transposed, and fully vitrified — thought to have the most appeal to commercial customers. Are these the crème de la crème of the older pieces? Not exactly in terms of design, but probably in terms of appeal.

It is worth remembering the company had no way of actually knowing if the proposed 1986 line would be successful: the acceptance of new Fiesta was certainly not the proverbial "bird in the hand!" Like the "bird in the bush," customers for this newly proposed ware had to be enticed and cajoled. Money was the bottom line. It was bantered about (because of a newspaper article posted on the wall of the retail outlet) that this "new" Fiesta was, at the beginning, viewed only as a money-maker to allow Homer Laughlin China to update equipment to fulfill commercial orders for white ware! (As reported in *Fiesta Collector's Quarterly.* Winter 1995, Issue 17, p. 6.) Remember three of the 31 Post86 pieces offered in 1986 were new to the line: the bouillon, the stacking fruit, and the 9½" platter.

The large disc pitcher (another signature piece, much more so than the ice-lip pitcher) was brought unaltered, and the small version was simply a heavier reworking of the popular and highly collectible vintage promotional juice pitcher. Recognition reflects the power of positive merchandising.

The sauceboat — an exact twin, barely distinguishable, old from new! The shakers, the bud vase, and the 10" vase, now known as the medium vase, proclaimed the rebirth, the reawakening, the phoenix rising from the ashes of a Fiesta dead and buried for an unlucky 13 years!

Twenty-eight pieces, plus three new ones, poised, ready, and quite able to entice a waiting public into proclaiming the new line the heir of the old!

And as years passed, other vintage pieces of high profile and necessary need bridged their way into the Post86 camp: the mug, the tumbler, the carafe, the rim soup, the AD cup and saucer, even a pie plate/baker. Those remaining behind, for one reason or another, seemingly have lost the chance for renewal!

There are interesting facts to be learned by carefully looking at the Post86 pieces. There are 36 Post86 pieces that are shared with vintage Fiesta, and then 35 the line calls purely its own. Seventy-one items have been available. When the five formally introduced as limited pieces are subtracted, there remain 66 pieces. And here lies a major difference in both marketing and artistic philosophy between the parent Fiesta and its burgeoning offspring Post86. Not one of the 66 pieces has been discontinued. Not so in vintage! As all old Fiesta collectors are aware, before two years had passed Homer Laughlin was in the process of discontinuing vintage items. The 12" compartment plate and the now famous covered onion soup had been dropped by the end of 1937.

To date, only one regular Post86 item has been officially discontinued: the pyramid candleholder, not counting limited edition pieces. A few others have been relegated to a limbo-like state of neither yes nor no: goblet and hostess bowl. These pieces are very problematic in the kiln, a situation which might or might not be solved sometime in the future. There has not been, to my knowledge, any piece discontinued due to public apathy. This can only speak well for Homer Laughlin's marketing research, and the admirable suitability of the designs themselves.

Another reason might be admitted: perhaps the success and continuance of Post86 Fiesta depends very strongly on the existence of an avid and devoted following of passionate collectors! In 1937, 1942, and 1946, Fiesta was purchased for use. Housewives with very little money to spend haunted Woolworth's for bargains, and bought colorful dishes for use, not to put in glass cabinets for display. Today, some 55 years later, the newest Fiesta items are acquired both for casual use and careful collecting. I believe the masters at the Homer Laughlin Company are wisely aware of the collectors in their thousands and thousands, and company decisions are made dependent upon this awareness!

Let us now disregard those decorated pieces aimed mainly at collectors, and that cute but awkward miniature disc pitcher, and weld ourselves to those large and impressive Post86 items well-designed by Jonathan Parry to reflect a new philosophy of potential use.

Bowls ad infinitum: bowls for hostesses, bowls for presentation, bowls on a pedestal, flat bowls for pasta, and oval bowls for mounds of food! Trays in glory: huge trays for pizza, trays (again) for hostesses, trays for serving.

And what about the welled snack plate, the range top shakers, and those tall and stately pedestal mugs, standing all in a row?

When asked, Jonathan Parry answered simply. These pieces were intended for informal home entertaining. Of course, some do fit quite naturally into commercial surroundings, shining with the same glitter in a restaurant as they do on a patio buffet table! But the thrust of many of the Post86 pieces — those pieces with no shadowy twin in vintage ware — is toward breezy, dramatic, and clever but mostly informal entertaining at home.

This, I believe, is the major change experienced by Post86 Fiesta. And it surely reflects the dining habits of Americans in the year 2000. Gone are bone dishes, quaint butter pats, toast racks, and oyster plates! Gone are newports and spooners, baked alaska plates, and tureens for sauces! Gone are comportiers and those innumerable nappies. Gone are those tiny individual open salts standing before each place setting. Gone, all gone.

And in the place of all this charm and all this grace, we are faced with the buffet table and paper napkins — arranged neatly, of course, in the Post86 napkin rings.

Buffet tables, trendy restaurants of all types, and earnest collectors are the backbone gluing together the existence of Post86 Fiesta.

Can we bewail? Can we try to resurrect the times of quiet family meals prepared by a woman whose life was her home? No, all this cannot, and probably should not, be recalled from the grave. We are what we are today, and for better or for worse, we face the future with a long line of Post86 buffet tables and TV trays stretching out before!

Vintage	Both	Post86
Ashtray†	Bowl, Cereal, straight-sided	Bowl, Bouillon
Bowl, Cream soup, handled	Bowl, Rim soup	Bowl, Cereal, stacking
Bowl, Fruit, 4¾"	Bowl, Serving, large	Bowl, Chili
Bowl, Fruit, large	Bowl, Serving, extra large	Bowl, Fruit, stacking
Bowl, Footed salad	Bowl, Mixing	Bowl, Hostess
Bowl, Onion soup, covered	Candleholder, Pyramid (Tripod)	Bowl, Oval vegetable
Bowl, Salad, unlisted (P)	Candleholder, Round (Bulb)	Bowl, Pedestal
Bowl, Tricolator	Carafe	Bowl, Pasta
Casserole, French (P)	Casserole, Covered	Bowl, Presentation
Casserole/Lid (P)	Coffee Pot	Bowl, Tripod
Comport, Footed		Bread Dish

Comport, Sweets
Coffee Pot, AD
Creamer, Stick Handled
Egg Cup
Lids for Mixing bowls (6)
Marmalade
Mustard
Pitcher, Ice
Pitcher, 2-pint
Plate, Chop, 15"
Plate, Compartment 12"
Plate, Compartment, 10½"
Relish Tray (compartments)
Syrup
Teapot, Medium
Tumblers, Juice (P)
Vase, Large 12"

Creamer, Individual
Cup
Cup, AD
Mug
Pie (Plate) Baker (P)
Pitcher, Disc, large
Pitcher, Disc, small (P)
Plate, Dinner, 10"
Plate, Luncheon, 9:
Plate, Salad, 7"
Plate, B & B, 6"
Plate, Chop (*)
Platter, Medium (11½") (**)
Sauceboat
Saucer
Saucer, AD
Shaker, Pepper
Shaker, Salt
Sugar, Individual
Sugar/creamer/tray (P)
Teapot, Large
Tray, Utility
Tumbler
Vase, Bud
Vase, Medium
Vase, Small

Butterdish, Covered
Candleholder, Millennium
Clock
Cup, Jumbo
Goblet
Lamp
Lamp, Teapot
Mug, Pedestal
Napkin Rings
Ornament, Dancing Girl (D)
Ornament, Holly
Pitcher, Disc, Miniature
Plate, Welled Snack
Platter, Large, 13½"
Platter, Small, 9½"
Saucer (for Jumbo cup)
Shelf sign (D)
Shaker, Rangetop, Pepper
Shaker, Rangetop, Salt
Spoon Rest (***)
Teapot, 2-cup
Tray, Hostess, 12¼"
Tray, Pizza, 15"
Tray, Round serving, 11"
Vase I, Millennium
Vase II, Millennium
Vase III, Millennium

†A number of Post86 ashtrays are known to exist as experimental deep within the HLC factory. Made from the bottoms of the teapot, they bear the Fiesta mark and are styled with one to four cigarette rests.

(*)We are considering the vintage chop plate analogous to the Post86 11½" chop plate.

(**)The vintage 12" platter and the Post86 11½" platter have the identical shape. The Post86 13½" plate is entirely different. See section on the platters on page 115.

(***)Officially, vintage spoon rests were made for Rhythm but were used with Harlequin, not vintage Fiesta.

(D) These pieces are decorated, but still considered true Post86 Fiesta.

(P) Promotional items in the vintage line.

Comparison of three Fiesta teapots in red. Left to right, large vintage teapot, Post86 teapot, medium vintage teapot.

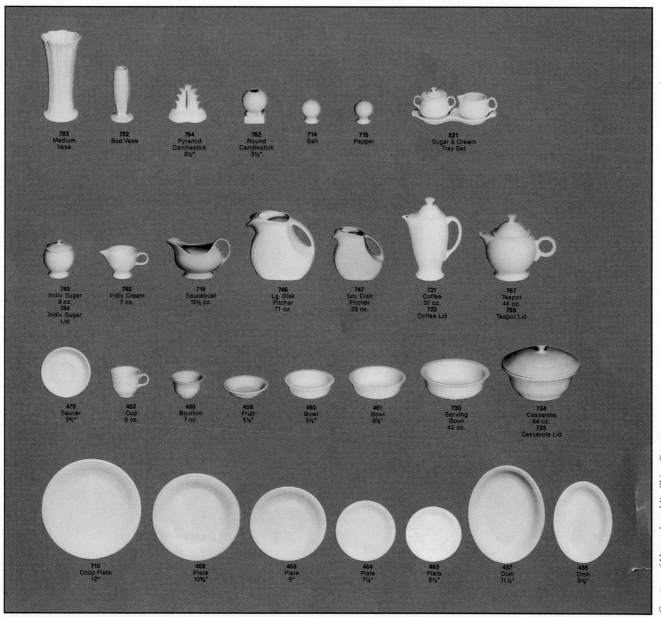

This advertising sheet from 1986, shows the assortment of new Fiesta originally offered that year. This is the only time actual photos of the pieces were used. Within a few years, some of the official numbers were changed. The bouillon, the fruit, and the 9½" dish (platter) were not available in the vintage Fiesta line.

Courtesy of Homer Laughlin China Company

F I E S T A ® S H A P E S

463 Plate B&B 6-1/8"
464 Plate Salad 7-1/4"
465 Plate Luncheon 9"
466 Plate Dinner 10-1/2"
467 Plate Chop 11-3/4"

760 Snack Plate w/well 10-1/2"

456 Platter No. 6 9-5/8"
457 Platter No. 8 11-5/8"
458 Platter No. 10 13-5/8"

468 Round Serving Tray 11"

753 Hostess Tray 12 1/4"

    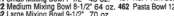 

470 Saucer 5-7/8"
477 Saucer A.D. 4-7/8"
293 Jumbo Saucer 6-3/4"

765 Pedestal Bowl 9 7/8" 64 oz.

460 Bowl Sm. 5-5/8" 14-1/4 oz.
461 Bowl Med. 6-7/8" 19 oz.
471 Bowl Veg. Lg. 1 qt.
455 Bowl Veg. Ex. Lg. 2 qt.

421 Small Mixing Bowl 7-1/2" 48 oz.
422 Medium Mixing Bowl 8-1/2" 64 oz.
482 Large Mixing Bowl 9-1/2" 70 oz.

451 No. 7 Rim Soup 9" 13-1/4 oz.
462 Pasta Bowl 12" 21-3/4 oz.

495 Covd. Casserole 51-1/2 oz.

459 Fruit 5-3/8" 6-1/4 oz.
472 Stacking Cereal Bowl 6-1/2" 11 oz.

450 Bouillon 6-3/4 oz.

452 Cup 7-3/4 oz.

453 Mug 10-1/4 oz.

149 Jumbo Cup 18 oz.
098 Chili Bowl 18 oz. No Handle

424 Pedestal Mug 18 oz.

487 Deep Dish Pie Baker 10-1/8"

766 Tripod Bowl

499 Relish/Utility Tray 9-1/2"

446 Tumbler 6-1/2 oz.

473 Fiesta® Clock

497 Salt 2-1/4" Pepper 2-1/4" Salt & Pepper Set

756 Rangetop Salt & Pepper

488 Round Candlestick 3-5/8"

469 Napkin Rings 4-Piece Set

821 Sugar & Cream Tray Set

498 Indiv. Covd. Sugar 8-3/4 oz.

492 Indiv. Cream 7 oz.

486 Sauceboat 18-1/2 oz.

494 Covd. Butter

489 Pyramid Candlestick 3-3/8"

476 Cup A.D. 3 oz.

493 Covd. Coffee 36 oz.

496 Covd. Teapot 44 oz.

764 Teapot 2 Cup

484 Disc Pitcher Lg. 67-1/4 oz.
485 Disc Pitcher Sm. 28 oz.
475 Miniature Disc Pitcher 4-3/4 oz.

448 Carafe w/handle 60 oz.

491 Medium Vase 9-5/8"

490 Bud Vase 6"

THE HOMER LAUGHLIN CHINA CO.

Courtesy of Homer Laughlin China Company

Future of Post86 Fiesta: An Essay

Way back when — in the last millennium — when Post86 Fiesta was first introduced, an acquaintance began buying the new Fiesta by the boxes and simply "laying it down." It was being treated like vintage wine, or ripening wheels of English cheddar to be broached some 50 years hence and sold. Wonder how many other collectors began to do the same; have the same approach, have the same philosophy of purchasing the Post86 line, and then, growing old with it, would open up boxes of now valuable dinnerware to sell as a hedge against the inflation of 2036?

It is hard to believe that in the depths of the Depression, collectors (if there were any back in those grim years) were buying red Fiesta, solely to figure out which pieces would be the most valuable in 1986. Which would it be? We all have exceptional hindsight. How could anyone, even the most astute, know that turquoise onion soups would be a flaming hot item some 50 years later. And yet, this is what my acquaintance, who resides on one of those long, thin barrier islands on the west coast of Florida, and others are now attempting to do. He is still a youngish man, and hopefully will be able, in 2036, to handle the brisk sale of his Post86 black, white, rose, and apricot dishes.

Well maybe!

This does not mean that I wonder if he can handle the sales: it means I wonder if

those sales will be brisk!

Would the new generation of collectors of American dinnerware be clamoring for Post86 pieces when the year 2000 reached middle age? Would the belief that to age along with ripening apricot dinnerware would sufficiently augment the personal bank balance in 2050? In 1988 and 1990, I thought not!

As a Depression baby, the grimness of the early to mid-1930s cannot be remembered. I remember only fighting an afternoon nap; having lunch with Margaret, my grandmother's black housekeeper; getting baby alligators sent from Florida by my aunt; and listening to "Jack Armstrong" and "The Shadow" on my small Philco radio. The problems of finance passed me by.

These were the introductory years of Fiesta; all I can truly remember is a rose Harlequin jug for milk. Nothing more! But as the '30s swept into the '40s, I can remember other things: the dramatic upheaval World War II had on my home-centered mother; the radio-centered living room with the Lux Radio Theater; the family-centered dining room with real china; and the dark pressing outside on the window pane.

These feelings could certainly not be duplicated in 2036 by those collectors looking back through the years to their childhood in the waning years of the second millennium!

So, it was decided, my friend's 1988 squirreling of unopened cartons of Post86 black place settings was futile. So I thought. But was it really?

After only some 15 years, having just broken the barrier into the new millennium, my rather elitist beliefs are now crumbling. My personal feelings for the '30s and '40s could never be duplicated, but perhaps with different trends and different remembrances, collectors, once young children in 1990, will in 2036 or 2040 or 2050, have their own compelling memories leading them to gaze back with yearning, propelled by their own nostalgia.

I cannot imagine what society will be like in 2050, and, as has been said before and will be said again: I will then be dead and have other more important things on my mind! My growing old with dinnerware is almost finished. I have the past, but how can I state that Post86 Fiesta will not be avidly sought in the future? Greedily be collected in 2050?

Perhaps, my friend whom I thought silly will smile (if he remembers me at all) and think of me as a fool for not having left behind dozens and dozens of unopened boxes of lilac and chartreuse, and most certainly juniper!

So why has my opinion been drastically altered? I do not pretend to predict the future in conjunction with anything as really unimportant (in the true scheme of life) as collecting American dinnerware, but I see trends.

These trends were natural, unpremeditated, in the years between 1936 and 1960. However, between 1986 and 2000, the trends, the plans, the schemes (if you will) for Post86 Fiesta vis-à-vis collectibility have been carefully choreographed and manipulated by astute marketing and definite decisions made by a few clever people at the Homer Laughlin Company.

Is this a negative statement? Is there a modicum of faultfinding in these words?

No, no, and no! The Homer Laughlin marketing and sales department and the art department are certainly to be admired. They have made Post86 Fiesta potentially a powerful and desired collectible in 2050.

How has this been accomplished? First, it should be remembered that Rhead developed some marketing and sales campaign schemes on his own: the individual sugar, creamer, and figure-8 tray of 1939 – 1943, the French casserole, the promotional pie plate and casserole, the 30-oz. juice pitcher. But these were items aimed to be cheap and aimed to interest any flagging consumers. They represented a one-time effort, not a determined and long-term philosophic approach presently emanating from the offices and corridors of Homer Laughlin China.

What is this philosophic approach? It is admirable, thoughtful, and based on clear and very clever marketing approaches. They are:

Limited color: Starting with lilac, Homer Laughlin China in conjunction with certain well-known retail mega-stores, has discovered the limited colors enflame the passion of potential collectors. Certainly limited colors can hardly influence the buying trends of restaurants and other commercial customers.

Exclusive Items: This approach ensures certain very highly desirable pieces — desired by the collectors, not commercial buyers — are hard to locate. It also makes ordinary pieces (the stackable fruit bowl and the 6" plate) very collectible in carefully selected colors.

Limited Exclusive Items: Not only are these pieces, i.e., the lilac round candleholder, made exclusively for one distributor, but they are produced in very limited numbers.

Clever Distribution: Charity items (i.e., the chartreuse coffee pot, the black Millennium I vase), and surprise sales (i.e., the scandalous retail outlet sale of the chartreuse sugar caddy) keep collector interest reeling and passionate.

There are other approaches geared to excite: we speak of the proclaimed "illegality" of certain Post86 "rogue" pieces in lilac and sapphire. And then the histrionic and over-dramatic disposal of shards of the raspberry presentation bowl! This announcement, complete with photographs, would curdle the sensibilities of Frederick Rhead. Yet all these approaches ensure future interest in many Post86 glazes and pieces. Collectors who disliked lilac and had the lilac ferry boat sail off without them are now determined to get duplicates of every piece produced in juniper. Collectors jump to gather those accessories both awful and admirable. (See the section on Fiesta Accessories.) Incidentally, I have been told the toaster, produced under Homer Laughlin license by Select Brands, is a disaster. It is an item being returned en mass by all the maiden aunts in the country!

But I am wandering. Suffice to say, my friend was wiser than I. Black has recently changed from a limited glaze to a discontinued one. Apricot has been discontinued for over four years. Lilac, sapphire, chartreuse, are also passed but not passé. The Homer Laughlin Company has, by many means, secured the collectibility of Post86 Fiesta for decades to come. So lay down boxes and boxes of juniper, scramble to get that elusive spoon rest or doggie dish, spend your tax refund on one dozen (if you can find them!) limited edition lilac bud vases before the price rises still further! Gather the original variations of the 9½" platter and the handled serving tray. It is all in the whirl we call the collecting game.

Unfortunately today, the rules of the game are set by Homer Laughlin.

Calmly, I will grow old with my Post86 Fiesta in blessed peace.

When Jonathan Parry died in late spring of the year 2000 (Friday, April 28), this very sad event started some wild — and not so wild — speculation. While he did not have carte blanc regarding the introduction of new items, he was in fact, the vital force behind each piece. He was single-handedly, albeit with very admirable and highly talented assistance, the creator of Post 86.

Now that this creative force is gone, it has been asked: will Post86 Fiesta continue in production? Will, or can, the deftly talented Judi Noble (if she indeed is named Art Director) carry the burden? Can new Fiesta exist without the special guidance of Jonathan O. Parry?

Of course, the company keeps mollifying and calming the collectors with soothing words and unctuous pronouncements, and we must admire them for their efforts. But words are easy, and Post86 collectors are learning to be wary.

There is nervousness, a quivering, frantic, frightened behavior among the powers at the Homer Laughlin Company. And a nervous and frightened dog bites. Time after time, decisions have been made that have rankled, disappointed, and angered the collectors who quite frankly have kept the interest in new Fiesta alive. Witness the outrageous action perpetuated against the estates of Mr. Parry and John Pittenger, HLC salesman and controller of Plant Four. Soon after these two HLC executives passed away, security guards went to both residences and blatantly confiscated trial and sample Post86 Fiesta ware! Sales literature was also taken, and all was justified by saying it was stolen property. This behavior severely damages the company's credibility and sent shivers of apprehension throughout the collecting community.

To sully the memory of Jonathan Parry with the word "stolen" is incomprehensible!

Will Post86 Fiesta be officially withdrawn as a wonderful memorial to a great ceramic designer? Or will the new Art Director be allowed to modify and change or return more closely to the design policies of Fiesta's originator Frederick H. Rhead?

Fiesta's retirement would be a magnificent memorial, but would Jonathan approve? Would he have approved of the invasion of his home? Would he have wondered at this treatment? After his existing sketches and designs have been realized as actual Post86 pieces (probably accounting for a good number of production months), would it be correct and wise to cease production and announce: Post86: 1986 – 2002?

Possibly, but I wonder if this announcement would cause Jonathan to smile or to frown.

But no matter my wonderment! The closing months of 2000 have caused a roiling tsunami to flood the Post86 collecting community. Barely one year after the successful introduction of the fourth limited edition color, juniper, suddenly, with little trumpeting and less whistling, cinnabar was announced. All existing pieces would be glazed in this red-brown color, and it would not be subjected to a time limit.

Then came official word that the spoon rest and an absolutely new bread dish would soon be sold through Linen 'n Things. Such events bespeak a continuing vigorous approach. The Homer Laughlin China Company must be healthy, must be in good shape, in good hands. Yet, the collector must remember, France was the leading and most powerful kingdom in the Western world just before the death of Louis XV. It bestrode and dominated Europe in the fields of war, the arts, literature, and even conversation. Yet as he lay dying, the king of this greatest of kingdoms reflected *Apres moi le deluge*! — I wonder.

Post86 Fiesta

The Individual Items

EXCLUSIVITY: A COMMENTARY

As readers begin to pore over the remaining parts of this book — parts dealing mainly with individual pieces of Post86 Fiesta — they will, on a number of occasions, plough into such terms as "exclusive item," or "limited edition." These two terms are two doors that lead ultimately into the exact same space: exclusivity. A piece of Post86 is exclusive either because it can be purchased only through one retail source, or it is exclusive because it is limited in number or span of production.

Exclusivity is a phenomenon unknown to older Fiesta, and bodes not at all positively on the future of the newer Fiesta. It seems to me that Homer Laughlin China is approaching the fringes of desperation, and responding with a franticness to enmesh all collectors (novice and sophisticated) in the "get-it-while-you-can" syndrome. Could it be an HLC marketing philosophy gone wrong? Or perhaps a series of selling decisions reeking slightly of carnival hucksterism? (For a detailed view of what I consider gross "hucksterism," readers are invited to check carefully the section on Fiesta accessories. Naturally, I am not expecting 100% or even 80% approval regarding these opinions, but these are my feelings.) If true, this is a sad, sad departure from the once calm greatness of the Homer Laughlin China Company!

This commentary is being written long after the main sections of the book were shipped off to the editors at Collector Books, although the idea have been nagging and whirling around in my mind for well over a year — taking a great deal of time to jell and settle! Without commenting or responding upon them, the words of other collectors (far more flamboyant than I) were noted, and filed away for reference. Flurries of collector anger, and tiny explosions of volcanic frustrations are beginning to dot various Fiesta message boards on the Internet — often later mollified by honeyed words from HLC's marketing management. All very genteel — as in a Victorian middle-class home where children were soothed with lemon drops and encouraged, gently, not to ask too many questions!

So it is believed that the subject of HLC exclusivity should be examined with objectivity — although this is very difficult, and I could be accused of presenting only subjective views. So be it! Since no collector or group of collectors really knows what goes on in HLC management (although a few might be encouraged by the company to think they do), the inner workings of the Homer Laughlin Company can never, never be publicly known, and thus any opinions expressed here are liable to all manner of refutation.

So, come along with me, and even if you do not agree with my opinions, we can try to sleuth our way onto some level of understanding.

A simple fact — in 1994, only eight years after the introduction of Post86 Fiesta, Homer Laughlin introduced a new and very brilliant glaze, lilac. Of course, the decision to introduce such a color had to be made some time before 1994 — let us say, early in 1993? Or perhaps late in 1992? We turn to the Huxford's words on new Fiesta in the eighth edition of their landmark book: in 1993, new Fiesta presented "a warm sunny Southwestern atmosphere. . . created" by apricot, new turquoise, new yellow, sea mist green. There were also soft periwinkle blue, a very pinky rose, neutral white and black, and a dark, dark, dark cobalt. If you will turn to the section on Post86 color palettes, the relative blandness of this combination can readily be appreciated. Was a change thought necessary? Was a little spice needed to enliven the stew? And if so, why? Could it be in 1993, sales of new Fiesta were slackening somewhat, so that a new color and a new approach were deemed necessary to relight the torch? All speculation, of course, but since the board room powers at HLC are loath to share information with inquisitive researchers and interested collectors, speculate is all we can do. Naturally, as a closed and private corporation, the company is deep within its rights to maintain an aura of secrecy.

Not only did lilac shatter the Southwestern pastel concept, it also introduced a marketing ploy never before known at Homer Laughlin — or at least not to such an extreme! Not only does lilac captivate the eye of the consumer with a pulsating almost psychedelic glaze, but the company also stirs up some shivery fears by proclaiming to the public: "Lilac is limited!"

The Huxfords state: "Lilac Fiesta has the distinction of being the first new Fiesta color to be discontinued." With all respect, this "distinction" is negative and misplaced! Lilac Fiesta's true distinction lies in the fact that it introduced a new, slightly wild and confusing marketing policy — a policy that is raging on today almost out of control: the HLC marketing strategy of "say it is exclusive, say it is limited, and the public (collectors?) will clamber to get it!"

Lilac worked! Even though a good number of the collecting and commercial public were polarized over the glaze, it worked — and now, some six years after it was discontinued, prices for lilac pieces are still escalating. Rumors also abound. Even though HLC officials declare that lilac is "gone forever," there is an influential group of Post86 aficionados which remains unconvinced — and harbors sincere hopes that lilac will appear again. Are there really vats of lilac glaze hidden in storage warehouses waiting to be reawakened? This is really a moot point, but it does show what Homer Laughlin says is not always taken as gospel. There is a growing concern that the company's public declarations are not always exactly correct!

The famous, although now somewhat forgotten, debacle of the chartreuse sugar caddies, further enhanced and strengthened the aura of mistrust. Today, the words of the HLC marketing gurus tend to be weighed and interpreted rather than accepted as gospel. The rightness or wrongness of this attitude is not the question, the fact of its existence is the important point.

Bloomingdale's, carefully noting the success of lilac, countered by arranging with Homer Laughlin to be the sole retailer of sapphire. This deeply saturated glaze was the first color to be both limited and exclusive: limited to only some 180 production days (1997); limited also to very few pieces; and exclusive to Bloomingdale's.

At this point — toward the end of 1997 — company management could have maintained some sense of equitable sanity, but perhaps forces unknown outside the well-closed Board Room compelled decisions on and on into the realms of befuddled exclusivity! Chartreuse popped onto the scene with a widely announced two-year limited run and a series of exclusive items. Probably the many individual retailers bid upon the right to various Post86 pieces. Collectors (and this decision had to be aimed solely at the collector!) excitedly dodged here and there to win the ultimate prizes of chartreuse tripods, medium vases, 9" oval platters. Lists, announcements, suggestions, and telephone numbers, fluttered throughout Internet cyberspace! Excitement, thrilling, questing, and only a few began to become aware of the long complicated marketing tunnel into which Post86 collectors were being led.

Pile it on! Wrap it up! Keep them going! Thus collectors continued to be led. Like a rollercoaster out of control, the approaching end of 1999 impaled before the reaching hands, Millennium Vase I, then Millennium Vase II, and Millennium Vase III — all absolutely necessary, all limited, and exclusive in some manner or another! Very "un-Fiesta-like" candlesticks, presentation bowls, disc pitchers — "only 500 made!" Exclusive, exclusive! Get yours before they disappear — buy two, get three, get them for resale later to those unfortunates not as quick and as smart as you!

Carnival tactics surely!

Everyone (well, almost everyone) became embroiled in this get, get, get! Bunny dishes for Easter, exclusive to the HLC outlet! Halloween pumpkin-faced pie plates in persimmon, happy little reindeer sets for Christmas celebration, planet plates and pitchers exclusive to the American Museum of Natural History! Dillard's mugs and pitchers, superannuated juice pitchers exclusive to a collector association, plates and tumbles, pie bakers and be-rosed vases, all limited and exclusive! All whirlpooling around dizzily to be snapped up and carried off as ultimate prizes by collectors — many of whom, unfortunately, were responding to the conditioned, well-Pavlov-ed, schemes of the HLC marketing board room. Introduce a new item, report it as a limited edition — and watch it sell!

All this well-choreographed planning works only if the public continues to lunge at the carrot. By summer 2000, thoughtful collectors were beginning to see the light and voice their complaints.

The Millennium Vase I was (1) exclusive to Bloomingdale's and (2) limited to 1,000 vases in each of 10 colors. Fine! Wonderful! If a collector purchased 10 Millie I vases in pearl gray (for Christmas gifts or personal use) from Bloomingdale's for $34.95 each, there would only be 990 other pearl gray Millie I's out there in the wide collector world!

Not so! To arrive at 1,000 vases suitable for Bloomingdale's shipment, Homer Laughlin produced hundreds and hundreds more — 1,400 vases, 1,800 vases, 2,200 vases in pearl gray, many with very minor flaws, and these "extras" (after the well-stated 1,000 were shipped to Bloomingdale's) were not destroyed to preserve the integrity of the original announced number, but sent to the Seconds Room of the HLC Retail Outlet to be purchased by dealers and sold via the Internet or in malls. Unlike the *Fiesta Collector's Quarterly* items (Moon-over-Miami and Sunporch), the Millennium Vase I was not numbered, was not controlled, and the announced number of 1,000 vases in pearl gray was meaningless.

However, it was noted that one thoughtful and intelligent collector came up with an explanation, and a refutation that Bloomingdale's was guilty of wrong-doing! In other words, Bloomingdale's announced that the Millennium Vase I (in pearl gray) was exclusive to them, and they would sell only 1,000 in each of 10 colors. And that was true! When pearl gray vase number 1,000 left the store, there were no more.

It has been reported that Bloomingdale's wanted to purchase more Millie I's to sell, but when the buyers approached Homer Laughlin, the company replied negatively. The mega-store had contracted for only

10,000 vases divided into 10 colors — no more would be shipped! Sounds great! But in the meantime, exclusivity for the Millie I shifted from Bloomingdale's to the HLC outlet where hundreds and hundreds of Millie I seconds (many in excellent condition) were being purchased for resale.

It seems the goblets and millennium candleholders underwent the same exploitation. Consumers ordering these exclusive and limited pieces — at quite substantial prices — waited months and months, undergoing so-called cancellations, and finally received bubbled, under-glazed, spotty, and otherwise defective items — while at the HLC outlet in Newell, West Virginia, so-called seconds in much better condition were available for anyone fortunate to be able to shop there.

In fact, the entire "shopping process" has become frustrating and sometimes funny. Goblets arrived from Bloomingdale's broken or in terrible condition, and replacements were promised. However, one commentator on the Internet remarks: "My friend was told she would receive another chartreuse goblet in December. In February, she called again and they (Bloomingdale's) said that they could not replace it. She told them that she wanted two cobalt ones instead. They agreed. A week later, she received the chartreuse one."

Consumers continue to chatter about the haphazard approach to exclusive Post86 Fiesta. To illustrate, I include some recent quotes from a popular public Post86 Internet message board — one with enough clout to have Dave Conley (HLC Marketing Director) as a reasonably regular reader! (Copies have been made of these postings, and they are available for those interested; for the present, the commentators will be anonymous.)

"I was told that 1,000 Millie I vases were made in each color, after which the molds were destroyed. Now it appears there were just as many, or maybe more seconds. Who knows. But that was wrong. . . All limited editions not shipped should have been destroyed. It is the same with the Millie candlesticks. From what I hear, the goblets have been a horror story for some as well. I decided to forego them altogether. [And] aren't we still seeing sapphire coming out of the [S]econds [R]oom years after it is supposedly discontinued. It's all become a game."

And then this perceptive writer nails the cover on tightly by saying:

"It is a classic and clever marketing strategy; create demand by limiting supply. Too bad it's a completely bogus limit. I have decided to stop chasing the exclusive and ignore the limited edition claims unless it is from someone like Joel @ FCQ [Joel Wilson, editor of the *Fiesta Collector's Quarterly*] where, I believe, the number is truly limited." (The *Fiesta Collector's Quarterly* sponsors a number of exclusive Post86 items: the Moon-over-Miami and Sunporch pieces plus the popular shelf signs.)

Another reader of this same message board adds:

"I guess the point I was making is just don't [HLC] lie to us — make as many as you want, but don't go advertising and saying only a certain number were made. I have decided not to buy anymore so-called limited either. I like Fiesta but something about the way they do business just rubs me the wrong way. It's just not honest and I would like to think of Fiesta as being honest American made, like apple pie, not just out for the extra dollar."

Wonder if the Homer Laughlin marketing pundits read and digested these comments — only two of many similar ones? No official rebuttal was posted, and the entire question of exclusivity continues to float in limbo!

Thus, exclusivity and limitedness — when pompously announced to create excitement and initiate a feeding frenzy among collectors — mean little and really signify nothing! Collectors (and I still maintain, new HLC marketing policies are aimed solely at the collector — this I repeat again and again) must become educated about a company's (any company's) sales gimmicks, and react with calm reflection. Yes, I do admit, my personal reaction to exclusivity announcements was not always calm and reflective: I grabbed along with many others. Remember, it took me over a year to come to these conclusions! But when I paused and asked why? — why am I buying Millennium candleholders in all available colors when I am not really sure that I like them? Why am I snapping up goblets when they have been known to explode when filled with hot liquid? If the answer is "because they are exclusive and limited," then the perceptive collector stops right there! I had fallen, like many others, deep into the sweet miasma of exclusivity!

Let Homer Laughlin and all the attendant companies that produce the accessories say what they will. It is their absolute right. But weigh their words, and analyze. Exclusivity? What's in a word?

Explanation regarding the individual item sections:

1. Pieces are listed alphabetically by category (i.e., Bowl).
2. The names of the pieces are those used in the Homer Laughlin China advertising sheets (i.e., Cup rather than Teacup).
3. For convenience, certain pieces have been placed together (i.e., Bowls, Stacking, Plates, Platters) and all saucers are listed with their cups.
4. An identification photograph appears at the beginning of each section.
5. Each section includes some vital statistics:

   a. Number: the official number given to each particular piece by Homer Laughlin China. If the number has been replaced by another, the original number is placed in parentheses, [i.e., Covered Coffee (721), Lid (722), 493]. If the number is not known, it will appear as 000.
   b. Mold Book: if known the date is given when the piece was last listed in the Mold Book.
   c. Introduced: the time the piece was first offered to the public. This date is often approximate (i.e., Spring of 1994).
   d. Mark: identifying stamp or indented or raised letter or word on item.
   e. Size: the official size is given.
   f. Liquid measurement: since the official measurement changes or can seem incorrect, each piece of hollowware was personally measured to the top. N/A means not applicable.
   g. Popularity: this is an objective listing, but please remember, some subjectivity is bound to be present. There are four categories:
   ❀ Exceptional: nearly all Post86 collectors strive to get this item in all available colors; some even pay exceptional prices for illegal pieces.
   ❀ Above average: considered a "must have" piece but not in all colors.
   ❀ Average.
   ❀ Below average.
   Popularity has nothing to do with use; everyone needs Post86 plates to use but not necessarily to collect.
   h. Color availability: only those colors officially produced. "Rogue" (illegal) items will be discussed in the text.
   i. Changes: refers only to changes appearing after the items were introduced as Post86. Any difference between vintage pieces and Post86 counterparts will be discussed in the text.

Bouillon Cup

BOUILLON CUP

Number: 450
Mold Book: March 26, 1986
Introduced: One of the original 1986 pieces.
Mark: Early examples have incised mark with dated stamp. In a few cases the incised mark can be barely noted.
Size: Height: 2¼"
     Width: 4"
Liquid Measurement: 6¾ oz.
Popularity: Exceptional
Color Availability: All colors except sapphire.
Changes: None

A lucky thirteen bouillon cups.

The bouillon cup was one of the 33 items to be offered in 1986, and, at that time, it was the only piece to be totally new to the Post86 line. The two other "new" pieces — 9½" platter and the 5¼" stacking fruit bowl — were not exactly, not technically new. Both had made an appearance in Fiesta Ironstone. So its uniqueness makes the bouillon somewhat special!

Also there is something enticing about when the bouillon was mentioned in the mold book. The date generally given for the reintroduction of new Fiesta is February 28, 1986. Yet the first mold book mention of the bouillon is March 26, 1986. There can be two explanations:

1. After the initial viewing of Post86, a retail representative made a suggestion about the inclusion of a very small bowl that would prove useful to the commercial (restaurant) customer.

2. Even if the Homer Laughlin China marketing

experts had definite plans to have the bouillon bowl, the time needed to produce the entire line in all its pieces took long enough to allow this bowl to be designed nearly one month after the formal reintroduction.

Watching in late 2000 and early 2001 how the new color cinnabar was introduced piece by piece, the second explanation seems logical. When a new color is introduced, it is usually first available in place setting, then platters and bowls and mugs: the essentials. Only after the customers have been enticed does the company begin to send forth bouillon, coffee servers, candleholders, and mixing bowls. This makes sense to me.

The bouillon does not appear in the mysterious 1986 brochure (along with stacking fruit, 5½" bowl, 9½" oval platter, and the 11½" oval platter). This brochure is discussed in another section. Even when the first official brochure was circulated, and all the above items were listed, the 9" luncheon plate was still missing. Thirty-three pieces of Post86 Fiesta could not possibly appear, full-blown, in a store's display rooms in one cataclysmic day! It takes time.

No matter if it appeared a week or so late, the bouillon quickly climbed up the ladder of success to become one of the most popular of the line. The reasons are mainly its small, slightly chubby size, its modest price, and its availability in all colors (except sapphire). The piece is homey, friendly, accessible, and, as a practical matter, very useable. Suggestions are said to have been made to the Homer Laughlin China moguls regarding a little lid modeled for the bouillon to adapt it for creme brulee, the burnt cream of Thomas Jefferson fame!

But the modest little bouillon has been around for many years, just doing its humble job, enjoying continual popularity, with no little lid yet to be seen!

Hostess Bowl

The catalog photographs were impressive, but as often happens, the difference between a photograph and the actual piece was monumental. This does not mean the bowl disappointed — no, just the opposite. It is a small, delightfully chunky bowl which, or so it seems, has an undetermined use.

And why a "hostess" bowl? In these days of political social correctness, it would seem the name is sexist. In fact, a number of "hosts" wondered if its use was exclusively feminine! Jonathan Parry once told me (and perhaps this has been mentioned before) Homer Laughlin shies away from naming a Post86 piece to imply a specific use. However, the term "hostess" (or "host") seems rather slap-dash! But it does imply this new bowl joined the growing number of home entertaining items now swelling the ranks.

What about the popcorn bowl? It seems ideal for this purpose. Or pretzel bowl? That is also appropriate. Or even better — snack bowl? I like that quite well. The piece is small for serving salad, the wrong size for mixing or tossing, and has a very unusual and distinctive shape — a shape that quite sets it apart from the usual bowl configuration. Note the deep lip giving a very high vertical rim. This might be considered "wasted space" in a more plebian bowl design. And the embossed architectural design (here four) that ranges about the sides harkens back to the presentation bowl and can be found on the goblets and the millennium candleholders.

And that brings up another interesting bit of news about the bowl! Simply turn it upside down and at once the collector notices that now the embossed design is pointing the correct direction — all the tips up! Also the high rim is now a very settled and sub-

---

HOSTESS BOWL

Number: 431
Mold Book: Not known
Introduced: January 2000. The first new piece of the year.
Mark: Incised and date stamped. See illustration.
Size: Height: 3¾"; Width: (top) 7⅝", (base) 4"
Liquid Measurement: 25 oz. (to the inside rim)
Popularity: Average
Color Availability: Seen in white, rose, cobalt, periwinkle, persimmon, pearl gray.
Changes: none

---

stantial base — securely binding the piece to the tabletop. The rumor being reflected among collectors is that the hostess (host) bowl is a clever redesign of the pillar candleholder. Yes, the base, now the top, would certainly hold (if a little deeper) one of those large single candles of the paschal type. Why the pillar candleholder was abandoned (if it really was) cannot be known at the present time. If the rumor is true, this new bowl — the first Post86 Fiesta piece of the year 2000 — is a wonderful example of clever adaptability.

The hostess bowl is not an upside down pedestal, although it looks very similar, and even might have suggested such an item. Why? Because actual Post86 pedestals do exist, but are only sequestered in the company's Art Department. They will probably never be made. However, who can really tell! Since Jonathan

Parry's death and until a new art director is named, there is no firm authority supervising artistic decisions. Mr. Parry must have been involved in the design of the pedestals, and now these two pieces languish without a champion. If, and when, some talented person is appointed to head the Art Department, it can be assumed he or she will champion new personal ideas and agendas, so it is quite possible the pedestals will be assigned to oblivion.

They come in two sizes and two different shapes:

large (convex) 7¾" base, 4¾" top
small (convex) 6¼" base, 4½" top.

These rather unique pieces have been glazed in turquoise and chartreuse. Collectors addicted to Candy Fagerlin's excellent website, fiestafanatic.com, should be able to recall seeing the pedestals in one of the photographs she posted some months ago: a scene of the Art Department's work room. The large pedestal was seen, holding a large paschal candle, on a display table.

For some reason, I believe Mr. Rhead would approve!

The underside of the rose hostess bowl. Notice it has the stamp and the incised mark.

An interesting "tower" of hostess bowls. Top to bottom, pearl gray, persimmon, cobalt blue, white, and turquoise. Note the large glaze slip at the base of the turquoise bowl. This fault is very abundant on the bowl — in fact, the HLC retail outlet is very well supplied with the hostess bowl with problems!

The only problem with the hostess bowl is that the points of the Art Deco design seem to be going in the wrong direction. Here the cobalt bowl is reversed and suddenly it looks like a base of something, perhaps the canceled pillar candleholder?

Vegetable Bowl

VEGETABLE BOWL

Number: 409
Mold Book: Not known
Introduced: Late 1999
Mark: See illustration.
Size: 12" x 9"
Liquid Measurement: N/A
Popularity: Below average
Color Availability: Not available in black, apricot, lilac, sapphire, chartreuse, juniper.
Changes: None

This is another late 1999 Post86 Fiesta introduction. This large, heavy, and potentially very useful serving bowl could easily take the place of the small, more delicate Fiesta Mate that until now was the oval bowl of the line. But perhaps there is still room for a smaller bowl of oval dimensions.

This bowl is so large there would have to be a considerable number of people sitting down at the table. So large, albeit well-proportioned, it really could be divided into two parts for more practical service. There have been a number of requests for a divided bowl and as yet none has appeared. This leads one to wonder about the kiln factors of this type of piece; perhaps it just would not survive in the super-heated firing process.

This might fit in superbly as a buffet item. In fact, many of the recent items in the Post86 line tend to be

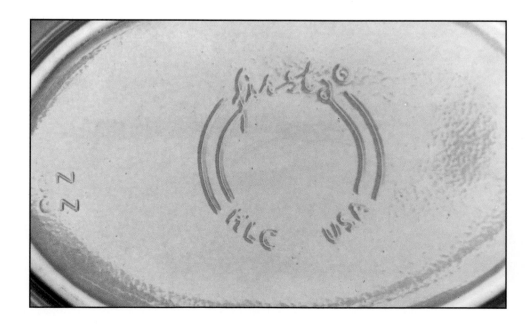

more usable for informal home entertaining. Mr. Parry was kind enough to reply when asked about this tendency. Yes, home entertaining was "in," and HLC was trying to fill this need.

At first, this large item was hard to locate and quite expensive; the price wavers in the mid $20s. It is difficult to contemplate the average collector gathering one in each available color — this would mean an investment of around $225.00. The piece simply is not that collectible which reflects in the below average popularity. Another condition might limit consumer enthusiasm; having seen more then 12 of these bowls, not one has been perfect! The open, nearly flat well is prone to bubbles, bursts, flecks, and other factory flaws. The public pulls back from such conditions, and this must be corrected before interest grows. Unfortunately, this piece is not cute as are the napkin rings, the tumbler, and the candleholders, so perhaps its size precludes much collector fascination.

This bowl was not offered in the two limited edition colors being produced in late 1999 and 2000, chartreuse and juniper, and yet was announced in cinnabar even before that glaze was available. The incised mark on all the examples examined is accompanied by additional initials referring to the modeler.

The HLC Retail Outlet has a new system to help customers ascertain which Post86 pieces are available in what colors. While just relatively easy to use, the site (hlchina.com) can still be helpful. Checking for glazes appearing on the vegetable bowl, the following chart appeared.

ITEM	PATTERN	DESCRIPTION	PATTERN NAME	LIST PRICE	UOM	PACK	WEIGHT
0409	0100	Oval Serving Bowl	Fiesta White	29.340	EA	4	13.000
0409	0102	Oval Serving Bowl	Fiesta Cinnabar	29.340	EA	4	13.000
0409	0103	Oval Serving Bowl	Fiesta Rose	29.340	EA	4	13.000
0409	0105	Oval Serving Bowl	Fiesta Cobalt Blue	29.340	EA	4	13.000
0409	0106	Oval Serving Bowl	Fiesta Yellow	29.340	EA	4	13.000
0409	0107	Oval Serving Bowl	Fiesta Turquoise	29.340	EA	4	13.000
0409	0108	Oval Serving Bowl	Fiesta Periwinkle Blue	29.340	EA	4	13.000
0409	0109	Oval Serving Bowl	Fiesta Seamist Green	29.340	EA	4	13.000
0409	0114	Oval Serving Bowl	Fiesta Persimmon	29.340	EA	4	13.000
0409	0118	Oval Serving Bowl	Fiesta Pearl Gray	29.340	EA	4	13.000

Pasta Bowl

PASTA BOWL

Number: 462
Mold Book: January 3, 1990 (as a big rim soup)
Introduced: c. 1990
Mark: Non-dated and dated stamp
Size: 12"
Liquid Measurement: 21¾ oz.
Popularity: Below average
Color Availability: All colors except sapphire.
Changes: None

The first point to note regarding the new pasta bowl is quite simple: it is not an enlarged rim soup. While superficially the same (except for size), once viewed together the differences are easily seen. The rim on the rim soup is much narrower in proportion and is slightly curved upwards; the pasta bowl's rim is wider and is absolutely flat. The drawing of the piece on the advertising sheet is of the pasta bowl, not the soup bowl.

The pasta bowl is very impressive and stately. The width (2½") and the flatness of the rim become a foil for the rings. They are presented marvelously, especially in persimmon with its opaque qualities. However, the rim does have one negative quality: it takes up a great deal of space!

Did Homer Laughlin wish the hostess to use one of these bowls for each guest? Could be, but the size works against this use. However where drama is necessary, putting this bowl in each place setting (with the chop plate underneath) would certainly catch the eye. Probably much more suitable in a restaurant where drama is in demand!

In fact, this bowl could have been generated mainly for commercial use. It really fails as any type of serving bowl (Post86 has so many others more suitable), or a centerpiece. I did see it once used as a base for a very elegant and formal Japanese floral arrangement —

with those gloriously smooth stones filling the center space and disguising the needle holder. There are some clever nonfood uses for this impressive piece.

The persimmon glaze allows the multitude of rings to display themselves with great beauty.

Pedestal Bowl

PEDESTAL BOWL

Number: **765**
Mold Book: **Feburary 5, 1997**
Introduced: **1997**
Mark: **Circular raised "Fiesta" with dated stamp within.**
Size: **Width: 9⅞"**
Liquid Measurement: **64 oz.**
Popularity: **Average**
Color Availability: **All colors except black, apricot, lilac, and sapphire.**
Changes: **None**

Post86 Fiesta is alive with bowls, all sorts of bowls: 14 of them if those who are in charge of the tally include both the limited edition presentation bowl and the chili bowl. In my personal estimation, the pedestal bowl is the most gracefully designed. Structurally, this footed bowl has no direct antecedent in vintage Fiesta unless is fills the same niche as did the 12" comport in the earlier line?

And what might that niche be? Certainly not for serving mashed potatoes or Lanttulaatikko (the earthy mashed baked rutabagas of Finnish fame) to a Sunday supper horde! The pedestal bowl can hardly be considered a serving bowl at all! The pedestal is approximately ¾" tall, and not only do four concentric rings appear on the bowl's surface, the pedestal itself has two distinct and decorative rings, just as did the vin-

tage comport! The pedestal is seen as a slight hollow within the bowl. All this obvious artistry leads the collector to believe a higher role was predestined here.

When dealing with the straight-sided bowls, I described the newest and the largest (#455) as a possible centerpiece float bowl. Now I am not so sure. The pedestal bowl, by reason of its more delicate design, is a more likely candidate as the table centerpiece, filled with fruit or with the judicious use of a flower frog as a container for a flower arrangement — quite Deco with callas and clivias in flame and orange! My crystal flower frog with the bulging eyes fits snugly within the interior hollow.

Yes, this well-proportioned bowl has many uses on table and sideboard, the least of which is serving!

Rim Soup Bowl

Just as the vintage deep plate (in more modern terms referred to as the rim soup) was not an original member of the Fiesta family in January 1936, so the Post86 Fiesta version had to wait for a while until it became available in the early 1990s; the vintage piece waited only a few months (August 1936), the new rim soup waited nearly four years. It was first mentioned in the mold book on January 3, 1990, and appeared publicly shortly after that date.

Not only is the new version much heavier, it is almost ¾" larger: fully 9" as opposed to the older 8¼". The reason for the enlargement cannot really be deduced. The Huxfords mention that the deep plate is often thought to be a salad plate, so perhaps a survey among the potential commercial purchasers of the new line hinted at a slightly larger shape.

Bowls for soup have always been part of all dinnerware lines, and there are two types of the shallow wide bowl: one with a flat rim, and one without, called the coupe soup. None of the Fiesta lines had the coupe soup,* although a number of other Homer Laughlin China lines did possess both types. However, collector excitement has never seemed to surround the Fiesta

rim soups. Never has a collector been known to wax enthusiastic over a colorful group of these flat bowls. They are usable, serviceable, prosaic — unfortunately nothing more. Like nice warm carpet slippers on a cold winter night, rim soups are necessary and welcome but often overlooked.

Since the HLC Rhythm shape disallowed any rim on any piece, its large soup bowl was automatically a coupe.

RIM SOUP BOWL
Number: 451
Mold Book: January 3, 1990
Introduced: Early 1990
Mark: A very few early bowls unmarked from 1992 with dated stamp.
Size: Width: 9"
Liquid Measurement: 13¼ oz.
Popularity: Below average
Color Availability: All colors except sapphire.
Changes: None

Tripod Bowl

TRIPOD BOWL

Number: 766
Mold Book: Not known
Introduced: 1998
Mark: Raised mark with small f
Size: Height: 2½"
Liquid Measurement: 4 oz.
Popularity: Average
Color Availability: All colors except black, apricot, lilac, sapphire. There have been rumored sightings of black!
Changes: None

Here is a cute little number! A tiny bowl masquerading as a candleholder. Or, perhaps, vice versa, a plump little candleholder pretending to be (on off hours) a little bowl! The piece can be purchased with or without the candle, and this depends merely on where it is bought.

It can be said that the smaller Post86 items are very adaptable — and perhaps more generally usable. Have you ever watched all those important TV cooks stirring and chatting on the Cooking Channel? One of the most thrilling questions appears to be: Does Martha really cook?

Most of these entrepreneurial personalities tend to have an agenda and rarely give the unqualified appearance of really loving to cook! Julia Child is the exception, and so are, I believe, the witty and somewhat naughty two fat ladies, Jennifer Patterson and Clarissa Dixon Wright! How those two English ladies could cook! Very sadly, Jennifer died in mid-1999, and never saw the dawn of the new millennium, but whenever the reruns are watched, I relish her saying, with a wicked little grin, as she beat raw egg yolks into a cake icing, "Just call me Miss Salmonella."

However, the point being that these two ladies used many, many small bowls for their grindings of nutmeg, shakings of salt, ground coriander seeds, pinches of pepper, shreddings of lemon zest, and moons of egg yolks. The delightful small Post86 Fiesta tripod bowl would work wonderously as a measuring adjunct in the kitchen. Martha, the Renaissance lady of kitchen, barbeque, and vegetable garden, would not agree as everyone knows she is basically antagonistic toward the new Fiesta line — but Jennifer, Clarissa, and most certainly Julia would, all three, love the color and the convenience!

And this stubby but charming bowl reinforces my belief in threes. It is a tripod bowl, with three short feet to give it its name, and to secure it firmly on the kitchen counter or the hall table. It can hold salted nuts, plain peanuts (shelled, of course), cinnamon and sugar for the morning toast, and, believe this, act as a very adequate handleless rum-laced eggnog mug. So much more unique than the regulation Tom & Jerry mug! It has the nutmeg dash of originality!

The tripod bowl is pleasantly versatile, refreshingly quaint, *delicieux*! But ending on a historical note — would Mr. Rhead approve?

Mixing Bowls

Having been told as a wee lad that the number three is unusual, almost magical, it has always been my favorite. Remembering the words now — "From the union of one and two comes three and the cycle is complete" — I cannot believe these words were completely understood by any of the children sitting around Sister Charles (that was, I believe, her name) as she told stories. But that is really not important. The words stuck in my memory, and the number three continues to be personally very important.

I mentioned this briefly when the three Millennium vases were discussed. Yes, it is a magical number! But, as a point of interest, all odd numbers are interesting. Add a third to a pair of candleholders and the table become more exciting. Six candles all in a row is too uniform and neat — add a seventh, and the setting sings!

Keeping this in mind (although perhaps only subconsciously), the designers at Homer Laughlin opted, not for the reissuing of six vintage Fiesta mixing bowls, but for the three Kitchen Kraft. The shape of the three Post86 bowls is much like the Kitchen Kraft pieces: wider than deep and gently curving. And also like Kitchen Kraft, the new bowls are very versatile. They do not need to remain mostly in the kitchen, perhaps as the pie baker must. Even though they are named "mixing," the shape, size, and sense of delicacy make them multipurpose: they can be used for serving, for display, and to grace the table or sideboard on numerous occasions!

Rumor states that the large mixing bowl and the casserole base are interchangeable, and that the rim

MIXING BOWLS: SMALL, MEDIUM, LARGE

Number: Small 421, Med. 422, Large 482
Mold Book: Small was mentioned May 8, 1997
Introduced: 1998
Mark: Small and Medium have the circular raised with small *f* plus dated stamp. The Large has only the dated stamp.
Size: Small: 7½", Medium: 8½", Large: 9½"
Liquid Measurement: Small: 40 oz., Medium: 52 oz., Large: 64 oz.
Popularity: Below average
Availability: All colors except black, apricot, lilac, and sapphire.
Changes: None

inside the latter was deleted to make the two identical. Some disagree, but after "playing" with an older inside-rimmed casserole base, the new rimless base, and the large mixing bowl, the last two named are quite identical, and the rimmed base is slightly different. Does this bit of information become vital to your enjoyment and understanding? Not really, just satisfying curiosity! Incidentally, the latest advertising sheet lists the casserole as having a 51½ oz. capacity and the large mixing bowl 70 oz. This bit of conflicting information sent me to my kitchen with a measuring cup!*

I do remember reading, not sure exactly where but it was a reputable, non-speculative publication, that in 1996, the Homer Laughlin Company was obtaining some new equipment to mechanically form the larger pieces. At this time, so the article informed, these mixing bowls were placed into a "waiting" state until the equipment was installed. It was thought the mixing bowls could then be produced in a deeper shape — more like the vintage examples. Obviously this never happened and the large mixing bowl is a mirror reflection of the newer casserole base. The two smaller bowls also remain more like serving rather than mixing bowls. In fact, there are general complaints, now heard more often, that HLC "missed the boat." These mixing bowls are not useable as such!

Rumor also speaks of three flat finialed lids. These have been seen in the art department offices, but have not yet been put into production.

I will not tell the answer. Check and see the next time you make and serve hot buttered rum in a large bowl — or even Kool-Aid for that matter!

Purchase the three mixing bowls in different colors. The contrast is vibrant.

Stacking Bowls

STACKING BOWLS

Number: Fruit: 459, Cereal: 472
Mold Book: Fruit: March 21, 1986,
    Cereal: March 30, 1986. Simply
    enlarging the fruit bowl.
Introduced: Fruit: February 1986
    (original item). Cereal: c. 1994.
Mark: Both stamped, two varieties.
    First non-dated, then dated.
Size: Fruit: 5⅜", Cereal: 6½"
Liquid Measurement: Fruit: 6¼ oz.,
    Cereal: 11 oz.
Popularity: Both below average.
Color Availability: All colors except
    sapphire.
Changes: None

Fruit and cereal bowls, one in mango red. Notice the cereal bowl from the Iron-stone line is very similar to the Post86 cereal, but there is a difference in the rings.

These two stackable bowls have an interesting background. One of the most interesting points is why they exist at all. This is, I believe, simply answered. Bowls with sloping sides are really much more convenient than those with straight sides — or better still, their use is different. A child, for example, finds a straight-sided bowl easier to use, trapping a spoonful of cereal against the side or a piece of peach, or an errant strawberry. If a child were trying to capture some food in the sloping-sided bowl, it would run up the slope and disappear onto the table. The stacking bowls are more adult-oriented!

The first stacking bowl to appear was the smaller fruit. It sprang to the public's notice as one of the 31 pieces within the original February 1986 reissue.

The original vintage line had nothing like the sloping-sided bowls. This shape was introduced when Fiesta was remodeled into Ironstone with Homer Laughlin China's strong hopes to revive the lagging interest in Art Deco dinnerware. But it has to be noted, the stacking bowls are not at all in the Art Deco mode: they are very standard with very ordinary shapes.

The larger and deeper stacking cereal bowl waited several years before being introduced in mid-1994. It is not really redundant to have two cereal bowls if the user remembers the child versus the adult idea. And there is a general belief that one can never have too many bowls or "a bowl for each chore makes Jill a happy girl!"

Do not be misled into believing these two Post86 bowls are merely Ironstone bowls wearing different glazes. Not so! There is quite a difference in the rings — both inside and out. The Art Department spent time on the changes and must have considered them worthwhile additions to the line. We all possess a penchant for bowls!

And someone else did also — at least for the stacking little fruit bowl — for it is available as a rogue item in sapphire.

And there is one very important fact about these sloping-sided bowls — they stack! Four, five, eight disappear into each other very conveniently and smoothly. They do look neat and colorful residing on a kitchen cupboard shelf. Cool!

Straight-sided Bowls

The four Post86 straight-sided bowls in periwinkle blue, juniper, turquoise, and chartreuse.

STRAIGHT–SIDED BOWLS

Number: Cereal 460; Soup 461; Serving 471; Extra Large 455
Mold Book: So: Not necessary, used only mold; EL: Not known
Introduced: So: February 1986; EL: Not known
Mark: So: Incised circular small *f*; EL: Dated stamp
Size: 5⅝", 6⅞", 8¼", 10¼"
Liquid Measurement: 14 oz., 19 oz., 40 oz., 64 oz.
Popularity: Average; above average; average; average
Color Availability: All except sapphire; all colors; all colors; all except black, apricot, lilac, sapphire.
Changes: None

Here under discussion are the four straight-sided bowls that are modeled after those offered in the vintage line, considered as quite unique in 1936. They were:

fruit, 4¾"
fruit, 5½"
nappy, 8½"
nappy, 9½"

Of the four Post86 bowls now available, three were listed on the 1986 advertising sheet. The sizes were a little different, and the stated names were different, but the unique bowl shape has remained.

cereal bowl, 5⅝"
soup bowl, 6⅞"
serving bowl, 8⅜"

The cereal bowl is nearly identical to the vintage 5½" fruit bowl, and the serving bowl is just ⅛" smaller than the vintage smaller nappy. These two are easily misidentified as the older Fiesta — at least by those just beginning to collect. The Post86 soup bowl appears in a new size and is offered as a part of the 5-piece place setting.

The Homer Laughlin Company — or at least someone in its Art Department — has an admirable passion for bowls. Bowls for every season and every use is the suspected motto, and the customers love it!

There is known to exist as a trial item a 6" pedestal fruit bowl. It could certainly be used for both cereal or soup. The pedestal creates a very distinguished item, rather elegant. While some critics maintain another small Post86 bowl was not needed, my personal opinion differs. The only photograph seen depicts quite a charming piece.

So early in 1999, a new bowl made its appearance — a very grandiose, very impressive extra large serving bowl measuring 10½" and holding fully two quarts. This bowl, even though based with exactness upon the 9½" vintage nappy, should really be considered a new item! Why? Because the eye plays tricks when the collector views this bowl: its proportions make it seem much flatter, shallower when compared to its three sister shapes — or the vintage pieces. The illusion of "flatness" lies not only in the one-inch added width, but more surely upon the narrow rim. In fact, this attractive bowl bears a resemblance to what might have been called (in the 1930s and 1940s) a float bowl, one of those delightful centerpiece creations whereby flat candles and wide blossoms were set adrift in perfumed water. The Post86 presentation bowl is another example of what might be deemed a float bowl!

All these straight-sided bowls must be considered hardworking, designed simply for honest use. They sit on the table top firmly, never tip, and are basically child proof.

The four vintage bowls: 4" forest green, 5" rose, 8" chartreuse, and 9" turquoise.

Note the similarity between the Post86 (left) and vintage small bowls in the gray glazes.

Covered Butter

Note taller finial. Pearl gray.

COVERED BUTTER

Number: 494
Mold Book: March 14, 1992
Introduced: Mid-1992
Mark: Three types, see text.
Size: Base: Length: 7⅜". Width: 4⅜"
Popularity: Below average.
Color Availability: All colors except sapphire.
Changes: Major change sometime during or right after lilac. See text.

The covered butterdish is an item with a rather tangled past. Many readers already will have knowledge regarding the various Fiesta butters: those people must kindly bear with my rumblings. Others might like to share my thoughts — anyone is welcome to read or to skip — the decision lies with the individual reader.

The butterdish, when dealing with the three great Homer Laughlin colorware lines (Fiesta, Harlequin, and Riviera) is more interesting for what it is not rather than what it is! Or perhaps more succinctly stated, what it is and where it is!

Vintage Fiesta has no butterdish — we all must know that fact (Some researchers now claim the Jade butterdish was sold with the vintage Fiesta line.), but it does have four types of vases, two teapots, pitchers to satisfy the most adamantly thirsty, and a covered onion soup (that did not last long), but no butterdish. Who among decision makers at Homer Laughlin concluded that Depression housewives would appreciate three sizes of vase, but nary a butterdish to sit in the center of the kitchen table! This fact is hard to digest!

And Harlequin was even more interesting. Here was a so-called "cheaper" line aimed at those who might find Fiesta a little pricey: those who shopped up and down the creaky aisles of the Woolworth five and dime emporiums! Those same Homer Laughlin sages decided the Harlequin line would possess the butterdish, but if a butterdish was to be had, it was not to be Harlequin's own. The ubiquitously seen Jade butterdish was to suffice, albeit glazed in all those rich Harlequin glazes!

And what of Riviera? Now if we have to rank the top color lines (and everyone is interested in rank, even Homer Laughlin collectors or accumulators), the position of Riviera is unabashedly third! (Perhaps even fourth if the Epicurean collectors of Epicure had their demanding way!) But here, equally unabashedly, Riviera has two butterdishes! One is the half-pound jade example and the second — well, it belongs to Riviera alone!

The Huxfords say it is so — so it is.

Yes! Riviera (a colorful line cloned from the earlier Century) has its own butterdish, quarter pound, but Fiesta did not even claim one! But, naturally, many homemakers purchased the Harlequin/Jade butterdish in glazes to match their Fiesta pieces.

This is true, but strange!

When the collector reaches "the brown Fiesta" Amberstone, a butterdish appears, but this finial-less piece cannot translate itself completely to Post86 Fiesta. The new Fiesta butterdish might be based upon the Amberstone example, but it is not an easy transference. Amberstone gives a rounded soft appearance while the Post86 butter is sharper, more angular, and, if the truth be told, even a little out of place when closely compared with the rest of the new line!

But sometime — and a date would be hard to determine without the precise purchase of a number of butterdishes — both the base and the cover underwent

Early rose butterdish.

slight, but noticeable changes. Using the rose butter cover (purchased in late '86 or early '87, I can't exactly remember) it is seen to be 6¼" long — fully ¼" longer than my sea mist green cover. The widths are the same (3"), but the sides of the green cover are thicker.

The 1986 rose butter base is 4" wide compared with 4¼" of the sea mist green base. The rose base is much more straight-sided; the green base swells gently in its center. The Art Department at Homer Laughlin China modified both cover and base to be more compatible with the Art Deco design of the rest of the line. Smart move. Or, as my friend comments, the change was purely to correct a firing problem! The one absolute in all these posturing is that my lilac butterdish base (1993 – 1995) is straight-sided. My chartreuse butter base (1997 – 1999) has the swelling sides. The design of the butterdish could have been changed during the run of lilac, or been introduced with persimmon (1997).

The only way the information could be dated with some accuracy is to ask the Art Department, or trace the glazes that appear in both the straight and curved sided bases. At this point, I would venture to say white through sea mist green could appear in both versions, lilac with only straight sides, and persimmon in only the swelling sided version. Wonder how goes the rogue sapphire butterdish? Can anyone tell me?

Oh, what a joy it would be to jostle the minds of those decision makers at Homer Laughlin China and to get straight answers! Now, this is not meant to say the managers and directors deliberately lead the researcher astray, but they inadvertently do so! The longer one deals with the HLC management, the more obvious it becomes that the general policy is to withhold information. Mr. Parry once told me information cannot be made available to the general public until the retailers are informed. This seems to make sense and assuredly is a legitimate reason. But often collectors and especially researchers fume under the shadows of mystery. Their minds are on (and this is commercially correct and has been stated before) making money, and they cannot really spend much time trying to remember — once a decision is reached, these dinnerware moguls look forward, never back! But I do pose a question. When the new line was offered to the consumer in 1986, there was no butterdish. By 1988, there was one. Oh, to be a fly on the boardroom wall and listen to the secret decisions! Did some executive suddenly shout: We must have a butterdish this time! And that was that!

On the second advertising list in my possession, there appeared a butterdish — with a tall finial (no sugar bowl syndrome here, originally button and then tall finial). But, I do surmise, if the butterdish had been offered in 1986, its finial would have matched the sugar bowl. But this is mere conjecture and does not have a real place in a supposedly serious discussion such as this. It seems that the Post86 butterdish was formed with an absolutely new design: it appears listed in the mold book in March of 1992. Thus, the price list mentioned above has to date from then, and there are seven colors available. It must be noted that official brochures can be misleading, due to the desire to save money, surely. The small brochure that introduced yellow in the Fiesta family of colors does not picture the butterdish, but be careful with conclusions! One cannot immediately say there was no butterdish because the two small photographs showing available Fiesta pieces are exactly the same in the yellow brochure as they were in the 1986 introductory brochure. A money saving decision?

What is known? The butterdish was modeled, and noted in the mold book March 14, 1992, and must have been offered for sale soon after that date. And the pie plate appears in the second trade listing. Two other newly listed items were the mug (#453) and the 13" platter (#458). Interestingly, the butterdish has not become wildly popular. Perhaps some inborn collector resentment explains why its appearance took place so late! Because in times past butterdishes were standard items in nearly all dinnerware lines, collectors tend to forget the absence of the butter in vintage Fiesta. It simply should have been there! The new butterdish for new Fiesta is literally new to the line, as new, for example, as is the welled snack plate or the 2-cup teapot.

Our new butterdish operates under the shadow of "what should have been."

It must be confessed, at times Post86 Fiesta has a few advantages over vintage. Everything tends to seem better the second time around. But one can hardly expect the vintage collectors to agree with this little premise!

This Post86 butterdish is a very modern looking piece. It does not have the lingering looks of the 1940s or 1950s. It is purely for quarter-pound butter or margarine sticks, not the solid pound butter sliced in half, to be accommodated in the Jade versions. No, the new butterdish is modern, snappy, and very useful. The identifying Fiesta rings work wonderfully in "oblong." Noticeable also is a variance in the height of the finials, but this is not deliberate and merely reflects differences in firing. There does however seem to be one minor problem: some of the covers of the earlier pieces tend to rock from end to end.

The first example I purchased was in 1992 in a local mall at a time when rose was being confused in the marketplace with its vintage namesake. This rose (pink) example was not marked at all and rocks with a vengeance. Nor was the black example marked when purchased one or two years later. But in 1993, I saw (but did not acquire) a yellow butterdish with an ink stamped mark. However, recently when my lilac example arrived in the mail, there was, again, no mark at all — and here we have reached the years 1993/1995. Now, when I received my chartreuse and pearl gray examples, it was noted that the mark has become incised. Thus, we have three available marks on these little charming butter holders, but the exact dates of each cannot be ascertained. Certainly, it cannot be stated that one mark is more valuable than the other. All that can be deduced is that some are stamped, some incised, some not marked at all!

And, naturally, all this interest in marks (or lack of them) is of interest only to the very exacting and serious collector.

What is truly interesting is the fact that the Post86 butterdish is really not very popular. One does not hear of collectors foaming to gather this piece in all available colors, such as happens with the AD set, or even the napkin ring. Perhaps butterdishes are all prosaically accepted by collectors and left at that? However, it must be added that someone or another loved this piece — for one or more Homer Laughlin China employees dared company vengeance and dipped the butter roguishly in the sapphire glaze.

Early base for butterdish (rose, right) contrasts with the swelling sides of a later butterdish base (pearl gray, left).

Pyramid Candleholder

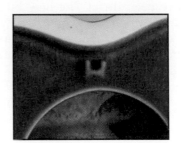

The "H" seen on some Post86 pieces to help collectors distinguish vintage from new.

Like its round counterpart, the pyramid candleholder moved directly from the vintage to Post86! It is much scarcer in the early line, but in Post86 is equal in availability.

But there the comparisons between the two shapes cease. The pyramid (known to vintage collectors as the tripod) is quite spectacular. It is nearly a unique shape — architectural, it repeats the thrust of that early '30s phenomena: the city skyscraper. Jutting upwards, the three sections of this candleholder are reminiscent of those high-rise apartment complexes built on marshlands surrounding New York City. Stepping into the future, these complexes were devoted to uniformity and anonymity and became cities unto themselves. Although on a miniscule scale, the pyramid (or tripod) candleholder with its stepped shape mirrors a futuristic design that in the 1930s belonged to Flash Gordon and Ming the Merciless!

Now the candleholder shape — any pair of candleholders for that matter — cannot really be considered with reference to the candles it holds. Candles are a fundamental and essential extension of the shape. This concept is often overlooked and is similar to the truth that a plate and its color can only be honestly viewed with food upon it. Just as the choice of food on a colorful plate is important, so does the choice of a candle — color, height, decoration — reflect positively or negatively upon the holder. For example, a short red spiraled candle would conflict with the vertical thrust of an apricot pyramid holder. The color would be conflicting also. The waxen spirals and red color

---

PYRAMID CANDLEHOLDER

Number: (764) 489
Mold Book: Not necessary, reused mold
Introduced: February 1986 (original item)
Mark: Indented, in one of the three base sections.
Size: Height: 3⅜"
Liquid Measurement: N/A
Popularity: Exceptional
Color Availability: All colors except sapphire.
Changes: None

---

would, however, enhance the more reflective curves of a black round holder. This is all rather esoteric, but details such as these separate the masterly host (or hostess) from those who are simply competent.

Both the pyramid and round Post86 holders are seen in sapphire, but these are considered examples of rogue items. Also the two appear in lilac, but the pyramid piece is much more rare in lilac. Wearing this glaze, they were exclusive to Bloomingdale's and only a limited number of pairs are said to exist. It is the distinctive shape and the occasional scarcity that projects the pyramid candleholder onto a high plane.

On May 25, 2000, word filtered down from Dave Conley. The pyramid candleholders were being discontinued: problem was the mold was not made for mass production and the company was losing money.

Several rather idealistic collectors spoke of starting a letter campaign to request HLC keep making these very popular items. This campaign aborted, and the dealers began to hoard like squirrels. These candleholders now have the dubious distinction of being the first regular Post86 piece to be discontinued.

Notice how opaque the persimmon glaze appears (right). It seems to shimmer next to the slightly larger vintage red (left).

Here is the new cobalt blue pyramid (left), darker and smaller than the vintage tripod in cobalt. Note the name change.

Round Candleholder

ROUND CANDLEHOLDER

Number: (762) 488
Mold Book: Not necessary, reused old mold.
Introduced: February 1986 (original item)
Mark: Indented, underneath two base sides.
Size: 3⅜"
Popularity: Exceptional
Color Availability: All colors except sapphire.
Changes: None

As with the sauceboat and the large and medium disc pitchers, this candleholder was an exact (except for height and weight) transference from the vintage line. Introduced as an original piece in 1936, the bulb candleholder was discontinued between 1944 and 1946 for eight or ten years. Can we assume they were not very popular? Not really, it can be thought that not all Fiesta purchasers in the Depression years needed or wanted candleholders, and once those who did want them were satisfied, the demand fell.

Later, as all Fiesta collectors well realize, both the bulb and tripod candleholders became very desirable, and this desire resulted in the inclusion of both pieces in the reissued line of 1986. Of the two, the bulb (now titled "round") candleholder has always been more accessible. However in the Post86 line, both are equally sought. While the round design is a little less dramatic or "deco-ish," it is often collected merely on its own. The small globe shape fits well on low and narrow shelves and lends a spot of brightness.

The delicate little snail-like curved feet of the rounded candleholder get lost in some of the early heavy glazes. All the original 1986 glazes are heavy enough nearly to obliterate those snail — or ram's horn — indentations. Yellow and turquoise are a little better, and lilac is better still. The best example of this candleholder is persimmon where the transparency of the glaze allows the original design to shine through.

But, as with the pyramid holders, this highly reflective globular piece can only be truly appreciated when holding a suitably designed candle.

Another interesting fact about this candleholder is the weight. While all are heavier than the 1936 examples, some Post86 holders are much, much heavier than others. The differences in weight are merely curiosities and do not reflect on a glaze or time of production.

Regarding the round candleholder with the lilac glaze: In issue 14 (Spring 1995) of *Fiesta Collector's Quarterly* there is a front page announcement that reads: "New items in lilac made exclusively for Table-Top Direct. Demitasse cup & saucer, Bud Vase, and Bulb (i.e., Round) Candleholders."

The article continues that the cup/saucer will be limited to 1,000 sets, the bud vase to 500, and the candleholders to 500 sets. It concludes: "As collectors will note, lilac will be discontinued in December 1995. These are items never before offered in lilac and are not available from other retailers."

Most sources give China Specialties as the exclusive retailer of these lilac items. When contacted, Table-Top Direct replied while they handled a majority (whatever that really means) of the round candleholders, the item was not made exclusively for them.

The round candleholder is appealing because it appears in all the colors except sapphire, but even here the collector with financial resources can with reasonable readiness obtain an example in sapphire. Even though the company lists sapphire round candleholders as stolen property, there are Post86 collectors who have no qualms telling everyone they have examples.

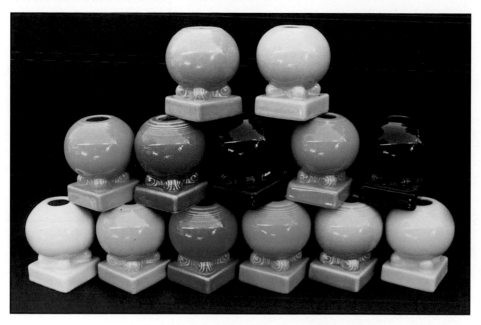

A wonderful collection of thirteen candleholders.

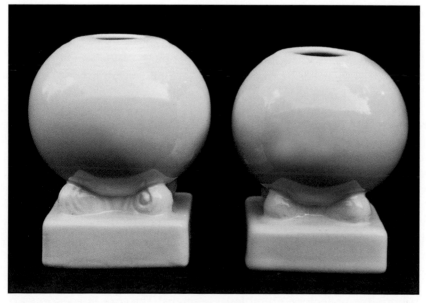

An example of how, at times, a Post86 glaze can look. The feet of the peri-winkle round candleholder (right) become mere "blobs" when compared with the "ram's horns" of the vintage ivory feet.

Carafe

CARAFE

Number: **448**
Mold Book: **January 8, 1996**
Introduced: **1996**
Mark: **Raised mark with capital** $\mathcal{F}$
Size: **Height: 7½"**
Liquid Measurement: **60 oz.**
Popularity: **Average**
Color Availability: **All colors except lilac.**
Changes: **None**

When an item of new Fiesta is a restyling of a very similar vintage piece, writing a critique is often problematic. Why? Simply because, I find, vintage collectors and devotees are always measuring and calculating the differences and similarities between the two, often to the detriment of the new Fiesta design.

So it is with the carafe. The vintage carafe must be considered a signature piece, and because of this rank, the Post86 carafe, during comparisons, oft comes out lacking. Unlike the new pieces with no vintage examples to which they can be compared, the new carafe is unlucky. Perhaps even the company was hesitant because the restyled carafe did not make an appearance until over ten years after the new introduction in 1986. In fact, a modeling log notation was not entered until January 8, 1996, when the carafe was listed as a new design.

And it is totally and completely a new design. When it was marketed, many collectors grumbled! Where was the distinctive stopper? What happened to the extended foot? Why was the opening widened to threaten the attenuated look of the throat after the perfectly rotund look of the body?

At the time of the new carafe's introduction, I approached, with caution (one always treads softly here), the HLC Art Department with questions regarding the stopper and received a rather sharply and

understandably exasperated reply: there was to be no stopper because the restaurant clientele who wanted the carafe — a redesigned carafe — demanded the opening be wide enough for ice cubes.

So the carafe was redesigned with ice cubes in mind!

Again, it was as simple as that! The Homer Laughlin Company was providing what the market desired, not what collectors thought artistic. With heavy use in restaurant dining rooms, the carafe needed to be more securely placed upon the table, thus the lack of the original extended foot. The new carafe was to be a hardworking member of the Fiesta family, probably pouring gallons and gallons of ice water or iced sangria or chilled Rhine wine throughout all manner of commercial settings! Harried handsome waiters (or even winsome waitresses) could not be expected to keep tabs on an elusive and easily lost stopper. Practicality reigns! The cork lined stopper became superannuated.

Physically, this carafe is almost perfectly designed for its work. The full roundness of the original has been replaced by a more sloping look: wider at the top and narrowing minutely at the bottom. A series of very well-placed Fiesta rings encircles the body close to the top; these are not present in the original piece. A second, much less pronounced, series of rings encircles the base. The handle is flatter, easier to grip firmly, pour rapidly, and disengage quickly, and most importantly, the new carafe feels and looks strong enough to be loudly "thump-able!"

And tray after tray of ice cubes can easily disappear into the 1½" opening! As a design well-contrived to do what needs to be done, the new carafe must have received high marks. As a copy of the more elegantly Deco vintage carafe, perhaps it fails. But now be honest, what really matters here?

Since it came into production after lilac, the new carafe should not appear in that color. But it does! It has appeared for sale on the Internet, and, hard to believe, the seller makes the following statement: "The existence of the lilac carafe is credited totally to unauthorized Homer Laughlin China insider activity. When it was discovered by Homer Laughlin China that these got out, rumor has it that they tried to locate and confiscate them as stolen property."

The entry included a photograph of the lilac carafe and an opening bid of $3,000.00! Now, as my Jewish friend would say — this seller has chutzpah! Wonder if Homer Laughlin China security guards ever located this one?

However, it is glazed in all other colors, including sapphire.

The piece, along with the disc pitchers, is a favorite to receive decorative decal treatments!

Notice the wide throat of this sea mist green carafe.

Casserole/Lid

This piece is monumental! As heavy and "ready for work" as a cast iron Dutch oven only much more beautiful. It floats like an impressive ship — a dowager dominating the dining room table!

But first, indulge me in a moment of subjective explanation regarding the term "casserole." Casserole should, to my mind, be correctly used only for those large lidded kitchenware pots that can be placed into a hot oven, filled with items such as beans and franks; noodles, cream and tangy cheddar cheese, or even a cassoulet of prodigious proportions — food to be cooked and then whisked to the table, placed on a trivet and served. In dinnerware lingo, "casserole" now refers to a serving dish for hot food: it is, in all honesty, a covered serving dish.

I have known cooks who love to experiment and "dance with some danger!" They swear the Post86 casserole is oven-safe!

In years past when middle-class families had cooks in the kitchen and serving maids in the dining room, the many pieced dinnerware sets included both a round lidded serving piece, and a sister piece in the oval shape. To distinguish the two, the round piece was called a covered casserole, the oval one a covered serving dish. The term "casserole" here is still not absolutely correct, but perhaps this is where the term became connected with an elegant serving dish with a lid. But enough of verbosity!

The Post86 Fiesta covered casserole has a very interesting history. Like any formidable dowager of grandiose pretensions, its history is a little shrouded and checkered. Even her official number and size have altered during her tenure as the central most impres-

CASSEROLE/LID
Number: (body: 724) (lid: 725) 495
Mold Book: September 10, 1995
Introduced: February 1986 (original item)
Mark: Indented mark with small *f.*
Size: Round: 9⁵⁄₁₆"
Liquid Measurement: 51½ oz.
Popularity: Below average
Color Availability: All colors except sapphire.
Changes: Two, see text

sive piece of the line. In the 1986 booklet depicting available new Fiesta items, the casserole body was number 724, the cover 725, and the volume held was 54 oz. Then in 1988, the number appeared as 495 for both body and cover, and it held 48 oz. From 1994, the number stood at 495 for both pieces, and the volume jelled at 51½ oz. The slight differences in volume reflect the changes mentioned in the mold book. However, there is a more important situation — in existing brochures for the introduction of the new line not dated, but obviously meant for late 1985 or 1986, this stately piece is pictured with handles and a knobbed finial, and glazed in the new apricot color. It is the revised 1969 Ironstone shape! (In this same brochure, the teapot, coffee pot, and both types of sugar bowls also appear as Ironstone Fiesta. See the section on this brochure.) The weight is said to be semi-vitreous!

Now do these pieces exist? There are rumors, and more rumors! Talk revolving around having a friend who has spoken to a collector who has actually seen an Ironstone casserole glazed in the new color rose. Some writers/researchers say the Post86 line does have a few semi-vitreous pieces floating about. One friend, Mark Gonzalez, states he saw an Ironstone coffee pot glazed in white, but, foolishly, did not purchase it! (See section on the coffee server.) The authorities at Homer Laughlin insist the use of semi-vitreous clay in new Fiesta was a trial only — a trial that did not meet expectations, and that Post86 covered casseroles in white, black, rose, apricot, cobalt blue, do not, or should not, officially exist! Yet we can see, very obviously, an apricot-glazed Ironstone casserole pictured in the brochure. Even if this brochure was only a trial run, obviously the apricot casserole had to exist to be photographed. Thus the collector can hope!

Within a very short time — days or a week or two — this Ironstone shaped new Fiesta was discarded, and with it any claim to "semi-vitreous-hood." All was vitreous ware. Yet, here is where another, more legitimate and obvious difference in the casserole and cover are to be experienced. The body of the casserole from 1986, until about 1992, had an inner lip. Then, some say, in anticipation of the largest of the three nested mixing bowls, the lip disappeared and the large mixing bowl and the casserole body became identical.

The casserole can be found in both versions (with and without the inner lip) in white, black, rose, apricot, cobalt blue, yellow, turquoise, and periwinkle blue. From sea mist green on to cinnabar, only the lipless variation can be located. At this moment in time, one version is not more valuable than the other, but personally, I would not dispose of any casserole with the inner lip!

Interestingly, the earlier casserole cover does not fit the later casserole body: it is slightly too small. Some dimensions for both variations:

Early example with inner lip: 9⅛" round, 3¼" high, 7/17" foot, 4 lbs., 9 oz. weight.

Later example without inner lip: 9⁵⁄₁₆" round, 3½" high, ½" foot, 5 lbs., 7 oz. weight.

The casserole, both body and cover, was "tinkered" with quite often — to soften the lines, adjust the fit. Just like any dowager — with a tuck here, a pat there, a push, and a pull! Such a monumentally magnificent sculptural centerpiece must remain in the best of shape.

Older casserole bottom with inside rim.

Revised casserole bottom, no rim.

Clock

Like the lamp, the clock was originally a J.C. Penney exclusive. Introduced in 1993, it, again like the clock, proved unpopular and was withdrawn within the year. But here the path traveled by lamp and clock diverge. The lamp took the narrow path, despaired of its future, and ended up dusty and forgotten: virtually unwanted and relatively uncollected!

The clock went its own way and, while it rested, it never despaired. In 1996, it returned, reinstated and refurbished, as a regular Fiesta item. The demand for the clock has been steady, but not furious. There are several reasons for this, the major one being its usefulness. If a clock is needed for the kitchen, or the screened porch, or a bedroom of dainty daughter or a stalwart son, then the Post86 Fiesta clock could be considered. Yellow for the kitchen, persimmon for the porch, rose for the daughter, and turquoise for the son. But remember, a little of the clock goes a long way.

Fitting in well when needed, the clock can easily be overused. It is quite evident in any room where it appears, and too many Fiesta clocks in too many Fiesta colors, and in too many rooms of the house, give rise to a very "spotty" effect. "Oh, here's another one," a visitor might think as a black clock is noticed over the commode in the downstairs guest powder room!

These clocks are too dramatic, too noticeable, much too conspicuous, to be scattered about the house

---

CLOCK

Number: 473
Mold Book: January 31, 1997 (a mold change?)
Introduced: 1996
Mark: Dated stamp
Size: Width: 10"
Popularity: Average
Color Availability: All colors except lilac.
Changes: Appears with and without the sixtieth anniversary logo. Also face can be concave, convex, or flat.

---

like so many large poker chips be-dotting wall after wall. Careful and cautious use is the motto here!

And then what can a clock do except tell time? This item, like some of those well-designed genuine Fiesta accessories, is better behaved in use. Or like a Rowoco bottle stopper without a bottle to stop, the Fiesta clock is lost with time to tell! The clock is really not a collectible; it is a "useable!"

There are wonderfully exciting exceptions to this statement, however. One of the most dramatic, clever and striking, original and fascinating, displays ever seen was in an entrance way about ten feet square. One wall held the front door, the wall directly opposite was an open arch into the living room. To the left was a console and ornately gilt wall mirror, but on the fourth wall to the right — on a blue-tinted white wall — were ten Fiesta clocks in ten colors. Each proclaimed a different time while underneath, engraved on a plaque matching the clock's glaze, was the name of the city where the given time was true. Sydney, Singapore, Bombay, Baghdad, Athens, London, Rio de Janeiro, New York, San Francisco, Honolulu. The display was so fascinating, such a well-conceived sophisticated use

of a collection (yes, collection!) of Fiesta clocks that the cities were jotted down to be remembered.

But, sadly, few of us have the simple open space for such a home spectacle, and most of us are limited to discreet and practical use of the Fiesta clock.

When the clock reappeared in 1996, it was the year of original Fiesta's sixtieth anniversary, and thus there are two prominent variations: with and without the sixtieth anniversary logo. Sapphire with the logo is probably the rarest of the clocks.

The regular clock also appears concave, convex, and even flat. This depends entirely on the mold used and does not yet affect the value.

Coffee Server

COVERED COFFEE SERVER

Number: (721), lid (722), 483
Mold Book: March 18, 1986
Mark: Indented, circular
Size: Height: 9¼"
Liquid Measurement: 36 oz.
Popularity: Below average
Color Availability: All colors except sapphire.
    Only 24 in chartreuse.
Changes: Radical changes very early in pro-
    duction. See text. Some changes in size of
    spout opening, but this was probably not
    deliberate.

This piece also falls into the same mysterious category of appearing in a very early Post86 brochure looking very much like an Ironstone coffee pot. As said before, this Post86 Fiesta disguised as Ironstone is so rare — in all those pieces in question — as to be nonexistent. However, a very reliable Homer Laughlin China collector (not given to unicorn sightings) tells me of an "Ironstone" coffee in white, and this logically is one of the extremely early Post86 coffee servers. Then the brochure depicts one in black — so there are at least two somewhere, some how!

A friend of mine who was raised in Newell just a block away from the Retail Outlet remembers going there, as an adolescent in 1986 and seeing a row of Ironstone coffee servers glazed in the five new Fiesta colors. They stood upon the same shelf as a row of the "regulation" coffee servers still being sold today. This observation is absolutely trustworthy because living in a small town dominated by the Homer Laughlin Company, he knew his subject clearly.

This anecdote clearly confounds the official statement that the Ironstone type of coffee pot was never produced. But, to allow for the political reasons surrounding the official statement, probably very few were

manufactured, and those that did come from the kiln and appeared in reasonable condition were sold at the outlet. Unfortunately, my friend had little money and did not purchase any! Even though, he recalls, the price was high, he still regrets not buying at least one!

This new Fiesta piece is not a personal favorite of mine. It has been described as one of the three "dismal" designs of Post86. A gentleman writing in *Fiesta Collector's Quarterly* states that the new style coffee pot can "pollute" the purity of [the new Fiesta] design. For my part, there is a tendency to agree: the new coffee server lacks the stalwart impressiveness of the vintage example. The smooth sides and smaller almost curvilinear appearance certainly is not very Art Deco! But then I am not a good one to discuss the matter objectively because the vintage example was not a favorite either. And most any ceramic coffee server, in my private estimation, rests quite a few levels down from the teapot. The teapot, any teapot in any dinnerware line, belongs in the inner circle of my favorites! Now, naturally, after reading my opinion, the reader can without hesitation say — who cares if he likes teapots more than coffee pots? And the reader would be correct. I just wanted to make my opinion known!

The same writer in *Fiesta Collector's Quarterly* opinions that the design of Fiesta Ironstone was moving strongly away from its Art Deco roots. It is true because the country, in one of its eternal design swings, was itself moving away from Art Deco. But, he observes, "it should be noted that even with … this horrific combination of flared bowls and ugly glazes, the line [Ironstone] managed to have a decent looking coffee pot."

Actually, my less than positive reaction to the coffee server is a question of balance. The vintage example is rather unsteady: a tall robust frame on a very narrow base. Yet if I were objective to the highest degree, it would be admitted the Post86 coffee server presents a much more sculptured outline — the entire shape flows with a symmetry not possessed by the vintage piece. Also, this smoothed out newer version, as mentioned above, lacks the pure and evident Art Deco qualities of the older! If the sauceboat is a Post86 item that most resembles its vintage forebear, then the coffee server must be the Post86 item farthest removed, even with its incised Fiesta mark — the resemblance between the two is there, but barely!

No matter — objective or subjective — this piece remains problematic.

However, at the end of this back and forth comparison, pitting one against the other, it must be observed the Post86 coffee server handles with more security, pours with more ease, and stands on the table with less pomposity — and its smaller size makes it very suitable as a demitasse coffee server. Two of the most often repeated pieces on the Post 86 collectors' wish list are the AD coffee pot and a larger regular coffee pot. Somehow I believe HLC will not acquiesce.

As the pros are matched with the cons, the readers can see my feeling for the coffee server is ambivalent at best, and a statement is required to close the case.

Can we accept the following? Standing alone, the Post86 coffee has a certain graceful charm and obviously handibility. Placed side by side with a vintage example, it pales and falls into deep shadow. When placed among a grouping of the restyled, but still Art Deco Post86 Fiesta, it fails to pass muster: it simply does not fit within the same category. Does it "pollute?" Perhaps that is a very harsh opinion, but it most certainly does not belong!

The brilliant vintage red coffee pot stands by the new example in white. Like the teapot, the wide lid of the vintage piece just could not withstand the fiery heat of the vitreous kiln.

Note the difference in the openings of the spouts.

Cup and Saucer

In every dinnerware line, there are always some pieces designed to catch the eye of the beholder/collector. In early Homer Laughlin China shapes, the pickle dish was the object of much fanciful imagination, and the large and dramatic items — teapots, toast holders, comports, oyster tureens — whipped up into a froth the creative juices of the designers of the day!

This we all know. But conversely, there are those essential, undramatic and uncomplicated items which are virtually impossible to make eye-catching and clever — plates, cups and saucers, and shaker sets are among the most prosaic and simplistic. A designer with a purpose can create a biomorphic ovoid plate, or an octagon plate, but that is about as far as that path can be followed.

The cup and saucer are even more difficult to design uniquely. Some designers are intelligent enough to leave this pair alone and expend energies on the other pieces in the dinnerware line. One of the most creative of all modern designers is Eva Zeisel: her work for Hall under the Hallcraft name tended toward the limits of acceptable avant-garde, but her cups and saucers for Hallcraft were conservatively traditional. She knew to over-design a cup was a disastrous mistake! Some ceramic designers attempt to "jazz up" the little cup with a trendy handle or a strange shape, but often these do not work.

CUP AND SAUCER

Number: **Cup, 452; Saucer, 470**
Mold Book: **Cup: November 16, 1985. Saucer: November 25, 1985.**
Introduced: **February 1986**
Mark: **Early cup unmarked. About 1993, the dated stamp was used. Saucers were always stamped, but about 1993, this stamp was changed to the dated example.**
Size: **Cup: Height: 2¾", Saucer: Width: 5¾"**
Liquid Measurement: **Cup: 7¾ oz.**
Popularity: **Above average**
Color Availability: **All colors**
Changes: **None. Although there is some disparity in handles.**

Ben Seibel's cups for Pfaltzgraff (Country-Time) or Roseville (Roseville Raymor) might possess flowing lines, but they function awkwardly.

There are tall cups and short cups, there are square cups and oval cups, but as perhaps Mr. Goldstone would agree, the best cup is the round cup, and the best saucer for serving his egg roll would also be a simple round! (Thanks to the song, "Mr. Goldstone" from Lerner and Loewe's musical "Gypsy.") The vintage cup and saucer were perfectly designed, and this perfection was carried — almost — in toto into the Post86 line.

Take a cup and saucer of the same color (this because the two will then function as a single unit) and study it carefully. It is best to do so through squinted eyes — for in this manner the forms and balances are easily seen. There is an obvious imbalance: obvious although it took me some careful viewing to corner the cause!

The size of the saucer is too small for the cup! So a like example was garnered from both the vintage and the Ironstone wares for study and measurement. The results were:

Vintage Cup	Ironstone Cup	Post86 Cup
Height: 2¾"	Height: 2¾"	Height: 2¾"
Vintage Saucer	Ironstone Saucer	Post86 Saucer
Width: 6⅛"	Width: 6⅛"	Width: 5¾"

It is strange how a mere three-eighths of an inch can cause an imbalance. Was this purposefully done to create tension between the Post86 cup and its saucer?

Top to bottom: sea mist Post86, avocado green Ironstone, red vintage late, green vintage, original handle.

The cups/saucers are available in all colors. Here are nine, including three of the four limited colors (second row).

AD Cup/AD Saucer

While the AD cup and saucer were two of the original pieces in the vintage Fiesta line, they did not make an immediate reissued appearance in 1986. This cup/saucer set does not appear in the 1986 or the 1987 official Homer Laughlin China sales document — but can be seen in 1994. They were actually introduced in the spring of 1993.

The AD cup is a very good example of what is meant when researchers state that Post86 Fiesta is truly a new line of dinnerware, strongly and obviously based upon the earlier pieces, yet still individual unto itself! To look at a vintage AD cup and then to negatively criticize the new piece is rather rude! Rather like comparing the body of a boxer with the body of a swimmer: they really should not be compared. There are similarities (the two athletic bodies both have arms, and the AD cups both have stick handles), but the tone and impression are absolutely different!

The newer piece has no foot and is slightly smaller — both in height and width. This results in a completely different profile. No matter, actually, all diminutive coffee cups appeal to all manner of collectors. They appear in many dinnerware lines and are very popular.

Here is a description of the new AD cup as it appeared in a very influential quarterly:

Like the old one, it has the distinctive stick handle. The cup is slightly more elongated in shape due to the fact that the foot is not turned (Homer Laughlin China has not turned or undercut the foot of cups since the early sixties. The old way of molding cups was after they were jiggered, the cup would be turned on a wheel and a V-shaped chisel would be turn the foot so that it would nip in, then flare back out. Soon after the medium green was introduced in the late fifties, the foot on the regular teacups was simplified and the rings on the cup interior were eliminated. The AD cups were not made after the late fifties so were never restyled). We

---

AD CUP/AD SAUCER

Number: Cup: 476. Saucer; 477
Mold Book: February 26, 1993
Introduced: Summer 1993
Mark: Cup: incised mark. Saucer: dated stamp. Note: Sometimes the above are very difficult to see.
Size: Cup: Height: 2½". Saucer: Width: 4⅞".
Liquid Measurement: Cup: 3 oz.
Popularity: Exceptional
Color Availability: All colors except sapphire.
Changes: Very minor changes to cup.

---

have been asking for the demitasse cup and saucer for a long time and Homer Laughlin China has (reintroduced) this very welcome item. (*Fiesta Collector's Quarterly*. Joel Wilson, editor. Vol. 2, Issue 3. Summer 1993).

There are two barely distinguishable versions of the new AD cup; for a few months the underside bore only the Fiesta incision. Then in early 1993, the Fiesta registered R and USA appeared. The handle received some minor design changes; you can see a slight difference in the swellings where the handle fastens to the body. Not of major or vital importance, but appealing to inquisitive researchers. Of much greater importance are the persistent rumors that the AD set will be discontinued, or if not as drastic an event, be restyled.

Dave Conley, Homer Laughlin China director of marketing and sales, spoke emphatically on the Fiestafanatic (http:www.fiestafanatic.com) message board: "We are not restyling the AD cup handle. What we are doing is adding to the line a Fiesta children's tea set called My First Fiesta Tea Set. We all felt that children would have a difficult time with the stick handled cup so we decided to give the tea set up a more conventional handle. It is very possible that the cup with the conventional handle will totally replace the stick handle. This is just speculation and we will continue to produce the stick handled cup as long as the sales volume justifies keeping it in the line."

So collectors can hope popularity will keep the stick AD cup in production, but perhaps to be on the safer side of wisdom, the careful collector should purchase at least two additional sets in each color now just in case the handle does change. Having seen some photographs of the My First Fiesta set, I can see however why the regular handled tiny cup might even prove more popular.

The chartreuse AD cup/saucer set was an exclusive for the Retail Outlet and is very desirable in that color. Lilac was an exclusive for China Specialties and was limited to 500 sets. In sapphire, the set is one of the rogue items in greatest demand.

Compare vintage (red) with Post86 (apricot).

The AD cup/saucer in sapphire was never officially made.

91

Jumbo Cup/ Chili Bowl and Saucer

The mark of the persimmon chili bowl — certainly not the Fiesta mark!

These three pieces are discussed together because they are, actually, one and the same set. The chili bowl is simply the jumbo cup sans handle, and the saucer is meant for both. But the major problem here (if indeed there is a problem) is, are they the same or not?

Elitists and Post86 purists can be disdainful of the category Fiesta Mates, although not exactly with the same flurry of disdain that can shower down on Fiesta Accessories. The Mates are not considered true members of the family: they are simply pieces garnered from other Homer Laughlin China lines and dipped in Post86 glazes — to be viewed aslant.

The jumbo pieces are handsome and beautifully designed with wide curving expanses that take the rich glazes as if they truly belonged. Very useful, albeit extremely heavy, the bowl is probably artistically preferable because the handle of the cup interferes with purity of line. Both sit beautifully on their own saucer.

But for those who continue to question the pedigree of the cup and the bowl, signature rings appear around their base, yet none on the saucer.

Of all the so-called Fiesta Mates, only these three items appear on the official schema of the Fiesta pieces, and all three have received a number. The skillet, ramekin, and even the extremely popular sugar caddy never have been so honored. (However, in a late 1999 Post86 listing obtainable from the retail outlet, the sugar caddy was listed as the sugar packet and received a number, 479.) Also, and this is a most important point, members of Homer Laughlin's Marketing and Sales Department consider these items full-fledged Fiesta members. In fact, an Art Department

> ### JUMBO CUP/ CHILI BOWL AND SAUCER
> Number: Jumbo Cup: 149, Chili Bowl: 098, Jumbo Saucer: 293
> Mold Book: N/A
> Introduced: c. 1992
> Mark: See above.
> Size: Height: 3⅜"
> Liquid Measurement: 18 oz.
> Popularity: Average
> Color Availability: All colors
> Changes: None

spokesman has said: "They [the cup, bowl, saucer] were never marked as such [Fiesta]. We keep saying we are going to do it, but never seem to get around to it."

All that is needed is the stamped or incised name to proclaim these three pieces as family members!

One final point — Jonathan Parry, the ever patient Art Director at Homer Laughlin, has more than once mentioned that the Mates are geared more for the commercial trade, and this is why they are not available in the limited edition colors. There is no skillet in lilac or sapphire or chartreuse! However, the three pieces under discussion do appear in the three limited glazes and are avidly sought.

What more does one need to recognize the jumbo cup, the chili bowl, and the saucer as Post86 Fiesta?

Goblet

GOBLET

Number: 000
Mold Book! Not known
Introduced: Very late in 1999.
Mark: A block lettered name shared with the millennium candle- holder.
Size: Height: 7"
Liquid Measurement: 12 oz.
Popularity: Not yet known.
Color Availability: Seen in rose, cobalt, yellow, turquoise, peri- winkle, persimmon, chartreuse, pearl gray.
Changes: None

These beauties were kept such a secret from the ordinary collector — the hoi polloi — that when they were offered in the Bloomingdale's by Mail Winter 1999 catalog many collectors gasped! Of course, those persons floating on the creamy top of "collector-hood" knew of the goblet, and one gentleman, very well privy to the ways of Homer, spread the information about a smaller goblet also being considered for production, but canceled for the near future. But that rumination is beside the point! Suddenly there were Post86 Fiesta goblets — a glorious surprise for the end of the millen- nium.

About the two sizes: Dave Conley, as marketing director at Homer Laughlin, did admit in writing (Jan- uary 25, 2000) that two sizes had been planned.

As soon as the advertisement was noticed, never were orders placed so quickly! Unfortunately, Blooming- dales had decided to sell them in sets of four — all one color. At $59.99 a set, not many collectors could rush to add all available colors. But, at the time of writing, it is still not exactly known how many glazes grace the 7" sides of the sleek goblet. Bloomingdale's showed only

four colors: chartreuse, cobalt, gray, and persimmon.

And then the anxious settled in to wait — and wait — and wait! When would the goblets be shipped to Bloomingdale's? When would they be sent off to those collectors who had telephoned orders? Were the gob- lets being produced at all?

Bloomingdale's sent out three "change of delivery date" notices until that date reached December 14, 1999! Then January 14, 2000! Rumors flew like crumbs scattered to scrambling geese! It was, everyone noted, getting very close to the end of chartreuse. In fact, orders for chartreuse ceased September 1, 1999. Was the goblet real? And if it were real, would one appear in chartreuse?

My order was placed the same day I saw the adver- tisement — early September, and on December 23, 1999, I finally received my chartreuse set. Impressive they were, and individually graceful, and as I experi- mented to gain insight, the conclusion was reached — a very simple conclusion, obvious to all — that these goblets would dominate any table setting in which they were used. One could never overlook the goblet! Thus,

The goblets were to be made in two sizes. These five are the larger size. The retail outlet in Newell is awash with these goblets, many of them in poor condition. The goblets have problems.

these ceramic goblets harked back to times medieval when all drinking vessels were clay. Ceramic goblets, regardless of their beauty, simply do not mingle well with true glassware. They are "occasional" items, chalice like, to be used by themselves or during informal celebrations. Perhaps they fit into the growing concept of informal home entertaining.

Meanwhile, the Fiesta message boards chattered worriedly: "I just received mine! Oh joy," one collector crooned. Another groaned: "Called Bloomingdale's! The goblet has been discontinued!" Both joy and sadness were equally represented.

So what is the story as it stood in December 1999? What is the situation: a few collectors received their orders from Bloomingdale's; many others were informed the goblet had been discontinued. The only known fact is the goblet is the last Post86 piece to appear in chartreuse. The sugar caddy and the napkin ring vied for that distinction, but the goblet is indeed the final splash of chartreuse! That should be remembered in years to come.

The goblet itself might hold the answer. Its stem wears the same three point deco design as does the millennium candleholder, and these two have the distinction of displaying a completely different raised mark — like a child's open block printing. The goblet base also bears the initials "JG" referring to Joseph Geisse, chief modeler at Homer Laughlin China. Does the Homer Laughlin Company consider the goblet as another millennium piece? Was it made in such limited numbers so that only a few — the ones who placed very early orders — will get them? Were there production problems unforeseen at first that literally halted the manufacture of the goblet?

Mr. Conley commented on the goblets. "The Fiesta

Raised mark.

goblet that appears in the Bloomingdale's- By-Mail catalog has been a production nightmare. We have not been able to deliver these in any satisfactory quantity, and this is the reason that so many […] have not been able to purchase them. Unless production yields improve considerably, the goblet will not become an open stock Fiesta item. Too bad, because we had planned to produce them in two sizes. " Even though the Bloomingdale's catalog still lists the goblets, this item has probably been unofficially discontinued. It does not appear on any of the Retail Outlet's availability lists.

Mr. Conley's statement leads me to suggest a modest acquisition of any goblets in any condition — especially chartreuse. Suddenly goblets have been appearing in tremendous numbers on the shelves and in the bins of the retail outlet's seconds room — a sure sign of production difficulties. The goblets look fine from the outside, but the glaze on the inside often is terrible. So whatever the technical problem, it does look very bad.

This is indeed a "bummer" — that medievally impressive piece of Post86 Fiesta — that a piece with such potential might be sickled down prematurely!

Lamp

LAMP

Number: 000
Mold Book: June 23, 1992
Introduced: 1993
Mark: Indented "fiesta" mark on base.
Size: Height (ceramic): 9¾". Height (including metal fixture): 14¼".
Popularity: Below average
Color Availability: Seen in the first nine colors — white to sea mist green. Apricot most desirable.
Changes: None

There are a good number of Fiesta lamps floating about on the secondary market, but most of them are homemade or specialty pieces. I am looking at a photograph at this time of a rather interesting red lamp. It consists of a carafe body (minus the handle) with a sweets comport base for a neck. Plump and attractive, but hardly could be called a true lamp. There are many others.

The only true Fiesta lamp — vintage or Post86 — is the one designed and produced exclusively for the J.C. Penney chain in 1993. It was, unfortunately, a limited item that did not sell well! The tall body, sloping in toward the bottom, was difficult for the company to produce, and these problems resulted in retail overpricing. Production worries and high prices do not make for a very successful product. So it disappeared very quietly in about one year.

The shape was also against it! There is little hint of the Art Deco background which has made Post86 Fiesta so popular. The lamp has been lumped together (by some) with the coffee server as the two most disliked pieces in the line. The lamp is sleek, modern (perhaps moderne), but hardly linked with any Deco design.

It came with a sloping sided shade in white. Since J.C. Penney pulled the lamp from their retail stores rather abruptly, dealers often locate mint caches hidden away in back rooms, dusty storerooms, forgotten warehouses — in fact any place where undesirable, rather embarrassing items might be sequestered. These lamps are purchased in groups, dusted off, and offered for sale.

Strangely, however, they are still not eagerly sought — even though scarce and accompanied with an anecdote to create a tiny bit of interest. Hardly do squabbles occur over their purchase, and whenever a lamp does appear in a mall booth, it seems to take a long lease on the site. Collectors — or at least many of them — forget that the lamp is a true, honored, and marked member of the Fiesta family — a fact often intellectually admitted, yet emotionally overlooked!

Teapot Lamp

Courtesy of Mike & Sharon Durik

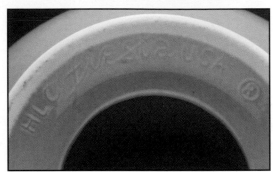

These lamps are extremely rare. Molded by Joseph Geisse, chief modeler of the HLC Art Department, these are legitimate Post86 pieces. Yet it is to be wondered if the decision to produce a lamp from the teapot shape was at all wise. The J. C. Penney exclusive is much more elegantly conceived, and even it did not sell well.

Noted in the mold book on August 12, 1997, these are not merely wired regular teapots, they are new pieces. The base and the lid are produced in one piece, and there is no opening in the spout. The original graceful finial has been reduced to a mere bump.

The finial has a hole and it goes right through! There is also a hole in the back and one was, it is supposed, to have purchased a lamp kit and make a funny little informal lamp of the piece. These lamps were usually sold without shades.

Was it popular? Hard to tell, for these lamps were produced for a very brief time. Technically, the teapot lamp was the second Post86 piece discontinued, second after the J. C. Penney lamp. I repeat, do these discontinuations really count? On a technicality, yes! But most researchers claim the spring 2000 discontinuation of the pyramid candleholder ranks as number one.

TEAPOT LAMP

Number: 000
Mold Book: August 12, 1997
Introduced: 1997
Mark: Rugular teapot mark
Size: Regular teapot size
Popularity: Not known
Color Availability: Rare in all available colors; not available in sapphire, lilac, chartreuse, pearl gray, juniper, cinnabar.
Changes: None

Mug

MUG

Number: 453
Mold Book: August 1987
Introduced: 1988
Mark: Indented, plus dated stamp. Some early mugs seem to have no mark.
Size: Height: 3½"
Liquid Measurement: 10¼ oz.
Popularity: Exceptional
Color Availability: All colors except sapphire.
Changes: None, except change in handle (white only).

While not part of the initial Post86 selection, the mug was in early evidence; by 1988 along with the butter dish and the 13½" platter. Unlike the last two named, the mug was not a new piece of Fiesta. It was based on the vintage mug and, like its ancestor, became immediately a very popular item.

The Post86 mug was beautifully redesigned, and showed itself to great advantage, proclaiming its Fiesta-hood for all to view! The vintage mug, similar to the vintage syrup, bore no distinguishing Fiesta design characteristics: its body shape was quite generic. No rings graced its side, and no incised name was to be seen on its base.

On May 19, 1987, the new mug appeared in the mold book with the comment to use the old Fiesta Tom & Jerry handle. It is again mentioned in June and in August of 1987, which leads one to believe alterations took place. The most important design feature of the new mug was the four rings near the pronounced flaring top. These rings were the proclamation that the mug was now a true unequivocal piece of Post86 Fiesta!

The mark of this mug was doubled: both an incised Homer Laughlin China Fiesta and the dated stamp that

Post86 Fiesta mug (left) contrasts with the vintage rose mug, smaller, less pink in color.

identifies much of the new line. The use of this incised name is curious indeed because the original mug possessed only the genuine Fiesta stamp, no incisement.

Form appropriate for the late twentieth century is evident also. The new mug is considerably taller and wider: so much better to fill with coffee, my dear! The price, the design, the practicality make this mug one of the more delightful and friendly of all Post86 pieces. It vies continually with the tumbler. Collectors like to acquire and then use both the mug and the tumbler: the two are very evident in both home and office. And here is one area where each member of the family can indulge in his or her color preference. One might quail at an entire dinner table laden with chartreuse new Fiesta, but a mug in bright chartreuse? Now that is another matter!

The appeal also widens because of the many varied decals that can be seen on the mug. The three tasteful designs from MegaChina are widely evident and admired. It is my personal opinion that the MegaChina design champagne is very beautiful and decorates the mug without overpowering it. One of the points of the popularity of the mug is its unofficial rogue appearance in sapphire.

The Post86 Fiesta mug can be colorful and sassy, personal and practical, comforting with fragrant green tea or intoxicating with hot buttered rum! It is the Everyman of the Post86 line!

The white mug has a changed handle. Supposedly designed for House of Pancakes to allow waitresses a better grip, it was available only in white.

Pedestal Mug

PEDESTAL MUG

Number: 424
Mold Book: Not known
Introduced: Early 1999
Mark: Circular, raised with capital.*F*
Size: Height: 6". Opening: 4"
Liquid Measurement: 18 oz.
Popularity: Average
Color Availability: All colors except black, apricot, lilac, and sapphire.
Changes: Three versions

This new Fiesta item is, as of mid 1999, the one of most recent introduction. The pedestal mug, or latte cup (as it is often designated) is a unique piece — and not unique in a truly positive context. Lately, subdued grumblings, understated rumblings, and apologetic murmurings can be heard, but it is admitted, these come mainly from the most conservative of Post86 collectors: those who have a deep and true fondness of real Fiesta (vintage and new), and critique all or most newly marketed items on whether Frederick Rhead would approve!

Would Mr. Rhead approve of the latte cup? Now it is time for me to confess that this new Fiesta piece is not a favorite of mine. It must also be mentioned that latte is an expensive yuppy drink, and very chic at the present moment. Very commercially recherché indeed, but, it is wondered, why should those in control of Homer Laughlin China's art department feel a need to commit themselves to the soigné scene? The original philosophy of Rhead's Fiesta was to bring colorful sparkle to the thirties Depression homes — to be solid and appealingly thrifty while still colorfully filling the dinner tables of the American working and middle classes. Vintage Fiesta was to be instantly recognizable and produced primarily for the home.

Now all Fiesta collectors know this information well, so forgive the repetition!

So here are Post86 collectors confronted with a tall mug, overly large, with a slight funnel shape so unlike existing pieces as to need the sides embossed with the coffee and teapots, the disc pitcher, and the medium vase. It is by these alone shalt thou know this mug as true Fiesta! These raised images and, of course, the recognizable glazes and the mark!

A pleasant little story made the rounds of "collectors-in-the-know" in late fall 2000. It was told by a man known as Fiesta Rick, and it bears repeating. Fiesta Rick informed, " I have had the privilege of visiting the Art Department twice before Jonathan's passing; we had several discussions about the design of some of the newer pieces. I remember one discussion about the pieces that were chosen to be embossed on the latte mug. My question was why did they choose the vase shape. The other items, disc pitcher, teapot, and coffee server, all hold beverages, and the vase doesn't. I was bold enough to add, 'The carafe would have made a better choice.' [Jonathan] called Joseph [Geisse] in and had me repeat my question, [without thinking a moment] Joseph looked me squarely in the eye and said, 'Because I have a life.'" Thus those who use the pedestal mug must accept the presence of the vase! The anecdote ended with the brief comment that Jonathan had been hurt by the public (read collector?) bashing of the new items.

There are three versions of the pedestal mug. *First version:* Modeled on April 14, 1998 by Joseph Geisse, this piece had a rather heavy beaded edge: quite charming, but unwise. The beading caused the rim to deform during firing. After a few trial runs done in the cobalt glaze, this version was abandoned. *Second version:* This is strangely known as the #2 pedestal mug even though it was entered in the mold book on June 3, 1998. The body was straighter, more like a Royal Guardsman — straight and firm.The raised figures of coffee pot and vase also stood straighter on the sides. This version was, in my estimation, more stalwart, albeit less graceful. Only a few of these exist in rose. *Third version:* This is the actual mug available today.

Seated alone or with verbally scintillating, sparkling friends a la mode at small French bistro tables in a fashionable mall where everyone must wear, at least, a shirt and sandals, one sips frothy latte from a pedestal mug in periwinkle or persimmon, and talks of art, the dwindling possibilities of free love, and the latest trends in designer jeans! If this is true, or near truth, then this mug is, in essence, a specialty item. An item not to be used in regular conjunction with family dining, but specially aimed at drinkers of coffee-flavored foam in commercial public surroundings.

Physically, the mug is impressive and not unpleasing. (Perhaps, however, it has strong competition from the more conventional Fiesta Mate Irish coffee that, unfortunately, is only available in rose, cobalt blue, turquoise, and persimmon.) Six inches from footed base to slightly rimmed top and four inches across, it must be speculated how much steam-heated froth must be present to fill this space. Certainly, no besotted coffee lover (no matter how devoted) could do justice to this mug filled with mocha java, Mexican Maragogype, Hawaiian Kona, or even the finest of Blue Mountain supreme! Enough is enough, and the presence of a whipped milky froth is required! Shades of Frasier and Niles in downtown Seattle!

Now, a final confession, this account is flavored with a soupçon of tongued cheekiness! But I cannot really take this Fiesta piece too seriously. It bears, please note, the raised Fiesta mark and must be considered a full fledged member of the family on the par with a sophisticated female cousin who is quite ready to flirt with a husband or a college boy son! I muse over the fact that the pedestal mug is accepted in the family, while the hard working, solidly designed and patiently rewarding jumbo cup or the plebian chili bowl are still not quite allowed to hold the Fiesta name — not quite come il fault? Could it be that glamour has befogged the issue?

Pedestals

These pedestals exist in two sizes, but have never been offered to the public. When, or if, they will be manufactured in quantity is not known. Since it is believed pedestals have some relationship to the hostess bowl, they are discussed there (see page 60).

Napkin Ring

NAPKIN RING

Number: 469
Mold Book: Sometime between August 1991 and January 1992.
Introduced: Summer 1992
Mark: Raised on base.
Size: Height: 2¾"
Popularity: Exceptional
Color Availability: All colors except sapphire.
Changes: None

The clever round napkin ring became a physical reality on May 21, 1988 (its first mention in the mold book), but it probably was not offered to the consuming public until a year or so later. The first official Homer Laughlin China advertising sheet listing was 1994, but, as I remember, my black napkin ring foursome was purchased more than a year earlier.

Napkin rings. Yes, these are partialities of mine. I am, and always have been, extremely fond of napkin rings. Yet, this piece rarely appears in ceramic. Ben Seibel presents them in a Mikasa line titled Potter's Art, but usually napkin rings are silver, wooden, bone, or Bakelite — rarely ceramic. This fact makes the Post86 Fiesta piece rather special. This piece is a full, firm family member of the Fiesta line. Full-fledged and flying, and, I would suppose, aimed at the retail market. Yet I have noted at a popular San Francisco bistro these rings in assorted colors gracefully holding well-starched serviettes in complementary shades and tints. But the setting was sidewalk informal — picnic or barbecue ambiance was the aim.

The piece is the handle of the teapot — with an extra dollop at the top — and never appeared in the earlier vintage colorware lines. Perhaps Frederick Rhead thought that competition was too heavy with all the Bakelite beauties abounding. Today napkin rings are rarely seen on the domestic table setting: just slightly rarer than napkins themselves. Both situations are supremely sad. For what is so rare as a napkin in its ring?

What is somewhat surprising is these sets of four are quite expensive. The prices, per set, range from $19.95 to over $25.00, and many sources (the Homer Laughlin China Retail Outlet for example) make one purchase the set in the same color. This unfortunately means, to get a color selection of six rings, the embattled hostess must purchase 24 at a price nearing $120.00 or more! What about the idea of including one napkin ring as part of each Fiesta place setting?

The rings are firmly identified as Fiesta on the solidly securing base, but this mark can be overlooked depending upon the glaze. In my experience, apricot allows for the clearest reading, persimmon second.

These items are certainly not necessary! They are the icing fillip on the cake of entertaining. They are charmingly clunky, intentionally expendable, yet notably special.

The napkin ring is available in all colors except sapphire. Originally, Homer Laughlin China did not plan to offer this item in its third limited color, chartreuse, but finally bent to the demands of collectors. In late 1999, the word was out: napkin rings were to be available in chartreuse, but only as an item exclusive to the Homer Laughlin China outlet in Newell, West Virginia. Then came the collector brouhaha over the chartreuse sugar caddy, and many despaired over the possible cancellation of the promised chartreuse napkin ring. However, in late November 1999, Homer Laughlin China kept its word and the Retail Outlet commenced shipping. This last moment decision seems to give the napkin ring the possible distinction of being the last piece to be glazed in chartreuse.

A colorful display of a dozen napkin rings! The only glaze not pictured is chartreuse, a color exclusive to the Homer Laughlin China outlet. The ring was not issued in sapphire.

Dish Deep Pie Baker

DEEP DISH PIE BAKER

Number: 487
Mold Book: December 20, 1993
Introduced: Late 1994
Mark: Raised round "fiesta," dated stamp in middle.
Size: Width: 10⅛"
Popularity: Average.
Color Availability: All colors except sapphire.
Changes: None

One of the problems of growing older is the haunting memories of the times past. Personally, the idea of a deep dish pie baker is pleasant, but is it part of the today crowd? When I was young, my grandmother made two pies and one layer cake every Saturday morning. Whatever the pies (apple usually) or the cake, they would be consumed by the following Saturday being liberally served to cousins, aunts, and members of her sewing circle, and then the process was repeated. But, I ask you, who bakes pies today? What need is there, in the line of Post86 Fiesta dinnerware, for a pie baker?

But, please do not misunderstand me — the pie baker is one of my favorites! Probably because it takes me back to my grandmother and the 1940s. In my personal collection reside pie bakers in black, rose, apricot, periwinkle blue, lilac, and chartreuse: and I have yet to bake a pie! I doubt if this feat would even be possible. However, I cannot but surmise that the presence of a pie baker (i.e., plate) in the 1990s line of dinnerware is merely for a collector ploy! And, is the question, if these pie bakers were really used to cook blueberry, apple, or rhubarb/strawberry pies, would

Notice how the shimmering Post86 glazes reflect light. The flat persimmon piece throws a glint of red onto the sides of the lilac example.

they be worth much as collectibles? That is the question! Admittedly, unused, they are beautifully designed with architecturally perfect arches about the rim. The indented rim on the inside makes me wonder about the practicality of the piece as a proper pie baker. (My grandmother used Pyrex, simple and pure with sloping sides.) And this reinforces the idea of collectorism versus practicality.

It is my personal belief that the decision-makers at Homer Laughlin today wish to combine the dinnerware line with the Kitchen Kraft line, perhaps to capture the interest of the all-consuming collector. There is a very strange overlap here that confuses me. The collector/user can buy a number of kitchen pieces that seem to be unrelated to a dinnerware service, but don't forget, old Fiesta did offer a promotional pie plate long ago. Yet, the pie baker is a true piece of Post86 Fiesta: it has the raised Fiesta mark and the stamp to prove it. A double identification whamee!

But, we really must not forget that this new Fiesta is geared for the commercial trade where trendy little restaurants try to duplicate the starched-curtain look of the '40s and '50s! This concept is pleasant and very commendable. It is doubtful whether this smartly designed piece is meant for grandmothers at home baking pies on a snowy Saturday morning.

Here is the pie baker to be available in the Looney Tunes series — Sylvester on his signature yellow.

Disc Pitchers

LARGE DISC PITCHER

Number: (746) 484
Mold Book: Not necessary, used old mold.
Introduced: February 1986
Mark: Circular, indented with small *f*.
Size: Height: 7¼"
Liquid Measurement: 56 oz.
Popularity: Average
Color Availability: All colors.
Changes: None

SMALL DISC PITCHER

Number: (747) 485
Mold Book: Not necessary, used old mold.
Introduced: February 1986
Mark: Circular, indented with small *f*.
Size: Height: 5½"
Liquid Measurement: 22 oz.
Popularity: Above average
Color Availability: All colors except sapphire.
Changes: None

MINI DISC PITCHER

Number: 475
Mold Book: December 7, 1992
Introduced: Summer 1993
Mark: Circular, indented with capital *F*.
Size: Height: 3¼"
Liquid Measurement: 4¾ oz.
Popularity: Exceptional
Color Availability: All colors except sapphire.
Changes: None

The large disc water pitcher must be considered one of Fiesta's signature pieces. When it arrived on the scene in 1939, there were already two large pitchers well ensconced: the ice pitcher, an original January 1936 item, and the 2-pint jug, just a tad younger, being introduced in August of the same year. These two appeared in typically rounded shapes. The ice pitcher was to become very collectible in later years as it existed until about 1944. The 2-pint jug held the Fiesta stage until mid-1956.

The shape of the disc pitcher, both vintage and Post86, is very atypical; it is a flattened moon shape (perhaps the metaphor is oxymoronic?). At least it is not rounded as a true globe, but appears to the eye, deceptively, as a sky-bound moon shape, the night sky's disc eye!

Comparison of Post86 large disc pitcher (front) with the same-named glaze in vintage (rear). Left is chartreuse, right is rose.

Why was it thought necessary to offer another large Fiesta pitcher? The answer will probably never be known. But we are aware that in August of 1937, Mr. Berrisford (one of the experienced Homer Laughlin modelers) was shaping a square jug for Fiesta — a piece never put into production, and in March 1938, Mr. Berrisford was again experimenting with a flat-sided jug which was to become the disc pitcher. It arrived and was soon coupled with the smaller juice pitcher (in the vintage line a promotional item), and the two remained solidly popular until all Fiesta ended in January 1973.

As proof of popularity, both sizes were aboard when Post86 Fiesta was launched at the end of February 1986: now designated large disc pitcher (746) and small disc pitcher (747). They were two of the 31 members of the new and newly designed Fiesta line. The ice pitcher and the 2-pint jug of vintage fame were not on the passenger list when Post86 Fiesta sailed into the world of commercial dinnerware. There is probably something inherent in their semi-vitreous shape that forbids translation into vitreous china! However I believe the ice-lip pitcher would be welcomed as a year 2002 Post86 piece.

Four friendly miniature disc pitchers.

But, by 1994, not only were the item numbers changed and the name altered, a new family member appeared — the baby — the miniature disc pitcher. The official family was now:

484 disc pitcher large
485 disc pitcher small
475 disc pitcher miniature
Poppa, momma, and baby disc surely!

What about design logistics? There is absolutely no problem with grasping the large disc; its handle is functionally easy to hold as all four fingers fit into the arch and the thumb opposes correctly. The small disc is more daintily constructed, and men might find it more problematic to life due to the narrowness of the handle opening. But the mini disc? Now this baby is a real problem! So much of a problem, we are wondering if it was not envisioned as a shelf piece. It really does not function as an individual creamer — absolutely not. Most people would have to grasp it by the sides to pour. While the idea of the mini disc works on paper, it definitely — physically and psychologically — is not in the same class as the vintage Harlequin novelty and individual creamers!

Nevertheless the mini disc is popular, and while not practical, is highly collectible. They march in varied colorful glazes across many a collector's shelf!

The large pitcher is available in every Post86 glaze. It is also a very popular item for decorative additions including Homer Laughlin China's sixtieth anniversary logo. The small pitcher, also used for some interesting decals, can be seen in all colors except sapphire. However, unofficially, some pieces in this limited color are known to have escaped the confines of the Homer Laughlin factory. The mini pitcher also dances in all the colors except sapphire.

The large disc pitcher exists in two versions, however one has been rejected by the company and exists only in a few persimmon examples. This rejected version was originally received as the Anniversary pitcher with the sides slightly bulbous; it looked somewhat pregnant. Just how "pregnant" can be estimated when it is realized the regular pitcher is 4" wide and this variation was 6". Again, like the #2 pedestal mug rejection, the researcher can only surmise about the reasons. Since the disc pitcher has become one the great signature pieces for all the Fiesta line, to tamper with a good thing was viewed as sacrilegious. My thought only!

When seen alone, the Sevilla small pitcher could perhaps be mistaken for the Post86 miniature. But put them together and any question disappears.

Two curious notes:

1. The vintage semi-vitreous disc consistently weighs 2 pounds, 12 ounces, while the newer version weighs closer to 2 pound 10 ounces. One of the rare instances where the older line outweighs the vitreous ware.
2. Be aware that a Sevilla miniature look-alike hovers in the background to confound those easily confused. It looks much like the Fiesta mini, but it is slightly sharper with a larger handle opening, and fewer Fiesta rings. It is quite charming, however, and fits well into the family. It has been seen in pink, light green, yellow, and cobalt. These colors are not exactly Fiesta colors, but near enough to snag and confuse the unwary.

Chop Plate

The pyramid candleholder shows the plate's size.

When first offered as an original Post86 piece, the chop plate measured 12". By 1988, its size had dwindled slightly to 11⅝", and then on a recent advertising sheet, 11¾". Not significant, but interesting.

This plate has only size — and that only 1¼" larger than the dinner plate — to distinguish it from the others, and perhaps it should be listed with them. However, it is the name of this piece which is fascinating. Some retailers list this as a "round platter" — indeed other manufacturers of the more modern dinnerware lines tend to disregard the term "chop" completely. It is this disregard of an old bit of dinnerware terminology that makes me insist upon giving this chop plate its due! Even *Homer Laughlin China* disdains the true name in some of its brochures!

What is a chop plate? In the summer of 1996 issue of *The Laughlin Eagle* there appeared an entire focus on Homer Laughlin China chop plates. Since I wrote the article, I can quote with impunity: "There are, in this confusing world of dinnerware, a number of terms over which linger a sense of ambiguity. Terms of jargonese used by those who wish to stress their knowledge of chinaware, or by those who feel safe and fulfilled when using words instantly known by others

---

CHOP PLATE

Number: (710) 468
Mold Book: November 25, 1985
Introduced: February 1986
Mark: Some early examples unmarked, later ones date stamped.
Size: 11¾"
Popularity: Below average
Color Availability: All colors except sapphire.
Changes: None

of their ilk: like secret passwords to allow entry into a special little boys' clubhouse!"

And along with nappy, 36s bowl, baker, and dish (meaning platter), chop plate becomes one of those useful, but esoteric terms. Technically, a chop plate is infinitely more than simply a large round platter. There is something elementally grand about this piece. Can any dinnerware shape be more grand than the vintage Fiesta 15" chop plate? They are ceremonious and glorious pieces!

Chop plates run from 13" to 15" — but there are a few just touching 12" and into this category the Post86 piece can fit — even if it is a tiny bit smaller. The Post86 chop plate has been reduced for modern convenience, but it does carry its lineage proudly.

These large plates were indeed used as platters, but no respectable cook would place a roast chicken or a duck de l'orange on a chop plate: the shape, either of the duck or the plate, would be wrong. A chop plate was meant for chops! Chops piled high into a sizzling pyramid! If you are against chops, then hamburgers (either meat or vegetarian) piled high; pieces of fried chicken, perhaps. The chop plate could also be called into service to serve delicately quartered cucumber or watercress sandwiches.

Toy with your gastronomic inventiveness and use the Post86 chartreuse chop plate to serve a magnificent chartreuse de perdreaux, an elegant entree invented many centuries ago by the vegetarian Carthusian monks at Le Grande Chartreuse Monastery in Grenoble, those same monks who invented, and still produce the luscious liqueur Chartreuse. The green/yellow liqueur gave its name, of course, to the color chartreuse. I am viewing one of these memorable creations at this very moment: a huge mound decorated with strips of green beans, orange carrots, petit pois, glazed white onions, and green pepper cut-outs.

However, now that this picture is confronting me, I suddenly realize that the Post86 pizza tray was designed to fulfill the needs of those who love chop plates of grand proportions. This queen of all entrees, this formidable chartreuse de perdreaux, would not fit on the 11¾" regulation Post86 chop plate. It demands the immensity of the pizza tray!

Perhaps the best use for the chop plate would be in the guise of a colorful charger framing the dinner or the luncheon plate. Imagine a turquoise chop plate underneath a persimmon dinner plate. Certainly a moment of dining drama!

Welled Snack Plate

Note how the transparent glaze on the persimmon example allows the well's circles to stand out.

Some critics (and here the word "critical" does not denote only negative reactions) of Post86 Fiesta proclaim the more recent pieces are straying quite far from Frederick Rhead's original conceptions. Thus it is being mentioned continuously. This is, of course, absolutely true, but can it be any other way? New Fiesta was not conceived by Jonathan Parry and the Homer Laughlin officials, as a mere refined reworking of Rhead's ideas: they most certainly cannot wish to sell only museum reproductions ambitiously aimed at the collectible market!

Or so we have been told! Dinnerware, all dinnerware, must be solidly seated in its own time, and reflect not only the best and most useable pieces of the past, but also a certain cleverness for the present. Admittedly, I personally am strongly rooted in the past — all people, not merely collectors, of a certain age suffer or sustain these backward glances yet realize the present is where things are happening. Sad, perhaps, for the aging, but very true.

Thus the Fiesta of the '80s and '90s cannot depend just on the designs of Frederick Rhead. Mr. Parry has done an admirable job in trying to maintain the integrity of Rhead's ideas, but with an updated dash of modernity. He brought along those vintage Fiesta items that "work" for today and jettisoned those that do not — not that I agree with most of these decisions, but neither do I have public surveys, marketing aims, nor financial goals nudging me on!

For example, in the 1930s, divided plates were very popular: a quarter space for peas and carrots, a quarter space for a baked potato and the remaining one-half for the meat — whatever that might be in Depression times. After thinking about this, and asking several

---

WELLED SNACK PLATE

Number: 760
Mold Book: March 20, 1997
Introduced: Late 1997
Mark: Dated stamp
Size: 10½"
Popularity: Average
Color Availability: All colors except black, apricot, lilac, and sapphire.
Changes: None

---

astute people, I have no real answer about why divided plates were popular, and why now they are not! This concept is still used in micro-waveable TV dinner plastic trays! But I do not think the divided individual dinner plate will be introduced again in the Post86 line. I might be wrong. The Homer Laughlin China Art Department keeps its own counsel. As did Jonathan before he died.

To compensate for those abandoned vintage pieces, or perhaps merely to add present day interest and give consumers, both commercial and collector, some choices, Mr. Parry designed three plates for specific and varied uses. The welled snack plate (760) was the second of these plates to appear; it is mentioned in the modeling log three times (12/10/96, 2/15/97, 3/20/97) so it underwent revisions, and since it does not appear in black or apricot, we assume it was available only after these regular colors ceased normal production. When questioned about the exact use of the snack plate, Mr. Parry admitted that it had nothing to do with TV, but was specifically geared to home entertaining which is still on a large scale, but in a more casual buffet style. It is not thought that home entertaining is its only use because the snack plate would work admirably at the buffet table in an exclusive golf club dining room, or at a flower club luncheon. However, these plates are extremely heavy and not meant for holding while chatting on the terrace — (even though this might have been the original purpose — to emulate the "party plate" of the '50s (Ben Seibel's party plate designed under the Raymor logo and produced

by Steubenville, early 1950s, is a near double of Mr. Parry's 1997 welled snack plate). The weight and size of the plates demand a table, or, at least, a very sturdy and seated knee.

Incidentally, the only Fiesta piece to fit securely within the well is the small bouillon bowl — the teacup fits but slips about. Strangely, the tumbler does not fit at all! Nor does the jumbo cup or the jumbo chili bowl! All three of these seemingly logical choices are too large for the well. And, needless to mention, a hostess would not offer the use of this welled snack plate unless the bouillon or the teacup was deemed necessary to the meal.

Here is a welled snack plate in sea mist (left) shown to compare its size with the hostess tray (yellow) and serving tray (persimmon). All three are considered useful for entertaining and look gracious on the buffet table.

The bouillon bowl fits the well. Delightfully specific in use and design or perhaps to people more logical in outlook, very utilitarian in use and design! The well is quaintly outlined in some famous Fiesta rings, and within the well, three rings are placed. I find this rather charming.

Plates

The five sizes of plates. Bottom: 10" persimmon, 9" periwinkle blue. Top: 6" rose, sea mist green chop plate, 7" juniper.

Plates! Is anything so prosaic as a plate? Yet they are — all sizes — the backbone of each and all the dinnerware sets! A set can do without a teapot — and a number of important lines do just this — but dinnerware must have a series of plates. No matter how fanciful, graceful, and unique are the jugs and casseroles, the comports and coffee servers, they are nothing without the unifying elements: the plates!

And many ceramic designers decided to make something "new and different" when designing a series of plates. And quite often, this dangerous approach results in a flat "quirky" thing sitting in front of the diner. Some have been lucky and developed a restrained different look; the mid-century modern designers had some success with this approach: Ben Seibel, Eva Zeisel, Russell Wright! But, however, the true essence of a plate is to be round — with a rim, a verge, and a well. Yet one of Homer Laughlin's most successful shapes — Rhythm — offers a plate sans verge, sans well. The Rhythm plate is one simple, graceful curve. The most difficult piece of dinnerware to design is the prosaic plate.

Some lines attempt to capture consumer interest, not by a triangle or octagon plate shape, but by giving the purchaser a wider number from which to choose. Homer Laughlin did this quite often in its decaled

---

PLATES

Number: Dinner: 466. Luncheon: 465. Salad: 464. B & B: 463.

Mold Book: The first mention of "new" Fiesta was a plate, November 4, 1985.

Introduced: February 1986 (original item)

Mark: With the exception of a few early plates, all are stamped. The earlier with "*Fiesta*," the later with "*fiesta*." The later stamps were dated.

Size: Dinner: 10½". Luncheon: 9". Salad: 7⅛". B & B: 6⅛".

Popularity: Average

Color Availability: All colors, but the B & B not in sapphire.

Changes: None noticeable

*The five original 1986 colors. The impression is soft, muted, pastel —
even with black and the dark color.*

lines: Georgian Eggshell for example. This lovely and
delicate shape of the 1950s allowed for the dinner, the
luncheon, the round and the square 8" plate, the 7" and
the 6", a selection of six, plus the impressive chop
plate. The latter was really more of a round platter
than a plate. Did the average consumer buy examples
of each size? Probably not — it was the choice that
impressively fanned the flame of acquisition.

Vintage and Post86 Fiesta disdained such a numbers game. Mr. Rhead counted upon four solid and
secure completely rounded shapes with discrete
ringed decoration, and color. He believed, I think, that
plates formed the background, the essential, the necessary, and thus, why tamper with the design of the
essential, the necessary? The consumers would feel
safe with the simple familiar rounds of the plates, and
from this dinnerware haven, could view the more
flamboyant and startling pieces without becoming
startled themselves! The prosaic plate in the role of a
security blanket.

The four plates are the central facet, the backbone
of the Post86 line.

As the research reads in the official Homer Laughlin China early advertisement sheet, the plates were
listed simply as "plates" (no use designation) with
sizes. For example:

Plate, 10⅜"; Plate, 9"; Plate, 7⅛"; and Plate, 6½".

In the second sheet, designations appear and sizes
(for all but one) change.

Plate, Dinner 10½"; Plate, Luncheon 9"; Plate,
Salad 7⅛"; Plate, B & B 6⅛".

When Mr. Parry was questioned regarding these
size differences, he said, in essence, there was no real
size difference. It was a matter of possible shrinkage in
the kiln, or even hasty measurement. Collectors should
not anticipate different sizes, nor think one possible
size might be more valuable than another.

Remember that the primary thrust of the Post86
dinnerware service was aimed at the commercial
world of clubs, restaurants, bistros, and diners. The
dinner plate is extremely impressive: it is grand, so
grand that the luncheon plate is immediately recognizable for what is is! In fact, each plate is quickly
identifiable — a very valuable trait in the busy world
of commercial food service.

Another anomaly surrounds the plates of any dinnerware line. One must conclude that plates are
always manufactured in great abundance; their existence far exceeds the numbers of sugars, creamers,
platters, and most certainly the teapot! They are everywhere. Yet, because of their common qualities, their
abundance, they are used to excess, broken with abandon, and discarded without regrets. A housewife of the
forties (or in 2001?) would certainly be more prone to

repair the broken handle of a teacup, or the finial of a pretty sugar bowl rather than mend a broken dinner plate. Sharded plates were heaved, and replacements speedily purchased.

Plates of all sizes were heavily used, considered as expendable, and over the decades (after they ceased production) became scarcer than would have been considered possible. Then, when a sadly diminished set of Fiesta was considered for vigorous retirement — melmac was the new "rage" — it was usual that the large platters, teapots, sugar bowls, and creamers be saved and stored, but plates went the way of all expendables — into the dustbin, or suffered to be used as dog dishes or cat plates! This will probably be true of the Post86 Fiesta.

There is nothing simpler, more dramatic, more purely imposing, than a sparkling dinner plate. All Post86 plates possess a subtle understated beauty — a beauty uncomplicated by decals or bobs or knobs at the edge or metallic trim or any other flashy diversion to garner attention. Each plate is a weighty, impressive bit of sculpture, finely honed and under appreciated.

Some later colors. The impression is vibrant and daring!

Platters

9½" redesigned. 11½" Post86. 13½" Post86. Notice the lack of uniformity of shape.

PLATTERS

Number: 9½", 456. 11½", 457. 13½", 458.

Mold Book: Remembering the trade name for platter is simply "dish," we read a good scattering of "dish" in the mold book. The last mention is May 10, 1994.

Introduced: The first two were original, the 13½" appeared about 1988.

Size: See above.

Popularity: 9½" above average, others average.

Color Availability: All colors, except the 9½" and the 11½" did not appear in sapphire.

Changes: Major change for the 9½" size (see text), none for the other two sizes.

Platters are usually the most prosaic pieces in any dinnerware set — unless they are the enormous variety stretching 15" or over. Strangely plates are viewed more positively. Then platters become very impressive and receive special protective treatment. Due to the care given them, platters can be relatively common: they are much more available to collectors than, say, the dinner plates or the teacups and saucers — these pieces are heavily used and sadly broken.

However, the three Post86 Fiesta platters move away from this usual humdrum existence, not because of size, but because of a surrounding intrigue that keeps the researcher busily surmising.

Follow along, and perhaps the reader will agree! The vintage line offered only one platter: 12½", but for convenience it will be labeled as "large." Yet when Fiesta was dramatically reawakened in 1986, a choice of two platters was given to the consumer, and neither size was represented in the earlier line. The sizes of these two Post86 platters were 9½" and 11½". These two cannot however, be considered "new" pieces — in the traditional sense. Please bear with me as I explain.

First: the smaller 9½" platter, while never appearing in the vintage line, did appear in the Ironstone Fiesta of 1969 – 1972, and exists in all three colors: antique

9½", 11½", 12" vintage cobalt. Notice the uniformity of shape.

gold, turf green, and mango red. Incidentally, please recall that mango red is exactly the same color as the original Fiesta red, and is often used by vintage collectors to provide an underplate for their red sauceboat. It could be called a "cross-over" piece and is quite scarce and always expensively priced.

Second: the Post86 11½" platter is, in my opinion, the replacement for the vintage piece. As explained below, the proportions of this platter are the same as the vintage platter — except it is one inch smaller.

In an unusual brochure (distributed before 1988, because there is no mention of yellow or turquoise), after listing the 5-piece place setting at a sale price of $14.99, and five other sale pieces, the brochure states: "Also available exclusively at Stone & Thomas," and proceeds to name six pieces. They are 12-ounce bowl, bread & butter plate, bouillon cup, fruit bowl (stacking), 11½" oval platter, and 9½" oval platter.

Interestingly, the last four named did not appear in the original Fiesta line. Is this merely a coincidence, or did Stone & Thomas exert some pressure to have these new items included in the new line? Will we ever know?

Exact measurements are vital to present the case when regarding the medium and the small platter. The former is 11½" x 8 ¾" — the latter 9½" x 6¾". Both are nearly perfect footballs in shape, and the proportions are the same, i.e., the medium platter is 2" wider and 2" longer than the smaller. Measure now, the vintage platter: 12½" x 9¾". Again a football shape and 1" wider and longer than the contemporary medium one. The general proportions of all three (two Post86 and one vintage) are exactly the same, and even more curious, the three nest perfectly!

When we submit the large Post86 platter to the same measuring scrutiny, immediately something is out of joint! To follow the same proportional growth, this third platter should be 13½" x 10¾". Alas it is not! The length is accurate, but the width? 13½" x 9½". Fully 1¼" out of alignment! And the three Post86 platters do not nest!

Why were the two "new" platters — assumedly designed by Jonathan Parry — made to conform to the earlier platter's proportions? And why, when Mr. Parry settled to design the largest platter to appear in the 1988 advertising brochure, did he not make it also proportional to the vintage example? Can we ever answer? Thus I maintain the origin of the three Post86 platters: 9½" platter originated from Fiesta Ironstone; 11½" platter was the vintage 12½" platter but reduced one inch; 13½" platter was an entirely new design. The 9½" platter has its own interesting history; it was one of the few new Fiesta pieces to undergo a radical change after 1986 — probably within a year or so after being introduced. Again, it must be repeated: changes to existing dinnerware shapes are not undertaken lightly. To redesign a handle, a finial, or a lid, or, as with the smallest platter, the entire shape, the change involves expense and time, and alters the entire look of the piece (with the possibility it may no longer "mesh" with the other pieces), such a change is never done on a whim, or, as has been facetiously implied, "to have something to do!"

Remember that the small platter was originally advertised as a "sandwich plate." I wonder if the curved shape of the first version did not really allow enough flat base for the sandwich use. The first small platter — with its curving sides — was really an

underplate for the gravy. Unfortunately, Mr. Parry had to make a choice: sandwich plate or sauceboat underplate? The choice fell to the sandwich plate, and the restyled small platter — with its completely flat well — no longer truly functions as an underplate.

But the redesigned piece retains its correct proportions, and as a sandwich server it still nests perfectly with Post86's medium and vintage's large. So much for ceramic decision-making! The 13½" new platter still must remain different!

Thus, the collector will locate both versions of the small 9½" platter in white, black, rose, apricot, and cobalt. Starting with yellow (1988), only the "flat-well" version will be found — although it could be that some yellow early versions do exist. There is, please remember, no official 9½" platter in sapphire.

A confusing discussion for three such prosaic items?

Two varieties of 9½" platters.

Sauceboat

Single sauceboat.

When new Fiesta was first introduced (1986), many of the individual pieces were strongly based on the vintage shapes, and thus, can cause the neophyte to blanch with fear of possible misidentification: is the piece an example of vintage or of Post86 Fiesta? But only the new sauceboat — so closely similar to its vintage forerunner — can give even the experienced collector some worrisome moments. The new sauceboat is a nearly exact replication of the old!

Why the near exact duplication, vintage to Post86? Probably because the sauceboat is nearly perfect in form and function just the way it appeared in the vintage Fiesta line, and why muddle around with perfection? Like the old disc pitcher, but unlike the carafe, the sauceboat needed no modern modification!

The sauceboat is the one piece where weight, thickness, and lack of detailing do not always play the identification game fairly! After weighing several of both lines, it was determined that the earlier sauceboat is barely heavier. Most vintage examples tipped the scales at one pound even. The Post86 pieces were rarely more than one pound, one ounce — close indeed! The identifier can heft or weigh sauceboats for a fortnight or longer, and the answer remains the same: weight is not a clear clue for differentiating between old and new.

The lip of the new is a little more narrow and

SAUCEBOAT

Number: 719
Mold Book: Not really necessary, used old mold.
Introduced: February 1986
Mark: Exactly like vintage piece — with small *f.*
Size: Length: 7¾" from handle to tip of spout.
Liquid Measurement: 18½ oz.
Popularity: Average
Color Availability: All colors except sapphire.
Changes: None

pointed, but to note this characteristic accurately an example of each line is required. And, almost ironically, the trademark Fiesta rings can be clearer, sharper on the contemporary pieces. So are we approaching an identification conundrum?

Now there are a few persons who could — and do — differentiate between these two at the flip of a wrist: their *dexterite* is to be admired.

Now is it to the glazes we must turn? Will the

Notice how closely the Post86 (left) sauce boat resembles the vintage (right).

*In both shape and color, the Post86 turquoise sauceboat
(left) is a near twin of its vintage counterpart (right).*

glazes prove to be the thing wherein we catch the conscience of the king? Or, in other words, will the glaze clearly separate the old from the new? In a number of cases, yes! Apricot and black, periwinkle blue and sea mist green will rarely cause a whisper of worry. In other cases, not always. Those bearing the same name are the ones wherein the neophyte can anticipate trouble and tremble. Cobalt blue is not overly worrisome, and the pinky sharpness of the new rose eases the possibility of a mistaken identification with the soft grayed rose of the old. Turquoise might be problematic for those collectors whose eyes are not turned to "teal" versus sky-blue.

Note, please, that I hesitate to say take the word of the dealer or the mall salesperson when a question arises. Alas, from personal experience, I hesitate! In 1986, as a New Brunswick goat farmer recently moved to the wiles of Florida, a set of pink Fiesta was purchased for $100.00. I knew nothing, but was assured by the mall owner it was old. Occasionally, the mall where this set of 49 pieces was purchased is revisited, and the owner still sits ensconced behind her counter. She does not remember me, but when I grimace and glower at her over my glasses, I wonder if she becomes worried. Actually, at today's prices, my 13-year-old purchase is not a disaster — I just dislike a blatant lie!

With (pearl) gray and chartreuse, the collector, even the most astute, will be wise to wonder. Words are hard to translate, and thus one can say the new chartreuse glaze is sharper, more brilliant, and wears a shinier surface! But what exactly does that mean? The new gray has more surface sheen and lacks muted softness. These words are true, but exactly how can the eyes register "surface sheen" and "muted softness." In the case of gray and chartreuse, it will be wise to hedge bets by having an example of both the vintage and the new lines.

But then, dear friend, you can simply turn to Homer Laughlin China for the answer. Yes, the company has taken to inscribing an "H" somewhere on the base of a piece where neophyte identification could be problematic.

Without this "H," identifying old and new chartreuse and gray may well have separated the men from the boys!

Chartreuse base with H.

Rangetop Shakers

RANGETOP SHAKERS

Number: 756 (two items, one number)
Mold Book: March 10, 1997
Introduced: Mid-1997
Mark: Raised, encircling the rubber hole plug.
Size: Height: 4⅞"
Popularity: Average
Color Availability: Probably not in black or apricot. All other colors except lilac and sapphire.
Changes: Enlargement of drain hole.

First mentioned in the Homer Laughlin China mold book on December 16, 1996, this set was revised on March 10, 1997, in order to have slightly larger drain holes. They were offered to consumers very soon after that date. Just as the regular shakers are considered two separate items, the Post86 range pair officially must also be numbered as two due to the S and the P shaker openings.

Incidentally, this set, like the napkin ring, carries the "raised" mark, thus making these pieces official members of the Fiesta family.

Remember that the vintage line sported a "kitchen" shaker set. Kitchen Kraft's large ball was usually confined to the kitchen, but the Post86 version's role in life is totally different. Very much an Art Deco shape, this tall 1990s set underwent a change of function which required a change of form. Jonathan Parry devised the range top shakers not only to sit placidly on a shelf above the stove (wonder how many modern ranges have that rear shelf?) but also to stand stalwartly beside the barbecue (portable or permanent) on backyard decks and patios, and also to function very admirably on informal, but chic, *haute bourgeoisie* buffet tables.

In the rough and ready world of outdoor dining, the tendency is to grab, rather roughly, at a waiting salt shaker! If the reader will experiment with the Kitchen Kraft shaker, it will be immediately seen that the ball shape generally will be grasped from the top, not the side! And who wants a series of sweaty hands pressing down upon the shaker openings? The form of the old large ball shaker no longer functions.

Whoever designed the new shaker was wise to the ways of barbecuing! Not only do the new shakers possess added height (the better to see you, my dear) but the handle cries out "pick me up here!" This fact delights the persnickety maiden aunt who happens to be in the buffet line behind a grubby and sweaty ten-year-old nephew. However, this handle does not quite rate an A+. It is rather small for a mature man's two fingers and must be grasped thumb on top, index finger within the handle, and middle finger supporting from below. Not a dire circumstance, but with just a quarter inch more, the handle would prove less awkward.

Indeed the Post86 tall, solidly designed shakers are a very welcome addition to the kitchen, the deck, or even the rusticated informal table.

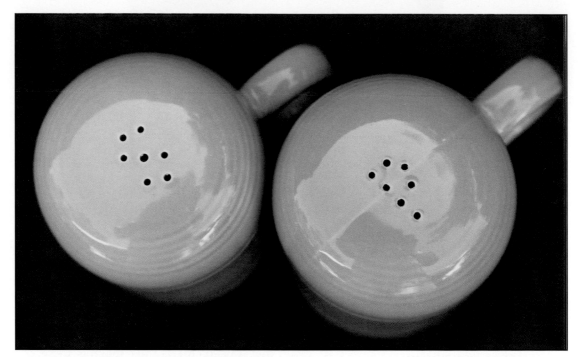

Technically both sets of shakers count as two pieces each because of the different holes.

Courtesy of John Iams

In October 2000, the Retail Outlet advertised a Halloween pumpkin design on a few persimmon Post86 pieces: the pizza tray, the pie baker, round candleholder, the mug, and the shaker set, shown here. They were very clever and became very popular. A photograph of all the pieces appeared on the Fiestafanatic website, and this pleasantly agitated the sales. More complete details about these festive pieces are on page 164.

Regular Shakers

REGULAR SHAKERS

Number: (714, salt; 715, pepper) 487
Mold Book: Not really necessary, used old mold.
Introduced: February 1986
Mark: None
Size: Height: 2½"
Popularity: Shaker sets are highly popular among generic collectors, but average among Post86 collectors.
Color Availability: All colors except sapphire.
Changes: None, unless cork to rubber stopper is considered a change.

Just as are the rangetop shakers, these little familiar pieces must be considered as two: the salt has the center hole — making seven instead of the six on the pepper. This slight different was reflected in 1998, when each partner of the set received its own official number. However, now they are both linked forever with one number, 497.

Naturally, this set was present when Post86 came into being, and it is nearly a mirror image of the vintage twosome! There are slight differences when examples of both lines are compared side by side. The vintage has a more graceful flare to the foot, is rounder, plumper, and a bit taller. The original set was used to make the mold for the new — this is assumed because, like other near duplications, there is no mention of the shakers in the mold book.

The regular shakers are never marked: there is little room, and when first produced, the base opening was plugged with cork, but now rubber suffices. Also sometimes the glaze (when it is thick) tends to obliterate the famous Fiesta rings.

These shaker sets tend to be overlooked by many Post86 collectors. Rarely are shakers the object of excitement or discussion — but interestingly, someone thought it worthwhile to risk censure at the Homer Laughlin China factory because rogue sapphire shakers are available and popular. Salt and pepper shakers are present in all dinnerware lines, and devilishly difficult to make exciting. There are a few ceramic designers determined to make the shaker somewhat "snappy," but invariably too much drama or cleverness in a shaker design leads to disaster. Bananas, polar bears, uddered cows and horned bulls, little boy salts seating on rocking chair peppers and their like are wonderful, for inexpensive remembrances of a trip to Honolulu, a walk along the Atlantic City boardwalk, a visit to the Grand Canyon, or a ferry ride to Victoria, British Columbia, but these clever tourist trinkets have no place in solidly placed dinnerware. Good shakers should be like old slippers — comfortable in doing what they were meant to do. Leave the cleverness to souvenir trash and the *haute* design to the teapots or the carafes or even the sleek, but problematic, goblets.

Individual Sugar and Creamer

SUGAR

Number: (Bowl, #743; Lid #744) #498
Mold Book: July 23, 1996
Introduced: February 1986
Mark: Incised mark.
Size: Height: 4⅜"
Liquid Measurement: 9 oz.
Popularity: Below average
Color Availability: all colors except sapphire.
Changes: Three. See text.

CREAMER

Number: (#745) #492
Mold Book: Not really necessary, used old mold.
Introduced: February 1986
Mark: Usually none.
Size: Height: 3"
Liquid Measurement: 7 oz.
Popularity: Below average
Color Availability: All colors except sapphire.
Changes: None

When we arrive at this sugar and creamer set, two of the original 1986 reissued items, there is a question regarding terminology. In vintage Fiesta, the set that fulfilled the same function was known as the regular sugar and the regular creamer. The term "individual" was used to refer to the promotional set: the smaller sugar and creamer on the figure-eight tray. No one knows the reason for the change. It confuses the issue just a little, but we Post86 collectors can live with that!

This cream has a very ordinary history: it is modeled directly from the vintage piece and encountered no problems in the transfer. The piece has been around since the first creamer — the stick-handled — was replaced in the fall of 1939. Until the restyling into Ironstone in 1969, the creamer retained the "ring" handle. Post86 keeps the vintage body and the Ironstone "ear" handle: it is a very pleasant, albeit prosaic marriage. Except for the handle, and a flatter, less delicate spout, the two Fiesta creamers are a near match.

But when we approach the sugar, the story is vastly different. This piece had a very complex transference, undergoing considerable change caused by the curves and delicacy of the vintage example. If the mold book is reviewed, alteration after alteration is noted starting in December 1985 and continuing to July 1996. The sugar was reworked in an attempt to perfect the design.

The arching and curving handles of the vintage bowl disappeared in 1969, during the redesign into Ironstone. It was this Ironstone shape that was first attempted for the Post86 sugar bowl. That brochure (so often touted as "mysterious") showed an Ironstone sugar glazed in Post86 white. When questioned, Jonathan Parry (Homer Laughlin China art director) denies that this sugar bowl form was produced, but there must have been a few around for it to have been photographed and also advertised for sale in the local East Liverpool newspaper! In addition, there are con-

*Notice how the new Fiesta sugarbowl (right in chartreuse)
was adapted from the vintage marmalade (turquoise).*

tinuing and persistent rumors it has been seen. Still, the official word from the company is that it never existed!

Whatever the reason or the answer, the Ironstone-shaped sugar just did not work. Before serious production started, it was scrapped.

In the rush to produce an acceptable and reliable sugar bowl, the art department chose the vintage marmalade, sans spoon opening, and it worked! But in the rush, the "nubbly" button finial was retained. This squat finial was soon scrapped, and the more typical flared tall finial appeared — and the sugar bowl was completed.

The above also gives the indication that the marmalade will never appear in the Post86 line.

To review: unlike the stalwart cream — faithful and trustworthy from the start — the flighty sugar has been seen in three disguises.

1. The Ironstone shape (very rare, perhaps a prototype).

2. Marmalade shape with button finial (first five colors only).

3. Marmalade shape with flared finial (all glazes except sapphire).

There is a questioning footnote regarding the sapphire glaze. Why did those Homer Laughlin China employees who surreptitiously glazed so many rogue items in sapphire overlook the sugar/creamer set? The pieces are small enough to conceal, carefully when leaving at the end of a working day, and the assumption is that a market would have been waiting!

The black sugarbowl (left) is "old style." Note the button finial. The sea mist green sugar (right) is the "new style" with the taller finial. For contrast, in the center is a vintage red sugarbowl. The high heat necessary for firing vitreous clay will not allow a high lid dome or the arching handles — they had to go!

Notice there was very little change in the creamer.

Sugar & Creamer Tray Set

SUGAR	CREAMER	TRAY
Number: 821	Number: 821	Number: 821
Mold Book: October 2, 1987 (to move handles down)	Mold Book: March 7, 1986	Mold Book: March 7, 1986
Introduced: February 1986	Introduced: February 1986	Introduced: February 1986
Mark: Circular indented mark with *f.*	Mark: Circular indented mark with *f.*	Mark: Entirely new, curved to follow base. Many trays have additional GG or C or O.
Size: Height: 2¾"	Size: Height: 2⅝"	Size: Length: 9⅞"
Liquid Measurement: 7 oz.	Liquid Measurement: 6½ oz.	Liquid Measurement: N/A
Changes: Early change in finial. Some adjustment in handles.	Changes: None	Changes: None.
		All Three Popularity: Average

There are a number of interesting little anomalies about this set, bits that make the collector a bit curious. The first, but by no means the most interesting, is how the last notation in the mold book for all three pieces comes after the regulation introduction date in February 1986. With the sugar, the problem is easily solved: the handles needed adjusting. If the reader will study the photograph showing the black Post86 sugar next to the yellow vintage example, it can be seen the handles of the latter are considerably higher. Yet I purchased this black sugar in late 1986 — it still has the button finial — so I cannot really explain the mold book entry of October 2, 1987 — over one year after known introduction.

The creamer and the tray were mentioned just a week after the introduction, and it can be assumed these were minor changes. Remember, the original vintage mold was used as the basis of the design, and there

must have been a number of minor adjustments.

Another curious change is the fact that the three pieces — from the very beginning — shared the same official number, 821. That does prove the set was believed to be a unit not to be dissolved. However, at the same time teapots and their lids, the regular sugar and its lid, received separate numbers.

The name proves interesting also. In the vintage line, the term "individual" was applied to this set: i.e., individual sugar and individual creamer on a figure-eight tray. In Post86 this term has been transferred to what was formerly the regular sugar and creamer. It took a conscious effort on my part to get this name change straight.

The older set was developed as a sales promotion from 1939 to 1943 and has always been the reason for much collector scrambling — especially in the more unusual colors. Perhaps the Post86 set has not quite kept up with this great interest, but I believe that if retailers allowed a "mix-and-match" philosophy, this unit would be considerably more popular. It is rather expensive to purchase, and if one wished a tray in cobalt blue, a creamer in persimmon, and the sugar in yellow (to try to emulate the vintage set), a cost of over $60.00 would be the price of this combination. Sometimes very obvious marketing strategy is overlooked by retailers.

Note how closely the Post86 (right in black) follows the lines of the yellow vintage piece.

The finial was later changed from button (black) to flared (white).

Like the sugars, the creamers in both lines are almost identical.

〜〜〜〜〜〜〜〜〜〜〜〜〜〜〜〜〜〜〜〜

(*Large Teapot*)

Many, many people, collectors and non-collectors, have a considerable passion for teapots. From the most elegant of fluted silver to the most " chubbly" humble of brown earthenware, teapots are a great source of pleasure for many people, much more so than the coffee pots and servers. Probably because there is nothing so satisfyingly secure as a hot cup of bracing tea in a cozy kitchen with the wind and snow battering the landscape outside the frosted window!

Until the summer of 1998, the collector could speak of the Post86 Fiesta teapot and be clearly understood: no confusion then. But now there are two sizes of teapots, and they must be distinguished. Officially there is no Post86 large teapot. Names are of great interest, and we remember a large and medium teapot in the vintage line — but no small teapot. Today there is a teapot which is physically large, but not so named, and a small teapot recently introduced.

The new (large) teapot belongs to the select and mysterious Post86 pieces that appear in a different guise in that mysterious 1986 brochure (see page 190). In this brochure it has the look of the vintage medium teapot — with a finial that looks very much like a tall slanting inwardly molded Jello dessert, or an elegant aspic. These finials/handles were very difficult to hold: they slipped from the fingers with relative ease. Since the medium teapot was manufactured much longer than the large vintage example, perhaps those making decisions decided to model the Post86 teapot after the more familiar and recognizable vintage piece. It is hard to tell, but it is known that for a time — a very short time — the Post86 teapot appeared in the guise of the

> ## LARGE TEAPOT
>
> Number: (teapot, 767; lid, 768) 496 (both)
> Mold Book: September 16, 1994
> Introduced: February 1986
> Mark: Incised, encircled mark
> Size: Height: 7¼". (The height of the vintage large teapot is 6¾".)
> Liquid Measurement: 44 oz.
> Popularity: Above average. There are many teapot collectors.
> Color Availability: All colors except sapphire.
> Changes: A possible three. See text.

vintage teapot.

Remember, the same design occurrence happened with the coffee server, the casserole, the sugar bowl, and to a small degree, the lid of the smaller sugar bowl in the tray set. Yet the company denies any such happenings: the Post86 teapot does not (so the official word is preached) exist in any such vintage/Ironstone shape, nor does this shape appear in any of the first five glazes (white, black, rose, apricot, or cobalt blue).

Yet there appears in a local East Liverpool newspaper advertisement a copy of this brochure stating that the new Fiesta so listed was available at the retail outlet. Why, it is wondered, would the Homer Laughlin China Company place an advertisement in a local

Two styles of sea mist green teapots. Left: the earlier version (1986 – 1993). The opening and lid, fired separately, often became distorted. With the introduction of lilac, all teapots and lids were restyled to provide more secure lids.

paper for some new Fiesta that — according to present announcements — never existed? I can hear the scenario now: Ring goes the telephone.

(Outlet salesperson): "Hello, Homer Laughlin Retail Outlet."

(Lady customer): "Yes, I have just seen your ad in *The Evening Review,* and I would be most interested in purchasing the teapot you show in white."

(Salesperson): "Sorry, Madam, but that teapot does not exist."

(Customer, a little upset): "What! It doesn't exist? Then why have you advertised it?"

(Salesperson, unctuously): "Sorry, Madam, but we cannot divulge that information!"

This conversation certainly does not ring true! Yet if Homer Laughlin China did advertise these items and if these items never did exist, then such a conversation must have taken place over and over.

Now to further complicate the "saga of the teapot," another occurrence must be discussed which has nothing to do with the existence of a Post86 Ironstone-like possibility. There are two variations of this large teapot: one running from 1986 until the advent of lilac (1994) and a second from, and including, lilac to the present day. So the careful collector will find two versions of the white, black, rose, apricot, cobalt blue, yellow, turquoise, periwinkle blue, and sea mist green teapots. But only one version of lilac, persimmon, chartreuse, pearl gray, and juniper. (No teapot in sapphire.) The first version — with a large, sometimes irregular, opening — is no longer produced (naturally) and yet no demand for it seems to exist. Is this an oversight on the part of collectors, or this version being kept a gentleman's secret? While there is presently no price difference between the two, I must admit this fact is a little puzzling. None of my five older version teapots will be sold for I am aware of the power of Post86 collectors to affect prices.

It would be wise, in my personal estimation, to keep any example of the discontinued teapot. Yes, technically, the teapot with the large opening has been discontinued! When my sea mist green teapot was received, the opening looked warped and the lid slid about like a puppy on ice! It was a bad form which did not function: the ill-fitting lid was dangerous.

In fact all lidded pieces are prone to the same problem, i.e., since the bodies and the lids are fired separately and vitreous clay demands extraordinary temperatures, the lids, being smaller and more vulnerable, often shrank so badly that, when put in place, they slipped through the body opening! If the lids did not happen to shrink to this degree, then they usually slipped about and rolled around, creating impossible social situations. According to a company anecdote, the decision to restyle the teapot came when English distributors complained vociferously about the new teapot mismatching its lid. The lid fit so poorly, the tea-loving British were removing the lid, discarding it in the dustbin, and using the teapot bottom for a vase. Time, certainly, for a revamped teapot!

So look carefully at your Post86 teapot. If it has a large, sometimes irregular opening, and the thin-flanged lid slips and slides, then it is the old style. You might want to purchase the new style (they are the only ones available now) and keep the older example — it might reward you in a few years.

Viewed from outside, the two variations are very similar — but if the collector remembers lilac and the colors that followed, there will be no problem.

A note of caution: these teapots are extremely heavy — so heavy that the frail-wristed elderly hostess should beware. A teapot filled with hot liquid carries so much weight "up front," a fragile grip is easily lost to dire, even dangerous, consequences.

Two-cup Teapot

The summer of 1998 saw the introduction of the 2-cup teapot, and immediately it became a favorite — a huge success. At the same time, there was the great fluster of the third limited color, chartreuse, and this compelled many devoted Post86 collectors to slip into Jaguars, Mercedes, and Porsches, or climb upon 9-speed bicycles to hunt down these exclusive little chartreuse beauties! They sold solely at the profits stores.

Some people wondered why this piece was thought necessary. There was already the small Colonial teapot residing among the Fiesta Mates. But that is just the reason for its appearance. Homer Laughlin China was seriously contemplating the cessation of the Mates, and this 2-cup wonder was to take the place of the Colonial pot. Also, when the two are carefully compared, like two young ladies lounging on a couch, the Fiesta teapot is plumply more compact, and, as one collector commented, much easier on the eyes!

While modeled upon the large teapot, this charmer has an eared handle that fastens with folds against the cute body!

Small individual teapots have long been greatly admired, vigorously collected, and lovingly used. Tea is known to have been "discovered" in China around 2200 BC, but only became available in Europe in the 1600s. Tea was first considered an herbal tonic, then when finally enjoyed on its own terms, was horrendously expensive — a luxury served ceremoniously. Because of the expense of tea, the early teapots were very small. Holding about 16 liquid ounces, the teapot

---

TWO-CUP TEAPOT

Number: 764
Mold Book: Not known
Introduced: Mid-1998
Mark: Raised mark with small *f* curving around other edge of base, usually under the handle.
Size: Height: 5⅛"
Liquid Measurement: 16 oz.
Popularity: Exceptional
Color Availability: All colors except lalic, and sapphire; rare in black and apricot.
Changes: None

---

was itself an object of admiration: the hot beverage was served in miniscule cups, quite often in the Oriental style (no handles).

Even though today tea no longer costs over $100.00 a pound, small teapots are still used in elegant situations. It is considered very cosmopolitan to present each guest with a personal small teapot (with matching cup and saucer?) after asking what type of tea is preferred. This can be done with the Post86 small teapot. What is your choice? Jasmine, Earl Grey, smoky Lapsang Souchong, or the special green tea, Mao Feng?

A wonderful assortment of sea mist green combined, for contrast, with a few pieces of vintage red.

The true Fiesta 2-cup teapot (right) replaced, in essence, the Colonial Fiesta Mate (left). Here they "face each other" in sea mist. The 2-cup Fiesta was modeled after an experimental individual vintage Fiesta piece never put into production. See Huxford, Collector's Encyclopedia of Fiesta 8th ed., *1998. p. 163.*

〔 *Bread Tray* 〕

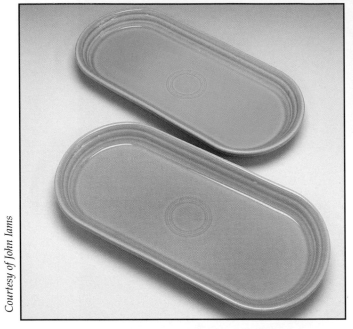

Courtesy of John Iams

The mark on the underside of the bread tray.

I owe my introduction to the bread dish or tray to John Iams. It is impossible for me to stress how much this gentleman from East Liverpool has helped with information and advice.

Rumors regarding a bread dish had been very quietly circulating for over a year. The item itself did not seem very exciting, so speculation was subdued and quite calm — unlike the frantic and tumultuous expectations surrounding the 8" vase. Then in late October, John wrote that he discovered some trays in the seconds room of the Retail Outlet. They had obviously been in production some time, and the seconds were being offered for sale.

John obtained turquoise and pearl gray examples, and soon persimmon and cobalt trays turned up, and the item was off and running. It can be assumed all available colors will be utilized.

Mrs. Laurie Holmes (to whom this book is dedicated) did some sleuthing in San Jose, California. The bread tray was found to be an exclusive for Macy's West, and sale advertisements had been already placed in California, Washington, and Oregon newspapers; the original price was $15.00, sale price $9.99. However, as Mrs. Holmes discovered, no trays had yet been delivered. Homer Laughlin production was again behind. Again assumption comes into play: it could very well be slated for a Christmas item.

Because the tray was an exclusive, no information could be gleaned from the Retail Outlet's catalog inquiry page, It was not even mentioned as a new item.

BREAD TRAY

Number: **412**
Mold Book: **Unknown**
Introduced: **Early winter 2000**
Mark: **See text.**
Size: **12" x 5⅝"**
Color Availability: **See text.**
Changes: **None**

The tray's shape is ideal for a loaf of ordinary bread — not too large and not too small. The piece resembles, in shape and proportion, the vintage Fiesta utility tray, but with an edging very similar to the pizza tray. This leads collectors to believe the piece was designed by Jonathan Parry before he died in April. It could be one of the last pieces this talented man designed; he continues to influence , but still one wonders when the Parry influence wanes, can Post86 Fiesta thrive under other hands — talented as they too may be! The utilitarian size and shape of the bread tray probably will prove more useful as a general table item than the pizza tray.

Hostess Tray

Three plates appeared in the mid-1990s, and all were centered around one fact: the rise of home entertaining. Naturally, these three had their uses in restaurants and country clubs — especially those serving buffets, but I believe the design of these three was a strong indication that Homer Laughlin China was aiming Post86 Fiesta more for the home — especially in the case of the hostess tray.

A very impressive piece (even larger than the chop plate), this tray would become the centerpiece of a patio buffet and used to serve items with a dip. All this is very obvious. About May or June 1997, the hostess tray began to grace the shelves of large department stores and smaller specialty shops. With a very wide ringed rim and divided into two sections (more for design effect than to actually separate food), this plate parrots the same handle design as the earlier round serving tray (#468). In fact, the third change of the serving tray was supposedly undertaken so that the two "trays" (serving and hostess) would more closely match. The straight-sided cereal bowl fits in the center circle and is sold separately. While this item created some interest among the consumer/collector at the beginning, it could never be termed "popular?" Were collectors adding one in each available color to their Post86 collection? Perhaps, but unlikely.

Now the following is probably an unfair comment, but of the hostess trays seen, all included "bubbles" and "pops." This might be coincidental, or it might be due to the design or merely the size. Until the advent about three months later of the pizza tray, this item was

HOSTESS TRAY
Number: 753
Mold Book: March 31, 1997
Introduced: Mid-1997
Mark: Dated stamp
Size: Width: 12¼"
Liquid Measurement: N/A
Popularity: Average
Color Availability: All colors except black, apricot, lilac, and sapphire. Some black or apricot trays may exist, but they are very rare.
Changes: None

the largest piece in Post86. A good friend reminded me how much this large divided tray looks like those large ceramic Art Deco ashtrays that stood upon wrought-iron stands. In the '40s and '50s every smoker seemed to have one standing next to a favorite comfortable chair. This tray begs for an arching aluminum handle to facilitate carrying it to the table.

The hostess tray exists as a rogue item both in lilac and sapphire.

Pizza Tray

In the closing months of December 1999 — as the second millennium breathed its last gasps — the Homer Laughlin Company, perhaps in a splurge of effulgent celebration or in an attempt to entice flagging collector interest, introduced some new items. The pizza tray was the first of these, and it popped onto the scene in September 1999. Surprisingly huge, heavy, and handsome, it filled the space long ago vacated by the vintage Fiesta 15" chop plate — although this pizza tray has a much needed protecting rim.

This tray is monumental and was received with considerable collector enthusiasm.

Fiesta websites and chat rooms on the Internet were bountifully engaged with commentary about this piece! It can, for example, actually be used in the oven for cooking pizza, and the glaze stands up to the regulation sharpness of the pizza wheel. It could be used as a centerpiece base, a tray for tumblers and pitchers, a joint of beef or a brace of game birds. This was a tray for many uses. And while its origins could be traced to regular restaurant ware, it was ringed as all legitimate Post86 must be and was dutifully stamped with Fiesta approval.

PIZZA TRAY

Number: 505
Mold Book: Not known
Introduced: Late 1999
Mark: Dated stamp
Size: Width: 15"
Popularity: Above average
Color Availability: All colors except black, apricot, lilac, and sapphire.
Changes: None

It sizzled and sang and received a much more explosive positive welcome than did, say, the hostess tray or the stopper-less carafe. Let us, you and me, hope that this enthusiasm will linger as the months pass!

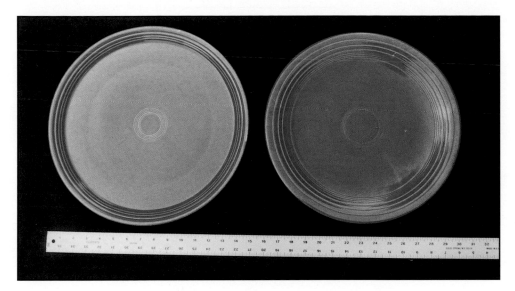

*Although flatter and with a true rim, the pizza tray
matches in size and use the vintage 15" chop plate.*

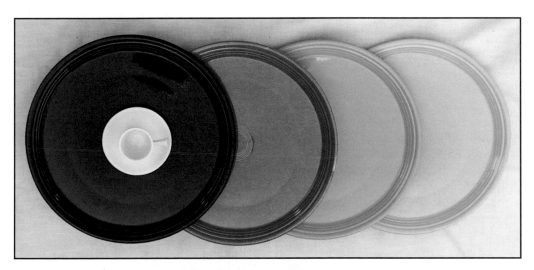

Four huge trays all in a row.

Relish/Utility Tray

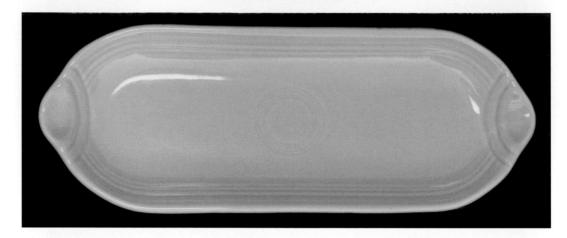

Remember, remember, remember! The American dinnerware collector is always remembering — stretching memory back into the past. This past might be long, long ago or merely last year. It all depends upon the age of the collector! Collectors, to be true, must have the ability, and the need, to remember. This is in our hearts and our minds. Nostalgia is vital to us. Even a 17-year-old Post86 Fiesta collector brings memories that influence the budding collection, Imagine then, the richly rewarding remembrances caught in the minds of those of us who are regarded as elders!

Remember now, summer barbecues of long ago when corn-on-the-cob was served fresh from the field and very hot from the boiling water. The corn was served on precisely designed hard plastic (could they have been plastic?) plates shaped like the corn ears which cradled them delightfully. The butter was kept ingeniously close, and little green handles with long sharp points were inserted at the end of each cob. Naturally, the children were disdainful of these "contraptions."

So what of this piece? Jonathan Parry comments: "(the) 499 relish was designed as a corn-on-the-cob dish — very '40s and '50s — but we prefer to use more general names for items to try and avoid type casting."

Thus the new title — relish/utility tray! But what's in a name? By any other name this item will retain its unique corn-on-the-cob shape.

Understandably, the name "utility tray" was attached to widen the use of this piece, but it cannot really be considered a redesigned vintage Fiesta utility tray! Actually, both as a relish tray and as a utility tray, the 9⅝" platter is better equipped for the job.

When handed the piece, and questioned about is "relishness," a friend casually remarked about its use for a few celery or carrot sticks with a scattered embell-

> **RELISH/UTILITY TRAY**
>
> Number: 499
> Mold Book: October 20, 1994 (called a corn tray)
> Introduced: 1995
> Mark: Raised mark with small *f.*
> Size: Length: 9½". Width: 3⅝"
> Popularity: Average
> Color Availability: All colors except sapphire.
> Changes: None

ishment of olives, and the fact that it would fit quite comfortably above the dinner plate at each place setting. However, the size (9½") would be too large for one guest. Neither would it be large enough to pass around the entire table nor small enough to serve one person. The implication here is that the size and shape make placing this tray on the formal dinner table quite questionable!

The piece does flourish greatly when one discusses the late '90s home entertaining phenomenon — the buffet. Homer Laughlin China has introduced a number of plates for this type of party. Buffet and barbecue have replaced the formal dinner: children and dogs racing about noisily, teenagers kissing behind the garage, birds flying overhead surprising all the guests, chair legs and ladies' heels caught in soft sod, and the smell of hot grease and charred animals. Daddy waving the long fork and the rangetop salt shaker. Mother carrying large bowls of salad and carefully watching her nubile daughter saunter off with a hormone controlled boy from down the street. Pulsating music from the radio, and the vigorous hooting of a maiden aunt on the loose!

No, no, too much noise, too much confusion! Give me this little tab-handled tray next to my solitary plate with one quiet stalk of celery!

It appears in all glazes, but is an illegal rogue in sapphire.

Candy Fagerlin, proprietor of a very popular and informative website on Fiesta who lives in California, reports that Macy's West sells the relish/utility tray under the name "bread dish." This makes sense if the bread involved consists of slices of small round French loaves and might account for the persistent rumor of a new Post86 item. All this proved misleading when on October 15, 2000, the actual bread tray was discovered in the seconds room of the Retail Outlet. So much for rumors.

The tray, no matter its eventual use, or name, is one of the most comfortable of all Post86 pieces to hold and carry. The tab-handles (originally designed as a space for the holders?) glove the thumbs to perfection, and the first three fingers slide beautifully, and automatically, into place under each end — the pinky floating free or steadying the dish. For all the questioning of the name or the use, as an example of pure physical design dynamics, this piece of new Fiesta is near perfection.

A turquoise Post86 relish nestles inside one from the vintage years.

Round Serving Tray

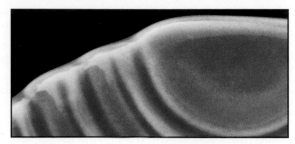

The older version of the serving tray's rim — no restraint here.

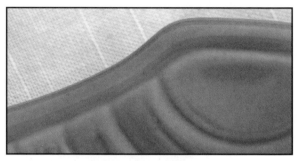

A sapphire tray with the new rim. Many collectors find the change constricting.

This tray was first sold as a "handled cake plate." It appeared so in the mold book, and it was under this name that I first purchased it in black. But since then it has always been officially entitled the "round serving tray, " and a tray it must remain.

The 1992 introduction of this piece seems to give it the distinction of being the first Post86 piece with no umbilical cord to the vintage line. Unlike some of the later pieces having no connection with the old Fiesta, the round serving tray is very compatible, very tastefully designed with an Art Deco approach, and quite in keeping with Frederick Rhead's Fiesta philosophy.

It also has another distinction: it appears in three variations; see color listing of the variations on next page.

The first variation existed from its introduction for one year until the advent of lilac in 1993. These trays can simply be known by their weight — they are awesomely heavy! When lilac was discontinued and persimmon popped up, the round serving tray became very much lighter with a different profile: smaller foot and less pronounced sides, variation two. The collector can pinpoint this change because it is reflected in a mold book entry (November 10, 1995): "Fiesta cake plate made lighter!"

Then with no warning at all, at the introduction of

ROUND SERVING TRAY
Number: 468
Mold Book: January 7, 1992
Introduced: 1992
Mark: Dated stamp.
Size: 11"
Popularity: Above average
Color Availability: All colors.
Changes: Three, see text.

chartreuse, another change was made, and many believe, not for the better. A rather thick outer rim now runs around the entire plate — including the handles. This third variation constricts the handles and contains them within the rim, the idea being (no doubt) to make the design conform with the hostess tray.

These variations have made the tray more desirable as collectors rush to get examples in all three versions. Also contributing to interest is the fact that this item is available in all the glazes — however, please remember, in lilac it was legally manufactured only with the Fiesta Club of America logo. Without the logo it is a rogue item!

Colors of serving tray in three variations

Variation one (heavy)	Variation two (light)	Variation three (rimmed)
white	white	white
black	black	rose
rose	rose	cobalt blue
apricot	apricot	yellow
cobalt blue	cobalt blue	turquoise
yellow	yellow	periwinkle blue
turquoise	turquoise	sea mist green
periwinkle blue	periwinkle blue	persimmon
sea mist green	sea mist green	chartreuse
	lilac (FCOA logo only)	pearl gray
	sapphire (both with and without logo)	juniper
	persimmon	cinnabar

Trivet

The inclusion of the trivet in this identification section could be questioned, but I believe no harm will be done. Actually the two sizes of pedestals should probably have their own entry also, but these have been covered somewhat adequately in the section on the hostess bowl.

Let the problem be summarized. There are certain categories of Post86 Fiesta items that are known to exist, but some float in that shadowy world of "will they or won't they?" (See listing below.) And, actually, it all lies with the decision making management at Homer Laughlin! The trivet was originally a real and honest Post86 piece, but now is no longer produced at the factory. Still the place of production cannot be exactly pin-pointed!

Ashtray: seen but with no official comment
Ornament, Round: experimental, never photographed, never produced.
Pedestal, Large: photographed, never produced.
Pedestal, Small: photographed, never produced.
Teapot lamp: modeled by Mr. Geisse, announced, photographed, produced, then allowed to lapse.
Trivet: modeled by Mr. Geisse, photographed, considered for production, then awarded to an overseas manufacturer.

These, the trivet included, could probably be introduced or reintroduced as Post86 items.

The trivet has a very distinctive characteristic: it is the only piece on which the HLC Dancing Lady appears in an HLC ceramic design. She is clicking her castanets in the center of a rather small plate-like vitrified ceramic disc. Actually, this would have been a marvelous decorative motif. However, either someone at HLC had an idea or some entrepreneurial wizard from another corporation spoke convincing words, and this lovely simple disc was placed within a wooden form depicting the large disc pitcher. A sad fate for such a classically clean item. The form of the completed trivet is not offensive, in fact the outlines of the large disc pitcher have been gently modified into a rather pleasing shape. And the function of this trivet is perfect — does what it is supposed to do.

After having tried to trace this trivet without success, it might be concluded it was only peripherally successful as a Fiesta Accessory and now has slipped back into oblivion. While originally modeled and manufactured at the HLC plant, it can be assumed once the production was awarded to another company, Homer Laughlin ceased actually making the ceramic disc.

But one fact can be assumed; the original model still is sequestered in the HLC Art Department with all production rights intact. Perhaps some day soon, the trivet will be another Post86 item — hopefully without the wooden frame of a disc pitcher, or a teapot, or even a circle.

Tumbler

```
TUMBLER

Number: 446
Mold Book: October 1995
Introduced: 1995
Mark: Three varieties: see text.
Size: Height: 3¾"
Liquid Measurement: 6½ oz.
Popularity: Exceptional
Color Availability: All colors
Changes: None
```

The Post86 Fiesta tumbler did not make an early appearance when the line was restyled and reissued in 1986. On the company's 1986 advertising sheet, 31 pieces appear; on the 1988 sheet, 34 pieces of Fiesta are available. It was not until later — when 42 pieces and nine colors were offered — did the tumbler make a belated 1995 reappearance.

The tumbler was not only tardy, it appeared late in "good" company. Other favorites to wait until later were the napkin ring (1992) and the AD cup and saucer along with the mini-disc pitcher (both 1993). Of course only the AD cup/saucer had secure connections with the vintage line! Remember the earlier tumblers were part of the original Fiesta offering, but were gone by 1944 — an existence of only eight or so years. With the well-deserved popularity enjoyed by the new, smaller tumblers, a life longer than a short eight years can be anticipated.

Where the vintage tumbler is 4½" tall and flares to a little over 3¼" wide, the Post86 tumbler is 3¾" tall and, with a much narrower "flare," is 2⅞" at its opening, a good deal smaller, much more solidly grasped in the hand. Even though lacking the petal grace of the vintage piece, the new tumbler became a hardworking member of the Post86 family.

This popularity is as solid as the piece itself — like an old friend, the tumbler is well-used, in great demand, and is put to a multitude of purposes. Those who acquire tumblers do so in the same manner as do acquirers of the mugs — for honest use, and at least two of each color seems the rule. They are expendable, dependable, useful, and indispensable — a well-deserved accolade for such a modest piece of dinnerware!

Probably one of the reasons for the consumers' fond thoughts regarding the tumbler is that it is available in all colors — including lilac and sapphire. A simple fact as simply stated and remembered as the piece itself! It is the only piece of contemporary Fiesta that can be acquired — in all the glazes — by people, that is, without endless bank credit. It is a wonderful pleasure to be able to state: "Yes, I have the tumbler in every color!"

Of additional interest, probably solely for avid accumulators, the tumbler comes with three different underside styles and marks. The tumbler with no mark presently is quite common, but is not limited to early production. These appear to have no bottom rings either — but in fact these rings have been over-glazed to virtual nonexistence. The second true mark is the regular circular Fiesta dated stamp. Remember the dated stamp was introduced about 1992. I have seen rose tumblers with no mark and with this stamp: the piece with the stamp was manufactured later.

A stack of tumblers — 14 colors (juniper, not pictured here, makes a total of 15). The tumblers are one of the few pieces available in all the colors.

Comparison of vintage (left), Post86 (center), and Harlequin (right) tumblers, all in turquoise.

The last variation we can pinpoint is the date: it is the 60th Anniversary tumbler stamped to go along with the Anniversary Disc Pitcher (1996). Since this Anniversary Set was produced in every glaze available at the time, the tumblers with this back stamp can appear in every color except chartreuse and pearl gray. Now, I have not personally seen tumblers with the 60th Anniversary stamp, but several sapphire 60th Anniversary large disc pitchers have been viewed, so the assumption is there were tumblers to match!

These sets (disc pitcher and four tumblers) were wont to get sadly separated and then just as able to be gathered together again. Only the most fanatic of contemporary collectors will insist on all the tumblers in their Anniversary Set bear the anniversary stamp. But then, there are a number of fanatics in Fiesta-land, and this is acceptable indeed. My only white tumbler has the anniversary mark — and it was a gift from a friend: perhaps impetuously wrenched from the set to which it belonged?

The Anniversary pieces were made dated 1996, and then production ceased. Perhaps the tumblers stamped with this mark are scarcer, but it does not seem they are more valuable. However, if you are a stickler and boast at being Fiesta proper when buying a 60th Anniversary Set, turn over the four tumblers: all should be stamped "Fiesta 60th Anniversary." (Please note, the disc pitcher bears only the regular incised Fiesta mark. No need for mark identification here — the proof is on the pitcher's side!)

Bud Vase

BUD VASE

Number: 490
Mold Book: Not necessary, reused mold.
Introduced: February 1986 (original item)
Mark: Indented like the original.
Size: Height: 6"
Liquid Measurement: About 4 oz. (The thickness of the vase sides and the weight of the piece vary greatly).
Popularity: Exceptional
Color Availability: All colors except sapphire.
Changes: None

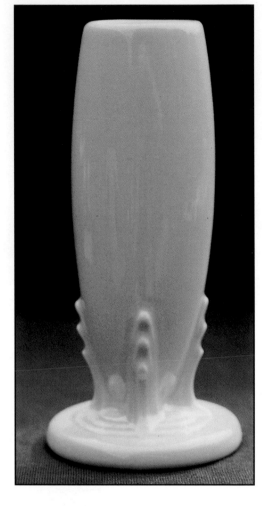

What can be said about the Post86 bud vase — except that it is one of the most popular items in the line, and was taken directly, albeit a bit smaller, from the vintage shape. Since it is not expensive, there are good numbers of collectors who make it a point to gather a bud vase in every glaze. Unfortunately, when dealing with sapphire bud vases, not only is the price high, but one dances dangerously with the law. Yes, there are sapphire examples known, but these are rare and illegal, according to the Homer Laughlin Company. Security at the factory has reached nearly the level of the Kennedy Space Center, with guards and security cameras preventing the unofficial glazing of Post86 pieces. So sapphire bud vases are very hush, hush!

This vase has always been designed perfectly for one bud or several: the opening narrows slightly from the sides to support the rose bud, or the single freesia stem. It is intimate, soothing, and rather feminine — suitable for a bedside or dressing table. The design genius of Frederick Rhead surely must be recognized in

this area — the area of designing individual pieces to be psychologically geared to certain uses in the home.

Now, naturally, the little bud vase ideally fits on hotel "breakfast-in-bed trays," and as home-like centerpieces on "tables-for-two." But, in general, this small vase belongs to personal spaces whether in home or hotel.

When it comes to decorations, this vase has received some very delicate, Art Nouveau designs of flowers, vines, and butterflies. These, in my opinion, are much more gracious than the rather blatant Sunporch, Moon-over-Miami China Specialties lines. But here I give my own opinion — which certainly is not the opinion of many Post86 aficionados.

While reading material on this vase in the lilac glaze, some curious information (to me) came to light. I found an early 1995 advertisement stating the lilac bud vase was made exclusively for Table-Top Direct, the well-known distributor. It was originally priced at $7.50. This same advertisement spoke of the AD cup and saucer, and the bulb (term used in the advertisement) candleholder in lilac. Up until this point, it has been understood these pieces were exclusively manufactured for China Specialties, Inc., a company ably directed by Joel Wilson — who also is the guiding force and editor of Fiesta Collector's Quarterly — the publication in which this advertisement appeared. Mr. Wilson could not be reached to answer if there was a connection between China Specialties and Table-Top Direct. In fact, no Strongville or Valley City, Ohio, telephone listing could be located with either Joel Wilson or China Specialties.

Just an interesting little mystery having little to do with the bud vase per se. Later the mystery was demystified! China Specialties disposed of its right to distribute Fiesta directly to Table-Top Direct. However Joel Wilson, head of China Specialties, continues to distribute specialty items in Sunporch and Moon-over-Miami.

The vintage red bud vase (right) is a little taller and a little thinner than the Post86 example (left), but they are nearly identical.

Medium Vase

MEDIUM VASE

Number: (783), 491
Mold Book: Not necessary, reused
    mold.
Introduced: 1986
Mark: The incised mark duplicated
    the vintage mark.
Size: Height: 9½"
Liquid Measurement: 32 oz.
Popularity: Exceptional
Color Availability: All colors
Changes: None

There is a reversal of roles here — somewhat a reversal might be a better phrase — between this vase and its vintage counterpart. The older line included three vases (that wonderful number three again shows itself) and I believe the smallest of the three (8") was the most popular. However, when the resuscitation of Fiesta began, it was the medium (10") vase that was chosen for rebirth!

Several reasons for this choice have been heard, but the most conclusive one was simply that the smallest was too small; it did not possess enough height to handle a nice bouquet of flowers. Thus the medium vase became one of the signature pieces of Post86 Fiesta.

It is collected in all the new glazes, and extremely coveted in the limited colors of lilac and sapphire, and, to some extent, chartreuse. Also, when a color is discontinued such as black or apricot, the price of the medium vase escalates.

The medium vase is simply an important piece! Due to its stately grandeur, variations of the vase have been noted — variations in height and weight — but it is generally conceded these are due to shrinkage in the kiln.

Strangely, the name continues as an exact transference from the older line. A "medium" vase most certainly implies that a "smaller" or a "larger" exists — to be linguistically correct the vase should merely be termed a vase. However, since the size was the medium vase in the vintage, the name was fly-papered to the new piece — and continues today.

The above was the first reason for the name. The second reason is slightly more subtle and depends upon knowledge — in 1986 — not widely known. In the early years of the 1990s when vintage items were being considered for rebirth, the 8" vase was seriously considered. The proof is the existence of a number of smaller 7½" vases appearing in Post86 glazes which occasionally appear in the secondary marketplace. These smaller vitreous vases were never put into production: these prototypes are most often found in white, but they also have appeared in black and cobalt. And they sell for very high prices!

Then, of course, in late 1999, the 7½" vase did appear. So the medium vase is not as meaningless as once thought.

Whatever the story surrounding the name, this vase remains popular. In the lilac glaze (a good example of the glaze the medium vase scrambles closely to the vintage vase prices. Would it be correct to state the lilac medium vase is the most coveted and most costly of all Post86 pieces?

Original Post86 Fiesta medium vases.

More stately medium vases.

Small Vase

Should this small Post86 Fiesta vase be here? I believe that it should! However, there was a rather declarative telephone message left on my answering machine some months ago regarding this small vase. The message was from a powerful person who is trying to influence the world of Homer Laughlin China collectors: the caller stated, rather calmly, very assuredly, and with considerable understated force, that the company would be very angry if the small vase was mentioned in anything I wrote! That is what I believe he said! Not only am I fearful of such messages, I cringed because confrontation is not my forte!

Dare I write about the vase? Should I submit to his demands? I felt a little like Dorothy when she first confronted the Wizard in the Emerald City's audience hall: The Wizard of Oz, the Great and Powerful! Dorothy being, of course, the small and meek. Just as the little dog Toto pulled aside the curtain hiding the reality of a modest looking Wizard, so my thoughts swept away my fears! This book is to present information, and the existence of a 7½" Post86 vase is information. As I held in my hands and studied one of these delightful vases, it was decided that collectors — all collectors not just a chosen few — must be allowed to see what I saw.

To publish a photograph of an illegally procured rogue item is to flaunt one's thumbs at Homer Laughlin. Yet photographs of these items have appeared with regularity in magazines and on the Internet. Unlike the powerful, I have no power to flaunt. To write about and to publish a photograph of this small Post86 vase cannot be wrong. It was, after all, my vase, given to me as a gift, yet its return was demanded — for what reason I do not know!

So with all that as introduction, let us continue!

Back in 1986, someone at Homer Laughlin China toyed with the idea of adding a small vase to the original reissue. This is absolutely within general public knowledge because a fair number of these early prototypes have been seen on the marketplace and have slipped to those collectors able to pay the prices. These have been personally seen but not actually handled. My sources report that this vase — never in full production — was semi-vitreous!

Another indication that a second vase was planned is the official name of the present vase: medium vase. It would hardly seem necessary to name this 9½" vase "medium" if there were not strong plans to manufacture a second vase of another size!

The prototype can be seen in white, black, and rose, and when offered for sale, the price range is extremely high. In fact, when it became known that Homer Laughlin China was planning to reissue the 7½" vase, an acquaintance reflected this decision would cause his $600.00 investment in one of the prototypes to plummet in value. Since such a prototype was and still is completely out of my financial power to ever own, my memory of his exact words is hazy, but this was my interpretation of the words.

The 2000/2001 introduction of a 7½" Post86 Fiesta vase — even if fully vitreous — could cause havoc with the prices paid for the 1885 – 1986 semi-vitreous prototypes. Is it possible that pressure was brought to bear on Homer Laughlin, and the plans to reintroduce the smaller vase was again scrapped? I would hardly believe such a grand and stately company — a leader in the production of ceramic and dinnerware for over 100 years — would, or even could, be so influenced!

Why all this bitter ruckus over the existence of a vase? Is not collecting supposed to be enjoyable and fun? Power politics should play no part! The smaller vase is in itself very charming and not just a lesser version of the medium vase. Its proportions are different: less flare to the top, less weight proportionally to the base. Its outline was much less "lotus-shaped" than the medium example with a resultant lack of gracefulness. It is a piece, however, well able to be appreciated for its own virtues.

Bloomingdale's was awarded the exclusive rights to this long-awaited vase, and on November 15, 2000, started shipping. On this date, the only colors available were white, cobalt, yellow, turquoise, persimmon, pearl gray, and juniper. The Post86 line now can boast having six vases — a status unequalled in American dinnerware history.

Note how similar are the Post86 (left) and the vintage (right) small vases. There is slightly more flare at the top of the older piece.

Specialty Pieces

As do most American dinnerware lines, Post86 Fiesta occasionally offers what can only be termed specialty pieces. There are two categories of specialty items:

1. Regular Post86 pieces decorated for a specific event.
2. Undecorated pieces specially designed for a specific event.

The first of these categories will be discussed under the section on decorated Post86 Fiesta.

The second, much smaller, category should be considered as a separate division. Presently there are five items to list as undecorated specialty pieces. They are:

1. millennium vase I (limited number)
2. millennium vase II (limited time)
3. millennium vase III (limited time)
4. millennium candleholder (limited number)
5. presentation or celebration bowl.

The fifth piece has nothing to do with the millennium and was the first of the specialty items. This piece was conceived to be glazed in raspberry and produced in very limited numbers. The other presentation bowls were limited as to time — all ceased production December 31, 1999.

Specialty items, limited items — call them whatever you wish — are quite honestly marketing ploys. They create great interest and excitement whenever Fiesta sales hit the doldrums and must be considered welcome and true members of the Post86 family.

A regular 5-piece place setting dominated by the rare color sapphire.

Presentation Bowl

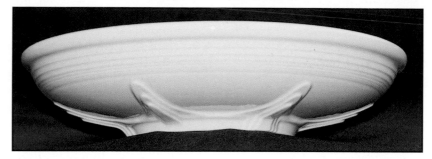

Note the architectural formation of the base. To see this, the bowl needs to be slightly propped. This example is yellow.

This bowl was officially unveiled at a celebration, December 5, 1997, when the 500 millionth piece of Fiesta was rolled out of the kilns. Designed in an Art Deco style by Jonathan O. Parry and originally produced in a raspberry glaze, these bowls were limited in this first run to 500 numbered pieces, of which only 15 were offered for sale to the general public. Two years later whenever an example comes to auction, the reserve price is over $7,000.00.

The Homer Laughlin Company mingled its burgeoning demand for security and secrecy with a heavy touch of humor when official photographs were distributed depicting the "destruction and disposal of the extra Fiesta collector raspberry (presentation) bowls." The photographs show the smashed shards being buried deeply at a very secret site. Mr. Conley — speaking at the HLCCA Convention in June 1999 — informed all present that the men shown in the photographs had to be killed so as not to reveal the location of the disposal site. It was assumed by the audience Mr. Conley was kidding!

This presentation bowl, often known as the celebration bowl, has the same philosophical availability approach as do millennium vase II and III or the new Fiesta limited colors; that is, all production will cease on December 31, 1999. The decision to make the bowl available in various glazes came after the cessation of black and apricot, so it is not generally available in these two colors, but then the company decided to pamper collectors by producing a limited number in black. These were for sale only through the HLC outlet in Newell, West Virginia. These were, I believe, rapidly sold out.

The physical aspect of the bowl is wide (12") and low (2¾"): it bears a strong resemblance to what was called in the thirties a float bowl. Incidentally, it shares

---

PRESENTATION BOWL

Number: 000
Mold Book: Not known.
Introduced: December 1997
Mark: Circular, raised with small *f* plus dated stamp.
Size: Height: 2½"; 11½" round.
Liquid Measurement: 64 oz.
Popularity: Exceptional
Color Availability: All colors except apricot, lilac, sapphire, juniper, and cinnabar. This was the only piece made in raspberry.
Changes: Three, see text.

---

this connotation with the large 2-quart serving bowl. Usually glass, but not always, a float bowl was filled with water — sometimes perfumed, often palely tinted — upon which were "floated" gardenias, water lilies, and other flat blossoms, sometimes interspersed with floating candles, again scented. This floral and candle presentation was used as a dining table centerpiece and was considered the height of glamorous sophistication. Unfortunately, the float bowl has gone the way of the extinct passenger pigeon and another dining table antiquity, the rose-petaled finger bowl.

The float bowl and the new Fiesta presentation bowl were both designed to be viewed from above, thus it is with surprise the layered six-pointed raised star design is viewed stretching up from the shallow base. This architectural decoration is a mixture of the Chrysler Building and a Flash Gordon skyscape! The Fiesta rings are in evidence about the outer edge, and also inside the bowl! — although the latter are not often

151

seen to advantage, because the dark heavy glazes sometimes nearly obliterate this inside decoration.

There are three versions of this bowl, but versions one and two each exist in only one color and in small numbers.

Version one: The original bowl had only three fee with three steps on each. Made only in turquoise, it was quickly seen that the weight of the bowl, just over four pounds, could not be sustained by only three supports; the design had to be modified.

Version two: Three more feet were added, but these had only two steps. These examples exist only in periwinkle blue, and when the Art Department realized the additions corrected the problem, these three feet were completely altered to have three steps.

Version there: The final version: six feet each with three steps. The collector can quickly see which three feet were added: they are not linked to the dry foot.

Thus, the flat open bowl has the unique distinction of being the only piece of Post86 Fiesta to be more advantageously viewed upside down!

As a specialty item the bowl does have its specific glamorous uses, but it does not really compete for practicality with the more plebian (yet perhaps more graceful) pedestal bowl.

Final word: Rumors are flying that five presentation bowls were made in juniper and then destroyed. Or were they?

Interest in this bowl is concentrated mainly underneath. The architectural motif was later used on the millennium candleholder and the hostess bowl. Black was an exclusive for the Homer Laughlin China retail outlet.

The grand prize of the June 2000 HLCCA conference exhibition was a cobalt presentation bowl with a special gold inscription and a reproduction signature of Jonathan O. Parry, its designer inside near the rim. Mr. Parry had died only two months before and this prize was very special.

Ten presentation bowls, all nesting in a stack!

Millennium Candleholders

MILLENNIUM CANDLEHOLDERS
Number: 000
Mold Book: Unknown
Mark: One of a kind, a distinctive FIES-TA in block letters with an additional Y2K.
Size: Height: 6¼"
Popularity: Average
Color Availability: All colors except black, apricot, lilac, sapphire.
Changes: None, a limited production piece.

Shaped somewhat like vases, these candleholders have an embossed design reaching up to the sides which is a reflection of the base of the presentation bowl and the hostess bowl.

Pile item upon item! The advent of the year 2000 spawned a good number of exciting new Post86 pieces: the pizza tray, goblets, the large oval vegetable, specialty vases, and the very classical presentation bowl. Too much of a good thing, perhaps, because the millennium candleholders created a fiery flash of excite-

ment, quickly followed by a yawn of acceptance.

When a single candleholder was placed in front of a person whose words I respect, he smiled: "I think they are trying too hard!"

The problem, as personally seen, is that the millennium candleholder has been design-stretched so far and wide from the Art Deco mood of Frederick Rhead that a return to the fold is virtually impossible! It is designed thoughtfully, but with a very pedestrian approach: this candleholder does not excite nor does it stimulate. There is an attempt to create interest through the three faint architectural shapes on the swelling pillar sides, but these "Chrysler-building" forms attract but briefly.

The best thing to be said: the millennium candleholder is soothing and holds a candle!

On an extremely practical note: American consumers have, in the past three years, paid $2.1 billion for candles, and another unbelievable $3 billion for candle accessories, such as holders, lighters, and snuffers. No wonder the Homer Laughlin Company decided to market a third Post86 Fiesta candleholder. After all, did not Dave Conley, the Homer Laughlin China director of marketing, once say — that as long as collectors ". . . keep buying. . . we keep our jobs. . . works for me." (A direct quote from the Fiestafanatic message board).

Well, no collector wants Mr. Conley to lose his position, so I just purchased two sets.

Through the spring and summer of 2000, more and more Post86 collectors were growing frustrated at what was being termed an "obvious deception." The Homer Laughlin company had announced Bloomingdale's would sell only 1,000 sets of these candleholders in each color. Seemingly, this turned out not to be true. Suddenly Bloomingdale's stores are awash with these candleholders — and at tremendous discounts. Many people expressed anger at wasting money on so-called HLC limited editions. This piece, plus the Millennium I vase, began to swamp the HLC retail outlet and other seconds stores.

The most memorable aspect of the candleholder is the unusual mark. Y2K appears only here.

The millennium candleholder is the only Post86 piece that had the Y2K mark. Here are six candleholders in assorted colors.

My First Fiesta Tea Set

A refashioning of the My First Fiesta Tea Set. Only the teacups, the sugar/creamer set, and the yellow 6" plate were originally part of the set. The two saucers (persimmon and pearl gray), the cobalt blue 6" plate, and the 2-cup teapot in sea mist green have been substituted to allow for a wider color assortment.

"What," they demand, "is this children's set doing in a serious book on Post86 Fiesta?"

My answer is boldly simple: The My First Fiesta Tea Set is here because it is interesting and sheds some light (albeit "candle" rather than "spot") on the Post86 line, and also because this book does not purport to be drearily serious.

This is a fun set that is well on to becoming extremely popular both with young ladies who like to dress up and have a tea party, and also with those older in years, but still young at heart, who simply like to collect the new line of Fiesta! Very simply stated!

The popularity of My First Fiesta has led to some frantic hunting and some unwise purchasing. By this is meant the fluctuation in the prices is probably the widest among all the Post86 line. The set has been seen at a very inflated price of $89.90, and it has been purchased for as little as $40.00 — less than half. For the time being, this set is not really rare, only difficult to locate. By the end of the year 2000, prices have equalized as collectors and doting parents realize "a dollar saved is a dollar earned!"

Arriving in a box nearly as exciting as the set itself, the wise papa or mommy will save this container, for it is charmingly and wittily drawn. On

The fascinating box cover design by Judi Noble.

either side of the sophisticated young miss serving tea to a granny doll, a well-dressed dolly, a teddy bear, and a floppy rabbit are two tall and thin cabinets portraying various new Fiesta items — all done in an appealing child-like manner. Needless to say, the artwork is done by the very talented Judi Noble.

Everyone will know by now the set comes in only one choice of colors: the teapot is yellow, the two teacup and saucer sets are in rose and periwinkle blue, and sugar and creamer are both turquoise and the small plates for cookies are both yellow. No choice here because what can be harder for a young lady to do except choose and choose again the colors she wants represented in her First Fiesta Set?

To capture the dreams of little girls and their collector daddies, Bloomingdale's in late fall 2000, slightly revamped the My First Tea Set. The colors are exactly the same, but the yellow teapot has the Dancing Girl logo in black and announces the date 2001. The price in the winter catalog was $79.00. How many "big daddies" will buy this for their "little girls?"

But there is some choice! Only the teacups, the sugar and the creamer are new items. And even then the body of the teacup is simply the AD cup — but the handle is new. It is meant for easy grasping by young hands. The other pieces already exist: the teapot is the 2-cup variety, the saucers are AD saucers, the plates are 6" plates. Thus of the nine pieces, five can be changed without harm done to the set or its philosophy.

Surely the Homer Laughlin China marketing department realized this and in realizing it, condoned it. So you could give to your little girl or lady-friend collector a set in two colors — rose and turquoise — or in a wide spectrum of color.

What fun! One should never be too serious about any Fiesta!

The only items newly designed — and at that, the teacups are really the regular AD cups with a redesigned handle. The sugar and creamer are absolutely new to Post86 Fiesta.

Three Millennium Vases

*The three millennium vases: III in pearl gray
(left), I in rose (center) and II in yellow (right).*

There is a story about the birth of the three millennium vases. The story starts with only one being planned. Note the lack of any number on the base of what has become millennium vase I. Then there were two, and finally three! Like the Three Pigs; the Three Bears; The Andrews Sisters; Tolkien's trilogy, The Lord of the Rings, and even Post86's disc pitcher threesome, the consumer was confronted with three millennium vases! All good things come in threes.

The following information was gleaned primarily through e-mail conversations with Jonathan Parry.

These were the last communications I had with Jonathan before his death. As he became more ill, a visitor to the HLC Art Department somewhat thoughtlessly turned this gentle man against me through the use of shadowy innuendos and half-truths. Could this be another indication that bitterness and spite are, like black clouds, beginning to overshadow the pleasant world of dinnerware collecting?

The millennium vase (it was not yet number I) was on the drawing board when a Bloomingdale's representative espied it and desired it for the store's millennium shop. And that was that! Mr. Parry designed the vase, basing it directly upon the carafe. It was modeled by Joseph Geisse.

Mr. Parry comments: "The two-handled millennium vase has been very interesting. There were a lot of comments about it on the forums of the Internet when the design came out. Many of the comments were less than positive — everything from it looked like a fat

lady with her hands on her hips to just plain ugly. It was even inferred that the majority had spoken [against it] and HLC should not make it. This was somewhat surprising since the design is based upon the carafe. On the other hand, I saw one go in eBay for $170.00 last week [mid-March 1999] which is very strange since [anyone] can still buy it at Bloomie's for $30.00 to $35.00. So I guess somebody liked it!"

Indeed a good number of "somebodies" like Millie I. It was produced in ten glazes limited to 1,000 each, and this total of 10,000 vases disappeared amazingly onto collectors' shelves: white, rose, cobalt blue, yellow, turquoise, periwinkle blue, sea mist green, persimmon, chartreuse, pearl gray. Later Homer Laughlin China produced a few black "Millie I" for a charity auction in June 1999.

By early spring 2000, prices for a black millennium vase I was reaching toward $800.00 and on eBay (mentioned above by Mr. Parry) prices for chartreuse examples hovered just under $400.00. It must be mentioned these pieces were largely inspired by bidding fervor! One merry wag on one of the Internet forums groaned (re: the price of chartreuse), "I should be so lucky!"

Then Mr. Parry, lucky and undaunted, started working on a second millennium vase slated to be a Homer Laughlin China general release. However, Macy's (Federated Department Stores) buyers were hunkering about the art department, saw Number II, and snap, it went off as a Macy's exclusive.

Mr. Parry continues, "Millie II was based on the

disc [pitcher] with a new top, of course. Some people hated that one also. Fiesta collectors resist change. They forget that we are in the china business, and our customer is the department store that sells it to their customer who buys it from them, not us." Shrewdly and bluntly, but a little confusingly, put!

All three were expertly modeled by Mr. Joseph Geisse.

A third design was attempted — this time again for general release. The scene arises of Mr. Parry and his staff working behind locked doors to discourage another set of buyers peeping about! And this final piece was based upon the morgue design. When Mr. Parry contemplated a third vase, he wanted a more classic shape, but one that still had connections with Fiesta. No doubt, Parry insists, this vase will be the rarest of the three because it was the last to appear.

As the year 2000 came to pass and the Y2K headaches failed to materialize, these three vases passed into the secondary market, and, after the first explosion of collector interest, fell into a period of hiatus — prices leveled. Chartreuse remains the most popular, and, as mentioned above, the millennium vase I in that glaze continues to appreciate. There is absolutely no logical reason why chartreuse is in greater demand unless it is purely that more people like it, or perhaps the term "limited" has erroneously been affixed to it? Pearl gray, being the "new boy in town," was the second most popular Millie I.

Readers who were shrewd collectors and filled their garages with a dozen of each vase need not lament. Even though demand has leveled, the collecting pendulum swings to music humans can rarely hear. Someday prices for these admirable, well-designed vases will — like the phoenix — rise from the dreaded doldrums.

Millennium I

The Millennium I vase was conceived by Jonathan O. Parry as an item for general distribution. It was still on the drawing board when it was spied by a representative of Bloomingdale's — the trend setting department store — and the entire run was contracted as an exclusive item. It was decided to make it a limited edition of 1,000 vases each in ten colors. The "limitedness" was energetically touted in advertisements.

The mark on this millennium vase is very interesting because there is no numeral attached: it is purely Fiesta Millennium. This is proof, of a sort, that there were no other "end of millennium" vases in the planning at this time.

Orders could be placed late in 1998. Because of the number limitations of Millie I, no color, except for per-

sonal taste, should be considered more desirable or more valuable. Yet psychologically, chartreuse was immediately sought with overt eagerness because the color was also limited. Pearl gray was purchased with overcharged vigor simply because it was the new color on the block. White, rose, and yellow remained available through a number of Bloomingdale's sources for quite some time. Still the continual advertising threat that only 1,000 vases were ever to be made in each color kept purchases snappy! Once they were gone, they were gone!

Prices reflected this philosophy: when first introduced in the Bloomingdale's catalogs, the vases cost $30.00. Then very shortly, the catalog price rose to $37.00. While on the secondary market, even while available through Bloomingdale's, the prices seemed to go berserk: chartreuse and pearl gray were being offered — and sold — for over $100.00. To some Fiestawatchers this willingness to pay was a wonderment — especially when the shape of Millie I (based on the carafe) was seriously ridiculed when the proposed sketches were first viewed by collectors some months before. However, very quickly, this vase was purchased, absorbed, and disappeared into collections and dealer inventories.

As the first few months of the year 2000 passed, this vase continued, very slowly, to rise in price. Even though it was the first to be offered, the fact that numbers were limited seemed to impress collectors. Also, in my opinion, Millie I, rotund and humble, possesses a very homey shape found irresistible by all but the most pseudo-sophisticated.

Millie I in black: continuing its interest in charity items, Homer Laughlin China made 24 numbered vases in black to be auctioned off by the East Liverpool High School Alumni Association in June 1999. The association provides scholarships to students from the area. The black vases were produced under very strict security, and when auctioned brought between $1,200.00 and $1,500.00 each.

Millennium II

After Bloomingdale's purchased exclusive rights to the 10,000 first millennium vases, Mr. Parry designed a second vase to take its place. The aim was general release. This second attempt was based on the large disc pitcher: flat instead of bulbous.

In a deja vu scenario, buyers for the Federated Department Stores were at the plant, and when this piece was seen, they wanted it to compete with Bloomingdale's. (Technically, Bloomingdale's belongs to the Federated Store Group, but has maintained its own buying department, and contractually acts independently.) For some contractual reason, the second vase was limited only to time: it would cease in December 1999, but would be produced in quantities to keep up with demand. The colors were chartreuse, persimmon, cobalt, rose, pearl gray, yellow, periwinkle, and turquoise (these colors have been listed in the order they appeared in Macy's advertisement).

Millie II was priced slightly cheaper in the primary market and was not very well received when first seen. Mr. Parry countered the complaints: "Some people hated it. Fiesta collectors resist change. They forget we are in the china business, and our customer is the department store who (then) sells it to the (retail) customer." This statement seems to be the official view taken by the company, i.e., "collectors are pleasant to have around, but our main concern is the department stores." While in many respects the statement is valid, but more and more, or so it seems, the company has become very, very aware of the power of the collectors — in fact, Mr. Dave Conley (marketing supervisor) has used the term "cult" when referring to Fiesta collectors on television. Homer Laughlin China and its marketing experts have, in many cases, played a "cat and mouse" game with all collectors — fanatics, cultists, and even those collectors who approach Post86 Fiesta in a state of calmness!

It is to be wondered how many restaurants really rushed to purchase Millie II vases. However, the sale to collectors was somewhat brisk, but not overpowering as was the demand for the first millennium vase. There is always an advantage to being first! Many Fiesta followers contented themselves to obtain one or two of Millie II — just to have an example.

The sheen and shimmer surrounding a commemorative vase were becoming just slightly less tarnished.

Millennium III

Still desirous of a vase — for general distribution — to celebrate the start of the third millennium, Mr. Parry designed his third vase after a classic beauty seen in the morgue section (The morgue is the room at the Homer Laughlin headquarters where unusual and important historical shapes are stored.) of Bob and Sharon Huxford's *Collector's Encyclopedia of Fiesta.**

While this vase, pictured in brilliant Fiesta red, is actually 12" tall, the redesigned piece is 9¾" tall. While never placed in production, the tall morgue vase has become a symbol of near lust on the part of many Fiesta collectors. Indeed it must be one of the most striking pieces ever to be contemplated by Homer Laughlin. Now that the dream has been partially realized, Mr. Parry confides that the morgue piece was conceived long ago in the Saturday Pottery School.

Millie III is modern and unabashedly Art Deco sleek. Its design remains very close to the original, and unlike I and II, this vase was not based upon any other Fiesta. But, for some rather murky reason, the beautifully clean lines of this vase prompted the unfortunately soggy idea of placing a long stemmed red rose to decorate. The rose appears only on the white and pearl gray glazes — presumably because the red of this rose would appear even more tasteless on the more brilliant colors, i.e., chartreuse or turquoise.

Sold primarily through the HLC retail outlet (or very occasionally on one of the Internet auctions), this beflowered vase was seen standing pathetically tall in row after row on a display table.

Technically there should be no Millie III vases in juniper. The former ceased production on December 31, 1999, and the latter came into production (supposedly) on January 1, 2000. However overlaps are allowed — even encouraged in some cases to create highly desirable items. Twenty-four Millie IIIs were glazed in juniper and those lucky enough to acquire one find themselves with a rather valuable piece.

This vase also appears in a very bright yellow announced as a trial color: sunflower. HLC promised this would be the only vase done in this glaze. The company donated it to a collectible association to be auctioned off to raise funds. The only other Post86 piece to be glazed in sunflower yellow was a dinner plate, also auctioned off in June 2000.

Like Millie II, this vase ceased production at the end of 1999. Spoken of as being the "rarest" of the three millennium vases, as the year 2000 settled into regularity, this vase slipped sharply in price, while Millennium I became more valuable.

*Now this tall red vase is locked in a glass curio cabinet in HLC's main offices. More and more Fiesta is being enshrined.

MILLENNIUM I VASE

Number: 000
Mold Book: Not known
Introduced: July 7, 1998
Mark: See below.
Size: Height: 8". Width: 8" from handle to handle.
Liquid Measurement: 66 oz.
Popularity: Exceptional
Color Availability: All colors except apricot, lilac, and sapphire. Only 24 made in black.
Changes: None, limited edition.

When Millie I was designed, no other millennium vase was contemplated, thus no "I" appears on the raised mark.

MILLENNIUM II VASE

Number: 000
Mold Book: Not known
Introduced: November 6, 1998
Mark: See below.
Size: Height: 8½". Width: Nearly 8".
Liquid Measurement: 96 oz.
Popularity: Average
Color Availability: Eight colors, see text.
Changes: None, limited edition.

MILLENNIUM III VASE

Number: 000
Mold Book: **Not known**
Introduced: **Mid-1999**
Mark: **See text.**
Size: Height: **9¾".** Base: **4¾" round.**
Liquid Measurement: **44 oz.**
Popularity: **Average**
Color Availability: **Not available in black, apricot, lilac, and sapphire.**
Changes: **None**

Decorated Post86 Fiesta

There once was a Boy known as Billy.
Decaled Fiesta drove him quite silly.
Wildly screaming he would
Get all that he could.
Billy sadly went mad willy-nilly!

Just what is, you question, the difference between "decorated" and "decaled?" The first term is broader than the second — i.e., all Post86 Fiesta with decals (Looney Tunes, Sunporch, etc.) is technically decorated, but not all decorations are decals. Thus there is a difference, and sometimes it is difficult to look at a piece and proclaim it is decaled. A moot point, but distinctions should be made. There are many more decorations that are decals than are not. Some hand-painted pieces perhaps, or pieces double-dipped in two glazes?

When first contemplated, this section seemed to present no problems, but that feeling was quickly "gone with the wind." There are many, many examples to be discovered in this category: some only one piece, others entire sets; some for a one-time event, others for an advertising campaign. Any piece of Post86 Fiesta enlivened with any type or kind of decoration belongs here. And this definition encompasses a goodly number of dishes! The decoration can be an elegant and simple series of stripes or it can be a very famous and well-known decal such as Sunporch. The decoration can advertise Dillard's Department Store chain or even the Homer Laughlin Company itself. The category "Decorated New Fiesta" is extremely large.

Perhaps a grouping scheme will help consolidate these items.

SPECIALTY ITEMS: These are usually limited to one or just a few pieces and are produced for a specific event. This is an ever-changing category. Those marked (*) are

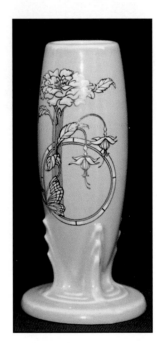

thought interesting enough to merit special notice.

1. General Specialty Items: Old Mother Hubbard, etc.

2. Specialty Items for a specific event: Fiesta Club of America, Homer Laughlin China 60th and 100th Anniversary, the Millennium, the Christmas Ornament (*) and plates, etc.

3. Advertising Specialty Items: Fiesta Shelf Display Sign (*), Dealer/Signature Plate, retail store advertising such as Dillard's, Mays, Macy's.

DINNERWARE: These are available in a variety of pieces and are usually meant for actual use or solely as collectibles, some as limited editions, others not.

1. Dinnerware sets produced by and for the Homer Laughlin Company: Cranberry, Aegean, Quattro, Holiday Fiesta.

2. Dinnerware sets produced by Homer Laughlin China for other distributors: Looney Tunes, Sunporch, Moon-over-Miami, MegaChina.

These dinnerware lines might not contain all the pieces in the Post86 line, but enough has been or will be made available to allow the customer to own a viable set of the treatment. It must always be remembered that some of these sets are not meant for actual dining, Sunporch, for example. Decaled Fiesta certainly is not new to Post86 — the vintage line boasted of many pieces with decorations. The above list, of course, is not exhaustive. It would be impossible to be complete because decorated ware is constantly changing as lines and pieces are added and deleted.

To continue in more detail —

SPECIALTY ITEMS

Decorated (or decaled) contemporary Fiesta falls gracefully into the two major categories outlined previously. The first consists of "specialty" pieces — either single pieces such as the Macy's "modern dancing lady" millennium plate, or as a set such as the Bloomingdale's millennium beverage set in pearl gray. The term "specialty" is merely my personal term for those Fiesta items ordered by retail stores for specific occasions or celebrations — or simply to capture purchaser interest. More examples might be the "American as Apple Pie" pie plate and mug (designed by Judi Noble for Boscov's), or another beverage set celebrating the 60th anniversary of Fiesta itself. The marvelous coincidence of the millennium allowed for a plethora of all manner of Post86 decorated pieces.

The Bunny Set, designed by Judi Noble, for Easter 2000. It is an exclusive for the HLC outlet. There will be a Reindeer Set appearing for Christmas 2000.

Hawaiiana

This line was produced for Lynn Krantz Dishware. The advertisement informs us that "Hawaii has always represented the ultimate island paradise, a respite from the headaches, difficulties, and trivial problems of everyday life." This is a combination set using several dinnerware shapes. The decorations are based on some of the famous Eugene Savage murals — murals which were used as subjects to grace the menus of the Mason Cruise Lines in the '40s and '50s.

But it might be better if the reader visited Hawaii to get the true flavor of the ceremonious pageantry of the Hawaiian royal past. Visit Mookini Heiau on the Kohala coast where the great warrior king Kamehameha I was born in 1758, or the Kopoloa Falls, or even meander down the touristic thoroughfares of Honolulu and dance the hula-hula on the beach at Waikiki. You might be better off doing all this than spending much money on this dinnerware.

But, admittedly, the pieces do look wonderful in photographs, but in the hand they disappoint with very little sharpness or definition. Hawaiiana Ware exploded with popularity when it was first introduced, but is now reduced to a soft back-burner simmer.

Halloween Pumpkin

Early in October 2000, when the many followers of Candy Fagerlin's website, FiestaFanatic at work, "tuned in," they were greeted by a charming smiling group of persimmon Post86Fiesta pieces wonderfully disguised as jack-o-lanterns. Since Ms. Fagerlin is a recipient of much of HLC's advanced notices, all viewers assumed these pieces would be available at the Retail Outlet.

The pieces were the pizza tray, the pie baker, the bulb candleholder, the shakers, and the mug. With eyes, noses, and grinning mouths in pure black, these items were in immediate demand for the upcoming season. So much in demand that the outlet severely limited the numbers to be sold to each customer: only one each. Even then the Halloween pumpkin was quickly sold out, and probably will become a very desirable collectible in years to come. These pieces have the most successful decorative treatment to appear on the Post86 line — at least to date.

John Iams, my very perceptive friend in East Liverpool, could not get any of this series for me, but he decided to contribute his own shaker set to be photographed for this book (see page 122).

Then there are the advertising items: "100 yrs in Florida" pitcher once available at Burdines, Mays' really exceptional "blue Christmas tree" plate and ornament, the New York sky line pitcher, and the innumerable plates and pitchers continually flaunting the name of Homer Laughlin. These pieces, most of which bear the name of the distributor, come and go with considerable speed. Some are purchased for household use, but most are gathered by collectors. Consumers tend to overlook these specialties when they are available in the primary market, but then, as soon as they are discontinued, collectors scramble to buy!

The millennium! Since humanity (in its swarming millions) has crossed the bridge into the third millennium, now is the time to tackle the millennium question. There is a gentleman on one of the message boards who is always kvetching about millennium terminology. He is, however, absolutely correct — the third millennium starts January 1, 2001. But let us follow the media's incorrect allocation. Fiesta followers have recently been subjected to a number of "third millennium" celebratory pieces: millennium plates, a variety of disc pitchers, accompanied by tumblers, announcing what we all know: we are in the year 2000! These are usually in the limited edition category and often have certificates proclaiming their valued position.

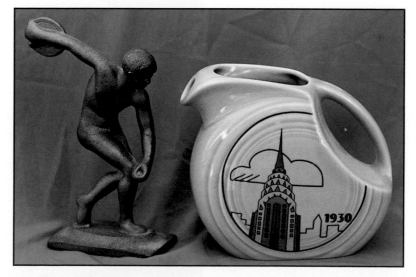

The Chrysler Building is the epitome of Art Deco architectural design — no wonder it appeared on the pearl gray small disc pitcher. This price was the first exclusive item for members of the Homer Laughlin China Collectors Association (HLCCA.) It was enthusiastically received and soon appeared on the secondary market. The second exclusive item — a yellow small disc pitcher with a Dick Tracy decal — was not as popular.

Bloomingdale's exclusive millennium beverage set.
This design was repeated for 2001.

A few pieces are worthy of more detailed commentary. Bloomingdale's pearl gray pitcher and tumbler set (officially known as the Fiesta 2000 commemorative beverage set) is tastefully simple and extremely attractive: 13 stars in 13 Post86 glazes — although some of the stars can scarcely be identified as the color they are supposed to be! The tumblers are cleverly done — one has a 2 in lilac, and three have 0's in persimmon, chartreuse, and a rather light cobalt blue. All bear the regulation Fiesta stamp. The mega-store's advertising copy reads: "Only at Bloomingdale's. Limited Edition of 10,000 sets. 5-pc. set includes the famous discus (Was the young man or young woman who wrote this copy a sports enthusiast? The famous "disc" pitcher was confused with the 4½ pound wooden and metal disk thrown about by straining athletes at sports meets!) pitcher in gray, decorated with thirteen stars, each depicting a color that made Fiesta an American classic. Four tumblers spell out 2-0-0-0. Certificate included." Bloomingdale's continued its exclusive beverage set at the end of the year 2000. Different colors, different words, new potential customers. The disc pitcher is now persimmon (incidentally, persimmon is very much admired by the consumers), the "2" tumbler in rose, one "0" turquoise, the other "0" periwinkle blue, and the "1" yellow. Will customers line up?

Macy's millennium contribution is not as attractive: a 9" white millennium plate that consists of a caricature of the dancing girl — this time a flouncy party girl whirling, with champagne bubbles bursting in circles about her! What makes this rather commonplace Macy's plate more exciting is there are two versions — either as a result of a manufacturing mistake or as a deliberate ploy. The most usual version has the words "The New" in barely noticeable chartreuse just above the much larger word "Millennium" (cobalt blue). The second version simply deletes the chartreuse words. Variations are born with amazing (or deliberate) rapidity!

Then China Specialties has a charming offering: a white presentation bowl consisting of a decal in muted grays and blues in the center which portrays various "men of importance" — the word "millennium" twice

Macy's exclusive millennium plate.

encircles the decal with the number 2000 in the middle. Quite an understated and tasteful contribution.

The three very important specialty millennium vases technically belong in this category, but since they have no decorations (except an extremely unfortunate long stemmed red rose on Millie III), these vases are discussed at the conclusion of the specialty Post86 pieces.

Homer Laughlin is responsible for adding a goodly number to the specialty category — and the line between "occasion" and "advertising" becomes very blurred. Most of the pieces offered for an anniversary or other occasion so obviously proclaim Homer Laughlin China itself that they really advertise the company.

And those occasional pieces seen on white depicting Old Mother Hubbard, her despondent dog, and her bare cupboard are quaint and unusual. Was some decorator dabbling with a desire to present a series of Mother Goose items?

Shelf Display Signs and Christmas Ornaments

There exist two Post86 specialty items hard to categorize, but because they bear decorations, the two are placed here: the Fiesta shelf sign and the Fiesta Christmas ornaments. Yet both are truly Post86 Fiesta, appear with some frequency in the mold book, and are very widely collected. Perhaps it would be more logical to place them with the regular Post86, but they really do fit the definition of a decorated piece.

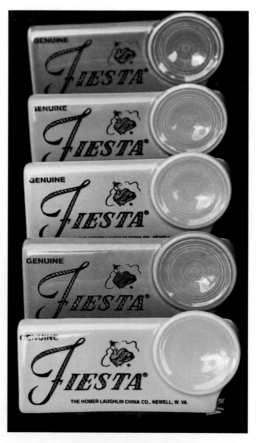

The five shelf signs.

In 1936, The Homer Laughlin China Company of Newell, West Virginia, introduced a new dinnerware line called Fiesta*. Its classic Art Deco lines and bright colors made it an instant success with the American public, and it went on to become the most successful dinnerware line in history. In 1986, Homer Laughlin reintroduced Fiesta* in a new, fully vitrified body in five new colors, Black, White, Cobalt Blue, Rose and Apricot. A number of other fashionable glaze colors have since been added as regular, full line colors, as well as, limited edition colors that are only produced for specific time periods. Chartreuse is being produced for 1998 and 1999 only and will be discontinued after December 31, 1999. This Fiesta* display sign was produced exclusively for members of

Fiesta® Collectors Quarterly
P.O. Box 471   Valley City, OH   44280

1998-99 Limited Edition Glaze Color- CHARTREUSE
*FIESTA IS A REGISTERED TRADEMARK OF THE HOMER LAUGHLIN CHINA COMPANY

The Fiesta shelf display sign was first mentioned in *Fiesta Collector's Quarterly* (Winter 96/97) as being produced exclusively for F.C.Q. members. The event was termed "historic," and it was stated Homer Laughlin China gave the *Fiesta Collector's Quarterly* (remember sometimes the lines are blurred between Fiesta Collectors Club and China Specialties) permanent rights to this sign. The announcement mentioned 600 signs were to be produced in each color. The original time of distribution was given as early March. However, there were production problems that caused the date to be advanced to mid-May 1997. The problem was the etched rings of the small featured plate disappeared with the heavy glaze; thus the art department had to retool all the molds to make the rings more prominent.

The display signs are a convenient size: 5½" long and 2¾" tall. They are issued yearly: 1996 — persimmon, 1997 — turquoise, 1998 — apricot, 1999 — chartreuse. It is not really understood how long the signs will be offered or in what colors. Presently, they are also available with Sunporch and Moon-over-Miami treatments. This fact emphasizes the connection with China Specialties. There is also available a periwinkle shelf sign which has been titled a mistake, and one in rose.

All Fiesta shelf display signs are marked with the raised "fiesta" signature.

The Christmas ornaments, while not quite as popular as the shelf signs, have quite a number of earnest people anxious to collect them. They also are issued yearly but in two variations: the holly design on white, and the Fiesta Senorita on selected colors. Christmas ornaments also appear with other designs made for a variety of distributors. The latter are considered by many to be more desirable. All are dated: all are stamped in gold "genuine Fiesta U.S.A." So the ornaments must be taken at their word — they are legitimate Post86 Fiesta! An ornament was first logged into the mold book February 28, 1991, reappearing on August 5, 1996 (directly after the next Fiesta piece — the shelf sign, July 25, 1996). Other mold book notations have been made on January 10, 1997, and May 9, 1997, and these will no doubt continue as each year demands slight changes.

Originally the ornament was made with a more open hanger. This proved very breakable, and it was modified into the present day hanger. Another type of ornament, a hollow ball, was also considered. Unfortunately, this piece proved difficult to produce and, out-

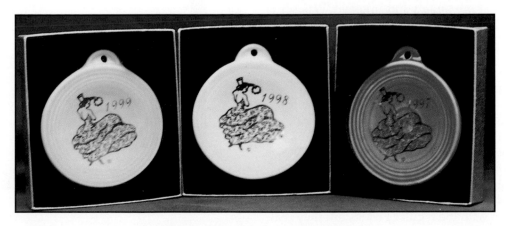

Three years of the Dancing Lady ornament.

side of few prototypes, does not exist.

Both these pieces should be considered specialty items for it is not determined how long they will be offered. Hopefully, the official Homer Laughlin China ornament will be a yearly event for a long time.

The 1999 Holly ornament.

Ornament exclusive to May's Company.

DINNERWARE

The second category of decorated Post86 Fiesta is much more broadly based, exceedingly more important as to number and variety of pieces, but perhaps not as widely collected. These are, after all, dinnerware lines in themselves, and as such are often purchased solely for use.

The most famous of these are the two offerings of China Specialties: Sunporch and Moon-over-Miami. These are all limited editions (usually 500 per piece) and are available most readily and directly by subscribing to the *Fiesta Collector's Quarterly*. In fact, it is believed, one must subscribe before one can purchase any of the Sunporch pieces from China Specialties. The Sunporch decal is probably the most desirable decoration on any Homer Laughlin dinnerware — collectors will snaggle and haggle and pay extremely high prices to add a piece to display on their shelves — and rightly so because on the older bowls, platters, plates, and vellum Century, it is warm and lovely. Not so sure am I regarding Sunporch on the stark white new Fiesta! The pure and gleaming white, unrelieved by any mellowing creaminess, makes the well-known colorful decal rather garish! Incidentally, Sunporch is also available on a vintage line manufactured by Harker.

However, I do not desire to insult or antagonize those who adore Sunporch on stark white! I accede it has a certain attractiveness — in a fresh and startling way!

Moon-over-Miami is also quite popular — a pink flamingo wading in a moon reflected pool and on cobalt blue, turquoise, or black Post86. One can be muddled regarding the night-time perambulations of these Florida flamingos! Usually all the Florida birds I know, except owls or a wandering member of the Nightjar family, tend to tuck their heads under their wings and snooze in the dark — not wander in shallow water under a moon-filled sky! Yet, readily it is admitted that MOM does have a dusky warm charm that can be very beguiling. The turquoise napkin rings are very attractive — and because of the collectibility of the Post86 napkin ring are very desirable.

The problem, as I see it, about these two lines is that many of the pieces cannot be used — or at least none whose decal comes in contact with food: plates, bowls, platters, etc. All decals are "over-glazed" and will scratch off. Sunporch and Moon-over-Miami are for decorative use only!

Looney Tunes Post86 Fiesta
for Warner Brothers

In 1994, Homer Laughlin China contracted with Warner Bros. stores to produce a line of new Fiesta depicting various cartoon characters popular in the forties and fifties.

Rather unusual Bugs Bunny mugs, different scenes and different handles, turquoise and rose.

Scooby Doo pieces are not easy to find. These shakers in sea mist green are unusual.

Unlike Sunporch and Moon-over-Miami, these friendly-faced dishes could be used with complete safety. When the group was first seen, I must confess my feelings were slightly negative. After all, who wants to spoon up mashed potatoes to slowly reveal the porcine face of Porky Pig? Or view the mouth of Bugs Bunny leering out from under a dollop of cole slaw?

But again, as often happens, a second thought, a more careful study, results in less caustic commen-taries. These pieces are really well designed. Rings of contrasting colors encircle each character and enrich the design. The teacup/saucer set is especially attractive as the cup sits directly upon the spreading circles of the saucer below. All have quite a charming look.

The Looney Tunes appeal mainly to those collectors who have been able to maintain a "child-like" approach to the world. Note, I did not say "childish" — which is to be slightly silly, vague, or immature. To be child-like is a strong positive condition extolled by the important English writer and mythologist C.S. Lewis. Lewis and his literary friend J.R.R. Tolkien (of Hobbit fame) maintain an emotionally mature adult retains a link with childhood. This link allows the adult to possess a sense of wonderment and joy: a sense of curiosity about and belief in the surrounding world!

True scientists own such an approach to the world — they are constantly searching. They are men, and women who continually express delight, who continually say "what if?" or "what now?" and do not dismiss as childish the possibility whereby other beings might inhabit the human world. These people relish in fantasy, and science fiction, are explorers and wanderers (both physically and mentally), and enjoy the Freudian depths of the folk and fairy tales of Grimm and Anderson. Their minds are open to all possibilities. The world could be inhabited by mischievous goblins, evil bogles, lob-lie-by-the-fires, and hairy footed hobbits, trusting Tweety-Birds, ducks called Daffy and Donald, mice named Mickey, and, most certainly, pigs with the unfortunate name of Porky. Many adventurous collectors find the Looney Tunes Fiestaware child-like!

Production of the line was very logically approached. Each character was assigned a color, and most years brought new items. Tweety-Bird appeared on white, Bugs Bunny on periwinkle blue, Daffy Duck on sea mist green, Sylvester the Cat on yellow, and

Porky Pig (the most popular) on rose. Granny, Foghorn, Penelope, and Pepe le Pew also appear but only very briefly.

Here is a list of the available pieces:

Tweety Bird (white)
10" dinner plate
rim soup
teacup/saucer
mug
teapot
large vegetable bowl
salt and pepper shakers

Tweety also appears on the rose teapot (with Granny 1994), an 11¾" mosaic plate (1995), a white Christmas set, teapot with Sylvester and mug (1998), and finally, in 1999, on a 10" white plate clock with Bugs and Sylvester.

Bugs Bunny (periwinkle blue)
10" dinner plate
rim soup
mug
teacup/saucer
sauceboat
small disc pitcher (Foghorn on the
reverse)

Bugs is also on the 1999 white 10" clock with Tweety and Sylvester.

Sylvester the Cat (yellow)
10" dinner plate
rim soup
teacup/saucer
pie baker

Sylvester appears with Tweety in the 1998 Christmas teapot and with Tweety and Bugs in the center of the white 10" clock (1999).

Daffy Duck (sea mist green)
10" dinner plate
rim soup
teacup/saucer
serving tray

Porky Pig (rose)
10" dinner plate
rim soup
teacup/saucer large vegetable bowl

Penelope appears on a yellow creamer and Pepe le Pew on a matching sugar bowl.

Holiday Post86 Fiesta

We reach an American favorite: Holiday Fiesta. There are two variations of this popular set. The first was introduced about 1987 and appears without the red entwining ribbon. At the same time, two Fiesta accessories were added: green and red Christmas flatware! After several years, the second holiday version

Holiday dinnerware. The bowl is the old version without the red ribbon.

appeared — with the red, and this version proved much more popular.

A confession: the earlier version has holly much more naturalistically portrayed, and because of this, I find it much more interesting. The former is, naturally,

quite scarce, and so more desirable — probably simply because it is no longer produced. Prices for the first version are exceptionally high — for example, $195.00 for the large disc pitcher! This was a price quoted to me by a very reputable professional dealer.

The Christmas plate, exclusive to May's some years ago, whose child-like quality of the Christmas trees made it very popular. There was also an accompanying ornament.

The holiday Fiesta decal appears, again like Sunporch, only on the white glaze (but here there is a better mingling of the white and the decal) and is limited to the following items:

plate, 10½"	cereal bowl, 5½"	salt and pepper shakers
plate, 9"	soup bowl, 6⅞"	individual sugar/lid
plate, 7"	serving bowl, 8½"	individual creamer
chop plate, 12"	serving tray, 12"	bud vase
oval platter, 11½"	large disc pitcher	sugar, creamer, tray
tea cup	small disc pitcher	mug
saucer	mini disc pitcher	

Twenty pieces, plus the jumbo chili with a different holiday decal, stylized multicolor pine trees. The set can be augmented by a few pieces from the cranberry striped white Fiesta.

Bouillon with a cranberry stripe works well on a cobalt welled snack plate.

Striped Post86 Fiesta

Stripes appeared on Fiesta long before 1986. According to the Huxfords, a spectacular set of eight red-striped covered onion soup bowls was discovered not too long ago, and this discovery put the appearance of the red stripes before 1937. There have been a few pieces of vintage Fiesta with dark-blue stripes, but the red predominates.

Thus Post86 is simply following a precedent. But still, Post86 with stripes is limited as to pieces available, and only the three major lines are mentioned here.

Table-Top Direct offers white Post86 in cranberry and Aegean, the former with a rich plum stripe and the latter with vibrant teal. They were touted as accompanying pieces for the holiday sets

Teal blue Aegean compliments a turquoise hostess tray.

or touches of lightness for the solid glazes. Currently, both lines can be purchased only in the bouillon, the cereal bowl, the luncheon plate (9"), and the mug. Table-Top offered a medium platter but no longer; these platters appear now in the secondary marketplace.

Far more interesting is the design called Quattro (or Quatra). This line was introduced in late 1997 exclusively for Macy's East — yet could be purchased through the Macy's-By-Mail catalog. Unlike cranberry and Aegean, Quattro boasted four underglazed stripes on the white glaze: the four colors that were the top-sellers of the time. They were (from rim to verge) per-

simmon, periwinkle blue, yellow, and sea mist green. The general effect is sugar-sweet — very clean, delicate, and extremely pleasant, reminiscent of cotton candy or volunteer hospital workers.

Like cranberry and Aegean, Quattro was meant to lighten the regular glazes. It can be used beautifully with any or all colors of the stripes.

The following pieces appeared in Quattro: dinner plate, 10"; salad plate, 7"; cereal bowl; mug; chop plate; and, only through the catalog, the large disc pitcher. Not a wide assortment, but enough pieces to add interest to the solid place setting.

Discontinued by the end of 1998, Quattro was still available through Macy's catalog at the close of 1999. Now it has reverted to the secondary market.

MegaChina

The closer I view the decorated Post86 lines, the more I appreciate them. Of course, some are appreciated more than others, and my opinions change. As said before, the Looney Tunes were once thought impossibly corny, but now these are looked upon with strong affection — a reflection of my childhood, perhaps?

But, holding onto the strongest of my feelings of affection are the products of MegaChina, a new company which produces the most charming, the most imaginative, and the most delightful of decaled treatments!

On September 10, 1998, the first meeting between the Homer Laughlin Company and the fledgling MegaChina took place with Dave Conley and Jonathan

MegaChina design Mystique, a delight on the rose coffee server.

Mark on MegaChina pieces.

Parry present as were Mr. Solito and Sam Collings. Three designs, the work of Mr. Collings, were offered for critiquing, and when the meeting ended, two had been scrapped: only the design Champagne remained. The others were too expensive or too problematic to produce. From this first meeting, the relationship between representatives of both companies has been mutually cordial, productive, and satisfying.

When he returned for a second visit, Mr. Collings was introduced to Judi Noble. While all the MegaChina designs have been the work of Mr. Collings, it is Ms. Noble who has translated these designs to the individual Post86 pieces. All work, artistic and production, takes place at the Laughlin factory in Newell, West Virginia. MegaChina has been incorporated into the actual production runs of Post86 Fiesta.

The public has greeted the offerings of MegaChina with enthusiasm. Because the new company is youthfully vigorous and conceptually innovative, this public can expect new designs in the future, and a growing expansion of their treatments on a wide variety of new Fiesta items.

The title which MegaChina has chosen for its concept is Today's Designs/Tomorrow's Heirlooms, a title definitely signifying their hopes for the product. Simply: designs purchased for use today, yet significant to be collected and cherished in the years to come.

Presently there are four patterns divided into two collections. A chart explains:

Today's Designs/Tomorrow's Heirlooms

The Art Deco Collection	The Silhouette Collection
Pattern: *Champagne*	Pattern: *Mystique*
Pattern: *Midnight*	Pattern: *Moonshine*

Midnight (black large disc pitcher) and Champagne (in white and chartreuse).

Moonshine pieces.

The difference between the two collections is obvious. The Art Deco designs are nonrepresentational, and as bubbly and light as the name Champagne. In fact, Midnight is a reverse of the first design — conceived in white instead of black to allow appearance on the darker glazes. Midnight was new in early 2000.

The Silhouette collection is just that: figures silhouetted on the lighter glazes. Mystique: young nymph-like creatures dancing with utter abandon surrounded by a sprinkling of stars. Moonshine: the mountain world of corn-mash whiskey produced in makeshift homemade distilleries deep in hidden forest glades. Shades of Snuffy Smith! There is also a variety of edge designs, but all fit perfectly within the categories.

Again it must be stressed how far this new company has traveled in such a short time. The first meeting was on September 10, 1998. On December 18, 1998, MegaChina sent its first order to Homer Laughlin. This order was partially received on April 12, 1999, and offered to waiting consumers, April 13, 1999.

Mr. Solito advises that all colors (except apricot, lilac, and sapphire, discontinued, or black and cobalt blue, unsuitable) will be used for Champagne, Mystique, and Moonshine. Midnight (remember, the reverse of Champagne) will be used on black, as long as it is available, and cobalt blue. In the future, the black designs will be used on any lighter glazes, the white Midnight design on dark glazes. It is as simple as that.

What Post86 pieces will be available in the MegaChina line is completely based upon the marketing decisions at the Homer Laughlin Company. There might be some pieces thought undesirable for decorating, such as the presentation bowl. As of this writing the following Post86 pieces are available to MegaChina devotees: large disc pitcher, covered coffee server, carafe, tumbler, mug, rim soup, straight-sided serving bowl (39 oz.), straight-sided soup bowl (19 oz.), 10" dinner plate, 7" salad plate, sugar and creamer, and the 11½" oval platter.

This number will certainly grow as more and more customers and collectors become enamored with the extraordinary delights portrayed in the MegaChina collections.

MegaChina offers its designs with or without rim decoration. Here is a persimmon 10" plate in Mystique (rim decorated), periwinkle 7" Champagne plate (no decoration), and the new Midnight 9" plate in cobalt (rim decorated).

Marks

Very rarely do pieces of Post86 Fiesta appear unmarked, and often when there seems to be no mark, the heavy glaze has just filled up the indentations. Larger early plates (luncheon, dinner, chop) were often not stamped. The only completely unmarked hollowware piece in my entire collection is a cobalt blue creamer: it has absolutely no mark! There must be other examples. Of course, the regular shakers are never marked.

There are three forms of marks:

1. Indented (or incised)
2. Raised
3. Stamped

There are variations of each form. In some cases there is a double mark — the stamp appearing with either indented or raised markings. At this time, different markings do not affect the value of any given piece.

When Post86 first made its appearance in 1986, the indented mark was nearly identical to the vintage, but the stamped version changed the small "f" to a rather scrolled capital "F." The

Early stamp on rose saucer

One of the first of the dated "lead-free" stamps, January 1992.

The date this tumbler was produced (LLD) translates to April of 1997.

Tumbler Anniversary stamp.

Dated back stamp (April 1998) and the incised mark seen on presentation bowls, mixing bowls, etc.

The mark of this chartreuse sauceboat carries the "H" to identify it as "new."

Napkin ring stamp.

Compare the incised mark on the vintage medium teapot.

The coffee servers have an interesting variation on the "e" and "s."

stamp appeared on the small items; the indented name on the larger. Thus not only were the early pieces based on the vintage items, the marks were also. This occurs even if the Post86 item was introduced to the line many years after 1986. The small 8" vase, known to exist but not available until late 2000, still bears the same indented mark as did its vintage ancestor in 1939!

A piece introduced with the indented mark usually still continues with the same mark: for example, a white teapot produced in 1999 will continue to have the same mark as one originally made in 1986. Technically these pieces cannot be dated. A pair of rose round candleholders was purchased in 1988. A pair of pearl gray round candleholders obtained in October 1999 will have exactly the same indented mark "fiesta made in U.S.A." as does the rose, sequestered underneath two sides of the square base.

The incised or indented marks are very prevalent today not only because they were continued from the older line, but also because if a different size is added to a unit — the straight-sided bowls — the new 2-quart size retains the same general type of incised mark. But the 2-cup teapot has a raised mark and does not continue with the indented mark of the regular teapot.

There seems to be no rule regarding what piece receives what mark. Some early cups have incised marks, some had no identification at all, and later cups show the dated stamp.

One of the most interesting raised marks appears on the base of an extremely late 1999 introduction: the millennium candleholder. A very clever designer incorporated Y2K, and forever added a bit of history to the piece!

The raised mark has numerous variations, and it seems to be reserved for large impressive specialty pieces (millennium vases, presentation bowls), or in cases where other marks would not fit (napkin rings, rangetop shakers).

Around 1992 the old "Fiesta" stamp was retired

and a new one introduced which included a dating and the words "lead free." This stamp appears on many pieces, either alone or in conjunction with indented or raised marking. It is from this stamp, interestingly always remaining the same size, that the collector can date any particular piece.

All dating of Homer Laughlin China ware commenced in 1960, and from that date all restaurant ware was so marked.

The year 1960 was given the letter A, and since the system did not start until May, that month was E. A piece of restaurant ware produced in May of 1960 would be marked A.E. How simple! But some 24 years later, the year letter had to be changed to AA, and when Post86 was taken into the system the year was GG. A dinner plate marked GG C was made in March of 1992. Still simple!

All items glazed in chartreuse will be numbered MM (1998) or NN (1999). A pizza tray manufactured in October 1999 will be marked NN J. Simple, very simple!

Anniversary pieces have a different stamp that does not contain the year since the date it was produced is well known. Regarding anniversary pieces, each piece of the set has received this special mark. If you are purchasing the Anniversary large disc pitcher and tumblers set, check on each of the tumblers. If one or more of them do not have the anniversary sign, the dealer has put together a bogus set. Purchase it if you want, but the seller should, I think, lower the price. Always let the dealer know you are an intelligent Post86 collector!

So except for some early pieces — usually plates — expect all Post86 to be marked in some way. But all this information regarding marks is quite peripheral to the enjoyment of your collection! To have knowledge regarding all the various marks is adding a dollop of cream to your mocha java coffee — nice but not necessary! As one collector observed: "While I could hyperventilate about 'did you ever notice that some ivory Fiesta is backstamped with black ink and some with brown ink' in a thousand word article and try to pass it off as newsworthy, I don't think the response of [any reader] would be anything other than a big yawn [and the question] which is worth more. . . the same? . . . then who cares?" (*Fiesta Collector's Quarterly*, Winter 1994/95, Issue 13. p. 8).

I tend to agree somewhat. Post86 Fiesta has not yet reached the stage where one mark is worth more than another, and quite frankly, sweet Scarlett, I hope it never does.

— Psst. But it is great fun to know! —

TABLE FOR DATING POST86 FIESTA

Year	SYM	Jan	Feb	Mar	Apr	May	June	July	Aug	Sept	Oct	Nov	Dec
86	AA	A	B	C	D	E	F	G	H	I	J	K	L
87	BB	A	B	C	D	E	F	G	H	I	J	K	L
88	CC	A	B	C	D	E	F	G	H	I	J	K	L
89	DD	A	B	C	D	E	F	G	H	I	J	K	L
90	EE	A	B	C	D	E	F	G	H	I	J	K	L
91	FF	A	B	C	D	E	F	G	H	I	J	K	L
92	GG	A	B	C	D	E	F	G	H	I	J	K	L
93	HH	A	B	C	D	E	F	G	H	I	J	K	L
94	II	A	B	C	D	E	F	G	H	I	J	K	L
95	JJ	A	B	C	D	E	F	G	H	I	J	K	L
96	KK	A	B	C	D	E	F	G	H	I	J	K	L
97	LL	A	B	C	D	E	F	G	H	I	J	K	L
98	MM	A	B	C	D	E	F	G	H	I	J	K	L
99	NN	A	B	C	D	E	F	G	H	I	J	K	L
00	OO	A	B	C	D	E	F	G	H	I	J	K	L
01	PP	A	B	C	D	E	F	G	H	I	J	K	L
02	QQ	A	B	C	D	E	F	G	H	I	J	K	L

Fiesta Mates
Much of a Good Thing!

An assortment of Fiesta Mates.

Here the collector or consumer has a good thing! These pieces are legitimate members of the Homer Laughlin family. Regular Homer Laughlin China restaurant ware they are — and by glaze only, not styling, linked to Post86 Fiesta.

An explanation was presented by Mark Gonzalez, a friend and fellow collectibles author: ". . . as for Fiesta Mates, the way I understand it is the Mates are regular HLC shapes made for the restaurant trade but have been dipped in some or all of the [new] Fiesta glazes." Believe this is as good a definition as one can get!

The company has announced the Mates have always been geared for the commercial trade: adding a mug here, a small creamer there, a rather stunning skillet serving piece somewhere else. They might reasonably be called "spot" items, to introduce a bit of color in a diner or a coffee house or restaurant! They were conceived to fill in when there was no counterpart piece in the new Fiesta. There is absolutely nothing cheap about them, in fact that skillet is unusually and intriguingly designed — and all the Mates are welcome at the most respectable dining table.

Since the Fiesta Mates are, by Homer Laughlin China declaration, commercially oriented, there arises some restrictions regarding color and availability. And since the limited colors are, conversely,

Close-up of the three Fiesta Mates mugs, (left to right), Denver (persimmon), Irish Coffee (rose), Tower (turquoise).

aimed at the collector market, purchasing Fiesta Mates pieces in those glazes can be problematic. Succinctly put: not all Mates are available in all colors. Restricting, but true! How Post86 collectors would love to own a skillet or a set of ramekins in chartreuse! These pieces were not officially glazed in chartreuse – but in actuality, roguery happens even with Homer Laughlin's ever tightening security measures: one can never be sure which unofficial pieces will suddenly, miraculously grace the shelves of the Fiesta pundits in power! There are a good number of "rogue" or unofficial items floating through the byways and back alleys of the collecting world.

The most popular Fiesta Mate* must be the sugar caddy. This piece ranks very high. The retail outlet has placed it on the list of Fiesta items that appears on its Internet website. The caddy has also been awarded a number (#479) and been renamed: sugar packet. But here is a bit of information that projects this piece, along with the jumbo cup, the chili bowl, and their saucer, into an entirely different category. These four items never were designed as generic Homer Laughlin China pieces! They were specifically created

In mid 2000, the sugar caddy "crossed over" and it is now officially Fiesta.

Colonial small teapot in sea mist green. It is much more delicately molded than the Post86 2-cup version.

for the Post86 line. Do not ask me why they have never been officially recognized, but this is surely the reason why these four (touted as Fiesta Mates) have long been known as "cross-over" pieces.

While my subject is the sugar caddy (packet), one event should be related. Many readers will already

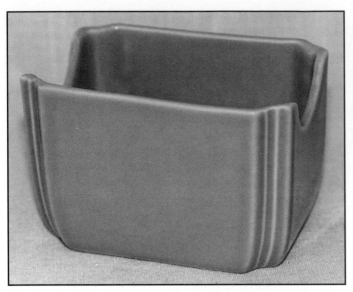

The desirable sugar caddy in discontinued apricot. This design is now a true Fiesta design.

know of what I speak. It is — The October 1999 Sugar Caddy scandal!

Yet again, the Homer Laughlin Company, nervous as a Broadway novice, pulled the old switcheroo and alienated (obviously not forever) many, many devoted Post86 collectors. Who, we may inquire, is helming the Homer Laughlin China ship of state? Those responsible for decisions should seek better advice.

Quite soon after the arrival of the chartreuse glaze, collectors have been requesting the company make the sugar caddy available in chartreuse.

The official announcement was broadcast to the waiting world of Post86 collectors: the sugar caddy would be glazed in chartreuse and available only through the outlet. This was extremely welcome and took place, as I remember, early in September, or perhaps in late August 1999. Those interested collectors were advised to place telephone orders. And many did — I was one of those malleable collectors who believed the announcement! On October 28, 1999, there took place an unbelievably insensitive and inconsiderate partial reversal of the official Homer Laughlin China decision. The usual crowd was waiting for the Retail Outlet to open for a warehouse sale, and here is what happened in the words of a person who was there:

"Re: Chartreuse sugar caddys, only 300 made? It was announced by the outlet manager over her loudspeaker right before they let the first 50 people in. In fact such a hub-bub was made about them that they had a sign put in the window pointing out to the crowd that said "Chartreuse Sugar Caddys, Limit 2 per Customer." Dave Conley was right there when she announced that there were only 300 made, and when they were gone that was that. [There] was [a] WQED filming [going on] for some type of special. WQED [is] responsible for the great programs that you see on public television that are reminiscences of old diners, amusement parks, etc. Must be doing a show on pottery or glass. . . ."

Such an arbitrary number — 300 — but we are beginning to realize how Homer Laughlin China works. Immediately — and I mean immediately — two of these chartreuse sugar caddys appeared separately on the Internet's auction site eBay and sold for well over $100.00 each. Another person commented: "It's a shame that most of us, myself included, have been so jaded by HLC. . ."

All collectors love and desire the sugar caddy: cute, charming, inexpensive, good for a myriad of uses. This is why there was much murmuring and dire disappointment when only a select few were permitted to purchase in chartreuse.

At this time, the napkin rings in chartreuse had been promised in the same manner. For a while, collectors wondered if the company would honor their commitment in the same manner! (Happily the napkin rings were sold in the announced manner.)

Both movie stars and manufacturers of dinnerware collectibles should never manipulate their fans!

Back to the other Fiesta Mates. If the collector craves a set of Irish coffee mugs in yellow or sea mist green, there will be disappointment as they are not available in these colors. Or if a beloved aunt (of the maidenly variety) lusts for one of those cute little handled cream jugs in pearl gray, she will be disappointed. Every glaze does not get sprinkled on every piece in the line!

As mentioned above, the jumbo cup and the chili bowl and the shared saucer really should be considered as Post86 pieces. They are so regarded by some Homer Laughlin China executives, even though they do not have the Fiesta mark. The cup and the bowl, very popular and well designed in a substantial manner, also have the Fiesta rings. These three pieces are now listed on the official advertising sheets, and they could be purchased in the three, to date, limited colors: lilac, sapphire, chartreuse. Strong indication that they are Fiesta.

Mark Gonzalez sent a series of photographs to collectors interested in the Fiesta Mates. These photographs are very enlightening, and a tad perplexing — to me! While Mark includes the commercial AD cup/saucer as belonging to this line, he also has several other pieces. In the listing on the next page, these pieces are marked with an (*).

When pearl gray was introduced in the middle of

1999, rumors began to float in and about the Fiesta message boards — was the line of Fiesta Mates going to be discontinued? The need for "filler" shapes has lessened due to some judicious true Fiesta introductions: the Fiesta bouillon (or custard) could replace the Seville ramekin, the jumbo pasta now has a Fiesta compatriot in the 12" rimmed pasta bowl, the individual Colonial teapot has become greatly overshadowed by the Fiesta 2-cup teapot, and the Mates oval baker has very recently found a replacement in the large (12" x 9") Fiesta oval bowl. And it can be easily assumed that the 14 oz. pedestal mug was designed to take over the role of the graceful 8 oz. Irish coffee mug once so important to the restaurant/coffee house trade. It will be sad if the Irish coffee mug is no longer glazed in Fiesta colors. This mug has always been popular; it is available in a nice selection of glazes: rose, cobalt blue, yellow, turquoise, periwinkle blue, sea mist green, and persimmon. A good sign of customer interest!

There are two Fiesta Mates pieces here by default — the ringed plate and the pedestal bowl. They were made specifically for the Red Lobster chain of restaurants but were not accepted. The plates were glazed in turquoise, sea mist green, persimmon, and a sapphire look-alike. Mr. Gonzalez states the glaze mix for this color is 60% cobalt blue with 40% clear, giving it more a muted shimmer between cobalt and sapphire. The small bowls were available in the same colors and were

This is the infamous chartreuse sugar caddy (#479). Only 300 were made, or so it is reported. Many Post86 collectors were upset at the rather unexpected manner in which this piece was sold at the Retail Outlet.

known as "Jung" bowls.

As Post86 Fiesta offers new items to fulfill special needs, Fiesta Mates necessarily must decline in importance, until they become mere useless shadows and fade away. A sad prospect for these attractive pieces.

Known Fiesta Mates

bowl, chili, 18 oz. (available in all colors)
bowl, jumbo pasta (to date seen only in persimmon)
bowl, oval serving, 10" (not available in limited colors)
(*) bowl, stacking (to date seen only in cobalt blue)
(*) bowl, pedestal (Red Lobster "Jung" bowl)
cup, jumbo, 18 oz. (available in all colors)
jug, handled, 5¼" oz. (available in cobalt blue, yellow, turquoise, sea mist green, persimmon)
mug, Denver, 8 oz. (not available in sapphire or chartreuse)
mug, Irish coffee, 8 oz.
mug, tower, 9 oz. (not available in limited colors)
ramekin, 3⅓ oz. (not available in limited colors)
(*) plate, ringed (Red Lobster)
skillet (not available in limited colors)
saucer (for jumbo mug) (available in all colors)
(*) saucer (dish-like) with sloping sides (to date seen only in sea mist green)
sugar caddy, 3½" x 2½" (seen only in periwinkle blue)
saucer (for jumbo mug) (available in all colors)
teapot, Colonial, 18 oz. (not available in limited colors, but rogue in lilac)

For some reason the Fiesta Mate AD cup/saucer are scarce. They are usually seen in yellow or turquoise.

Fiesta Accessories

Simply Too Much!

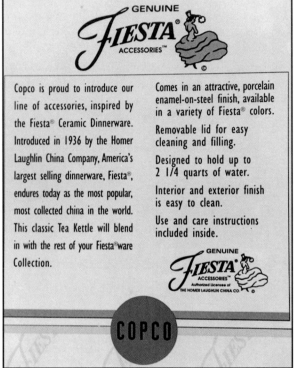

Note how both these items use the Fiesta name. Most accessories have a poor to fair quality and really could not exist without Fiesta.

With great pleasure, I embrace the line of Fiesta Mates. They are true Homer Laughlin shapes, and the standards maintained are high. Wonder if that statement can apply in general to the genuine Fiesta Accessories?

Not really! But before my detractors heap more abuse and fuss and fume at my opinions, it must be recognized that Fiesta Accessories can be divided into two distinct groups. The first group consists of well-designed, well-balanced, useful, and beautiful pieces. They are a joy to behold, and a pleasure to own and use. The second group consists of gimmicks, and do-dads designed like little bits of flotsam and jetsam floating merrily along on the name and colors of Fiesta! There is possibly a third group halfway between the good and the terrible. I simply use the term "not-so-good."

The problem with all these categories — the well-designed, the tawdry gimmicks, and the in-betweens — is the three befog the tentative Fiesta purchaser into believing that they are really needed to fill out a Post86 collection! The collector is befuddled and misled into believing all these extra pieces are necessary. They most certainly are not!

Let me comment carefully as to my personal opinion. It is better to proclaim succinctly a belief or two or three in a very simple way. Thus the reader will know exactly where I, as the author, stand regarding Fiesta Accessories.

There are three types of Fiesta Accessories: the good, the not-so-good, and the tawdry.

•I like the good types.

•I dislike the not-so-good types.

•I find the tawdry types a sad blot on the name of Homer Laughlin.

•But in relation to any of the three types, I deplore the fact that some manufacturers and some dealers try to inveigle collectors into believing that Fiesta Accessories are collectible!

If the cook needs a colander or a 7-quart Dutch oven or a dishwasher safe 4-quart casserole — enamel on steel, with aluminum handles and stainless steel trim, then by all means, look into the purchase of the really attractive Fiesta-colored cookware. These sleek, modern items are available through catalogs and in a variety of fine stores. They are well-constructed and beautiful!

If the householder is meandering through the marketplace for a new orange juicer or a Waring blender, a tea kettle or even a Belgian waffle maker and a deco-designed ice bucket, then look at these well-styled items sparkling in Fiesta colors and prominently sporting the Fiesta name and logo, fun and colorful!

Buy discontinued Dakotah linens, Fiesta striped glassware, and those snappy modern flatware sets — each stainless steel piece chiseled with the Fiesta name, and the knife also boasts the Dancing Lady: put there especially for the same consumers who purchase expensive clothing or designer bedclothes with the name Tommy Hilfiger (or Ralph Lauren) emblazoned upon them! Even our own Martha Stewart lends her name to K-Mart sheets and frilly towels for a price. Does she actually design them? I think not! Neither does Homer Laughlin design the Fiesta Accessories. No disappointment hovers here! Perhaps just a little over-priced.

But, beware, these should be purchased for practical reasons — for personal use and personal enjoyment. These are the correct functions for the Fiesta parasites. Now it is acknowledged that "parasite" is a strong word, and conjures up all sorts of negative images. But, please digest carefully what the accessories do! They make use of, and feed upon the name Fiesta! They worm their way into the public's mind and try to convince that they are really a part of the wonderful Fiesta family. They become parasitic upon the Fiesta name and reputation. They never should be considered true collectibles. The Belgian waffle iron in persimmon, while attractive and perhaps useful, does not belong on your display shelf — in all its available colors — next to your Post86 pizza tray or millennium I vase. No, no! This cookware, glassware, flatware, textiles, cookie cutters, and whatever, augment and extend, enhance, the appreciation of your Post86 Fiesta dinnerware. But they are not, in themselves, collectibles!

The greatest of the supreme satisfactions of bringing together colorful pieces of Post86 Fiesta dinnerware — mixing and matching as moods descend or depart — is its preeminent usability. So mix and match and mingle the dinnerware with all those lovely stylish accessories. Pile a persimmon colander high with pine cones and holly for a holiday centerpiece! Make luscious waffles with a yellow waffle maker as you leisurely contemplate breakfasting on the balcony of your Palm Springs condo! Or even fill a five-quart metal cobalt ice bucket with delicacies such as rabbit pate, beluga caviar, artichoke hearts soaked with balsamic vinegar, in discretely proper containers, or kumquats in Cointreau and present to the lady with whom you lunch. These are excellent, albeit tongue-in-cheek, uses for a few of the genuine Fiesta accessories. They will playfully sweeten your sense of high style! Treat the accessories with a light, merry touch; take them too seriously and their tawdriness will become self-evident.

The wise hostess does not spend even ten minutes choosing which swizzle stick to use. And it is not necessary to corner the market in Fiesta colanders.

Do not emulate an elderly friend of mine, a retired librarian of impeccable respectability, who foamed with the desire to obtain the $40.00 Fiesta oval roaster in all the eight available colors. When she learned it could not be purchased in chartreuse, she fumed and threatened a nasty letter to the Homer Laughlin China factory in Newell, West Virginia. Such events do not a calm collector make.

Above we have discussed those genuine accessories which possess some sense of style, a dash of beauty, a sense of usefulness, and an abundance of light charm! What about the Coney Island travesties that clamber onto the coattails, and ride along free and easy? Does the Post86 collector really need three-dimensional 3" candles depicting a softly modeled coffee server, disc pitcher, and teapot? Or a space-consuming tabletop spice rack, or a mug tree, or a teapot trivet*, or a vertical paper towel holder? Swizzle sticks, gummed wall hooks barely strong enough to hold a chihuahua's lead, a paper-napkin dispenser, or one of those tiny picture frames in the shape of a teapot. Buy a set of these frames (in graduated sizes) for a friend's housewarming, and I doubt if you will be asked to warm that house again!

What about the Fiesta canape set with four top-heavy cheese spreaders in assorted colors? — four spreaders stuck into a poorly modeled Fiesta teapot. Style out of a Lillian Vernon catalog! You can purchase a plastic "disc pitcher" timer if you wish, and if you do, let us wait for the possible, but improbable, introduction of a ceramic musical toilet paper holder, available in all 12 Fiesta colors, that tinkles out "Climb Every Mountain" every time it is used!

But here is a confession! I did purchase, out of pure

curiosity, a persimmon disc pitcher timer. I thought to use it daily to remind me to turn off the lawn sprinklers, or turn down the stew pot, or make a special telephone call: I am not a clock watcher. But when it arrived it was amazingly cheap, poorly made, with no bell. One is, supposedly, to run back and forth to see if the timer is finished. Either this, or my example, at $15.00 plus shipping, was defective. No matter, it is away in a drawer sharing space with the super duper tin egg separator, and the magnetic pin-picker-upper given when I retired from teaching!

Knowing my interest in Fiesta, a neighbor gave me a fantastic set of those little refrigerator magnets. Since I never write messages to myself, these charmers bespot my refrigerator door in great abandon! Even though lacking style, they are funky and fun!

Again the admonition — given with gentleness — approach even the worst of the accessories with a spoofy lightness, and they can work — at times.

According to Dave Conley, who monitors marketing at the Homer Laughlin Company, these accessories are all approved and licensed by the company. Homer Laughlin China does not actually manufacture them, but keeps strict quality control, and limits how and where they can be sold. Manufacturers come to the Homer Laughlin China head office presenting ideas and sale pitches for a wide variety of products and proclaim a possible link with Fiesta. While the income flowing into the Homer Laughlin coffers by licensing the right to use the Fiesta name and logo — on everything from egg timers to aprons — is economically understandable for the company, I simply wonder about necessity!

Because these Fiesta accessories rise and fall with as much frequency as pins at the end of a bowling alley during a Saturday night tournament, a definitive list is impossible to give. Copco has manufactured some respectable pieces, even though their teapot is too small at the bottom for rapid heating and very difficult to hold when filled with boiled water. Other manufacturers produce a Cool Touch toaster in the shape of a Romanesque arch which has proved so disastrously malfunctioning that consumers are returning it in droves, drawer knobs, plastic cookie cutters, napkins with huge paper tags proclaiming "genuine Fiesta," and a cutlery set ensconced in an oak storage block — on and on they come, are bought, and drift away! Prominently displayed on each of these accessories is the Fiesta name and logo in order to prove the item is Fiesta. Over and over, the collector is bombarded and bulldozed with the announcement "be the first to get your hands on this new Fiesta collectible!" "Oh dear, Auntie Maude, I must, must, have that fifteen piece cutlery set in all the colors." Balderdash! Buy what you want for practical use, not as a collectible.

So, please remember the Fiesta accessories are a very mixed lot. Repeat: I am not against this category per se. Some are perfectly designed and worth the price, many are cheap bandwagon baubles. The problem, as I see it, is when these accessories are touted as items absolutely necessary to a new Fiesta collection. They are meant to be used, not collected. But, naturally, that is totally and absolutely the personal decision of each and everyone who loves Post86 Fiesta.

Not the Dancing Lady trivet discussed on page 141.

The disc clock timer and the water kettle.

LIST OF THE MAJOR COMPANIES
LICENSED BY HOMER LAUGHLIN

This list does not claim to be complete. nor does it claim to list all the HLC licensed items available now or in the past. It merely shows the vast array of specialized products now linked with the genuine Fiesta name.

Anchor Sales and Marketing: (800-525-0852)
  Quilted protective covers for kitchenware and dinnerware.

Audry, Inc.
  Kitchen textiles (tablecloths, napkins, placemats)

Bailey Board Company: (509-453-8407)
  Kettle settles
  Tempered glass boards
  Cutting boards

Creative Imaginations: (714-995-2266)
  Miniatures
  Drawer pulls
  Hook racks
  Thumb tacks

Copco: (800-563-6000)
  Cookware
  Kitchenware
  Tea kettle
  Thermal carafe
  Plate display rack
  Hurricane lamp
  Paper towel holder
  Napkin holder
  Coaster set
  Canape set
  Small teapot clock
  Tall salt shaker and pepper grinder
  Short salt shaker and pepper grinder
  Revolving spice rack
  Mug tree

Culver Industries: (724-857-5770)
  Acrylic drinkware
  Glassware

General Houseware Corporation: (800-545-4411)
  Magnets

InterContinental Art: (213-770-8875)
  Framed photographs of Fiesta dinnerware and accessories.

Metrokane: (800-724-4321)
  Hand juicer
  Ice crusher

Metro Marketing: (800-367-0845)
  Cookware
  Colander
  Thermal gravy server
  Bowl set (eight pieces)

Rowoco: (800-576-9626)
  Cookie press
  Wrought iron cooling tray
  Pasta set (four pieces)
  Salad set (two pieces)
  Spoon set (two pieces).
  Swizzle sticks
  Bottle stoppers

Select Brands: (800-557-9463)
  Toaster
  Belgian waffle iron
  Warm-up burner
  Iron

Shadle Enterprises: (800-876-1125)
  Napkin dispenser
  Paper napkins
  Disc pitcher timers

Stanley Roberts: (973-778-5900)
  Stainless flatware
  Cutlery in block sets
  Plastic handled flatware

Weston Gallery: (800-593-7866)
  Ceramic frames

POST86 FLATWARE

The one Fiesta Accessory that is widely purchased by both vintage and Post86 collectors is the flatware. There are two lines. The first one has no official name; it has been called for years simply "Fiesta Flatware." It is, by far, the better of the two. Clean, well molded acrylic handles fit securely and comfortably in the hand. Not awkward, not overly heavy, these pieces are designed as Art Deco modern, but still they add a colorful note to more traditional tables. However, it might be best to say, the 5-piece place setting, the steak knives, and the hostess set fit into the general category of being best designed for home entertaining. This new thrust of use for the Post86 Fiesta has been discussed elsewhere in the book.

The colors are quite faithful to the dinnerware glazes, and the pieces are available in all colors except sapphire. They are no longer thought to be in production, however the Bloomingdale's-By-Mail catalog still carries them, and the 5-piece place settings can be found on a number of Internet auction houses. Primary market prices range from drastic sale prices of $4.50 a set up to $15.00. Auction prices can be much higher. Lilac and rose seem to be in good demand.

Late in 1999, a 15-piece cutlery set appeared, including a variety of knives and a pair of kitchen shears, all housed in an oak storage block. Since the steel runs the entire length of each piece, the knives will hold up to continual use.

Recommended.
****

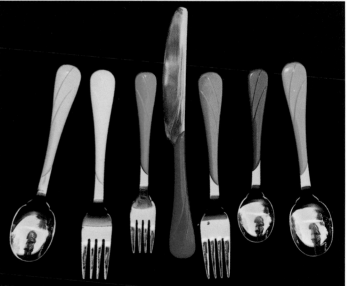

POST86 FLATWARE – CYCLES

Cycles, the second line of flatware intended for use with Fiesta, appeared in the latter months of 1999. Its introduction was a Bloomingdale's exclusive and was first sold through their catalog. Its description read "bright bands of Fiesta color race along these handles of high quality stainless steel."

Well, these words might be true literally and when the potential customer looks at a photograph of the 5-piece place setting, it seems actually true. But, wait until they are held and seen. The handles have no substance; they are merely thin steel, very awkward, and so insubstantial as to make each piece too heavy toward the utensil end.

Unlike the first flatware set (which was produced exclusively for the Homer Laughlin China Company), Cycles was manufactured by Stanley Roberts, Inc. of New Jersey, an authorized licensee of Homer Laughlin China. If it is true that the first line of flatware is no longer in production, then Cycles seems to be the official replacement. Unfortunately, Homer Laughlin China made a mistake. Just wishing to be sleek and modernistic does not mean that a design actually lives up to the wish! High-tech chic? Not at all.

Cycles is available in cobalt (navy), periwinkle blue, rose, turquoise, yellow, persimmon, and pearl gray.

Not recommended.
****

The Cycles flatware in persimmon. Note the awkwardness of the knife, which feels very difficult "in the hand." The box looks identical to the older, more acceptable flatware.

Back of the box. Notice the prominence of the Fiesta name. It seems that the purchaser is getting actual "genuine Fiesta!"

The Mysterious 1986 Brochure

An advertising brochure produced by the Homer Laughlin Company was printed shortly before the reintroduction of Fiesta in February of 1986. Much thought is expended upon this one brochure, and much wondering controversy emanates from its existence.

Depicted in this color brochure are 21 pieces of the new Fiesta line, divided between two picture panels.

Left picture: Large disc pitcher (rose), medium disc pitcher (cobalt or black), sauceboat (black), coffee server (white), casserole/lid (apricot), sugar/cream tray (apricot), pyramid candleholders (a pair in black).

Right picture: teapot (cobalt), medium vase (white), chop plate (cobalt or black), sugar/cream (white), large serving bowl (cobalt), shakers (salt and pepper in white), bud vase (white), round candleholders (a pair in cobalt).

The front of this tri-fold brochure shows a pink 10" plate on top of a stack of fourteen other plates. One side of the fold presents to the readers a five-piece place setting of each of the five available colors: white, black, rose,

apricot, and cobalt blue. Counting candleholders as one piece, we are presented visually with 24 of the 31 originally offered items. Not shown are seven pieces: the bread and butter plate, the 9" lunch plate, the bouillon, the sloping-sided fruit bowl, the straight-sided fruit bowl, and both platters, 11¼" and 9¼".

Potential purchasers have a visual picture of nearly all the pieces available in the early Post86 Fiesta line!

So, what is the mystery? Five of the new Fiesta items are shown in a form unlike what was sold almost immediately on the retail market. We are not discussing design changes that took place later. The coffee server, the casserole/lid, and the sugar bowl are in the shape of Fiesta Ironstone — a line that weakly flourished from 1969 until late 1972. The teapot looks very suspiciously as if it were molded in the shape of the vintage medium teapot, and the sugar lid of the tray ensemble sports a small insignificant button finial of rather unknown pedigree!

There was also a rumor that some or all of the Post86 line were first produced in semi-vitreous ware, then almost immediately changed to vitreous because Homer Laughlin China was now aiming to corner the commercial market. This rumor has been adequately debunked by comments from the Homer Laughlin China art department. All the Post86 line was, from the beginning, made of vitreous clay.

Let us drop for this discussion, the sugar bowl on the tray. Its little finial is interesting, but not vital – it had nothing to do with the Ironstone shape!

Because they were photographed, the following pieces have to be in existence — somewhere, somehow. Even though their existence is denied, they had to have been molded, glazed, and fired in order to be photographed.

1. Apricot Post86 vitreous casserole and lid in the Ironstone shape.
2. White Post86 vitreous coffee server and lid in the Ironstone shape.
3. White Post86 vitreous sugar and lid in the Ironstone shape.
4. Cobalt blue Post86 teapot and lid that appears to be molded after the vintage medium teapot.

Now the mystery is that those in positions of authority at Homer Laughlin China or those Fiestafanatics involved in Post86 research deny having seen any of these pieces. Such statements are heard as: "A friend of my cousin once knew a man who saw a white Post86 coffee pot." Nebulous and indistinct. So where are examples of these four pieces? No examples seem to exist even in the Homer Laughlin China morgue or the Homer Laughlin China museum. Strange!

Interestingly, the prominent leader of an influential HLC collectors association, when asked, denied having seen any Post86 Fiesta pieces based on the Ironstone shape. Yet on the cover of the quarterly newsletter that his group publishes, there appeared an apricot coffee server. The identification reads: Fiesta apricot coffee server — early Post86 design based on Ironstone shape (*The Dish*, Vol. 1, No. 4, 1999).

Those of us who do not have the power and the pull, or the need to dissimulate, are very appreciative to be allowed to see such an interesting Post86 piece. But, sadly dissimulation, mistrust, and suspicion have become routine among a number of (not all, of course) HLC dinnerware collectors. This was not true of the atmosphere just eight or so years ago.

But then a friend of mine who lived in Newell remembers something quite different (see section on the coffee server).

An official of the Homer Laughlin art department once replied to a direct question by intimating these early brochures were never really published, and they were never distributed. They were "test" brochures? Doubly strange that!

Courtesy of Mark Gonzalez

The last chapter (to date) in this saga is the existence of an advertisement appearing in a May 1986 issue of *The Evening Review,* an East Liverpool, Ohio, newspaper. This black and white advertisement is headed: "Homer Laughlin China Presents Genuine Fiesta Available in Assorted Colors." And it promptly and shamelessly used a photograph of the two-sectioned photo. These Post86 pieces so advertised were available at the Retail Outlet. Either they were actually available and being sold, or the outlet sales staff had a mountain of explaining to do!

Customer (with hauteur): "I would like to purchase a white coffee pot like the one shown in the newspaper ad you are presently running."

Saleslady (cringing slightly): "Sorry, Madam, we never had the coffee pot seen in the ad! But we do have this coffee pot in white!" Saleslady presents the redesigned white coffee pot, and the customer stalks out? (See the section on the large teapot for another imaginary Retail Outlet conversation.)

The last chapter has yet to be written — the ending is not yet known! Are there examples of Ironstone-shaped Post86 Fiesta floating about in the collectibles marketplace — enough to make any attempt at collecting them feasible?

Sources for Post86 Fiesta

A bevy of beauties — the Post86 bud vase is extremely popular.

GENERAL SOURCES

When the Homer Laughlin Company introduced the concept of "limited colors," it also began to toy with the additional idea of "exclusivity," that is, certain selected retailers were given exclusive rights to market specific Post86 items, usually in one color. At this time (and perhaps never) it is not known if these individual retailers bid on the right to sell exclusive items, or whether the company initiated the suggestion.

The gracious awarding of exclusive rights to various individual stores started in earnest with the limited color chartreuse. A list was required to keep track of which retailer was selling what item. Very confusing. The situation is very reminiscent, at least in my mind, of a medieval all-powerful sovereign scattering largess among scrabbling courtiers. This image does not work perfectly because I honestly cannot see Homer Laughlin China as the powerful monarch ruling all it surveys, nor can mammoth Bloomingdale's be cast in the role of a scrambling petitioner.

But let us leave this image, correct or impossible, floating about in the ether of my imagination.

This philosophy of awarding exclusive rights has been discussed in other sections of the book, but the crux of the problem lies with one, or perhaps two questions: It is absolutely necessary to know "who is selling what!" And as an adjunct, "who is selling what where?"

This marketing approach is sheer genius. It keeps a variety of commercial groups very content, and it creates a frantic desire to find and acquire the goodies among collectors and customers. Suddenly the "hunt, hunt, hunt" syndrome begins to function. This in turn impels the Fiesta message boards on the Internet to start flashing announced sightings. At the end of December 1999, these sightings consisted mainly of where to find the new glaze juniper, where sales on chartreuse pieces were to be found, and, in the last week of the year, interest abounded as to where to purchase the very new Post86 hostess bowl!

Thus merely to find a certain new item or glaze can be problematic! These Internet message boards are an excellent and invaluable source of information — although one has often to sift through considerable silliness and effusively clever camaraderie. Who can sustain an in-depth discussion of what food can be best served on the large pizza tray? Or why the My First Fiesta Tea Set is sold only in pastel colors? However, among all the froth there does appear concrete information and where to get what is important knowledge indeed!

Now if the reader does not have Internet access, message boards are not accessible and the approach must be completely different. Probably it is best to have two plans of attack. A very wise friend who was also a very astute shopper once gave me a suggestion: get on the mailing list of all major Post86 distributors, i.e., Bloomingdale's, J.C. Penney, Macy's, and Betty Crocker. By receiving retail catalogs, the collector/accumulator can instantly order desired items. However, be prepared to wait for delivery. Most of these large stores and mail-order houses list the item long, long before Homer Laughlin China can ship from the factory.

The Post86 goblet, exclusive to Bloomingdale's, was a classic example of the "wait, wait, wait" syndrome. First one hunts, then one locates, then one orders and finally one waits! And, be warned, there is many a slip between the ordering and the waiting!

While you are waiting to receive your mail-order catalogs, you will find the Homer Laughlin retail outlet is an excellent source. Situated barely minutes from the main Homer Laughlin China office in Newell, West Virginia, the outlet can provide information and be a source of Post86 items. But sadly, it has been reported that different salespeople will offer different answers to your questions so it pays to double-check. Also, at busy times, the outlet turns off its telephone and customers from outside and faraway must try again. During the Christmas season often the telephones are turned off for days!

At the retail outlet there is a long, plain, and simple room called the Seconds Room. There are roughhewed stall like compartments where Post86 and other dinnerware are stacked in piles. All the knowledgeable hunters rush into this space because while called "seconds," many of the pieces offered are in excellent shape. There are two problems — one for the actual outlet visitor and the second for the telephone inquirer. The contents of the Seconds Room changes quite often, and the sales staff will not go into this room to look for any item.

Treasures can be accumulated by scrounging in the outlet's Seconds Room, but at times your treasure can be confiscated! A friend had an experience with a periwinkle shelf sign. This ceramic sign had no printing or decal on it — it was only glazed. When he took it to the cashier, this vigilant lady refused to sell it. It was a "mistake" and Post86 mistakes are carefully guarded.

The telephone is the greatest hunting machine and can be used with dramatic results. Never be afraid of telephoning anywhere! Most sales staff (non retail outlet) are pleased to get a long distance query and are helpful and knowledgeable. Of course, this approach does not always work — but it's worth a try. I treat the entire event as an exercise.

For example, calling Bloomingdale's in Manhattan: "Hello, I am calling from Texas (or Illinois, or Florida) and I used to live in Manhattan, and shop at your store. I still miss it and like to keep in touch. Do you happen to have any Fiesta pyramid candleholders in the new color juniper?"

The above remarks — in my case true, but that does not really matter — tend to change the harried or bored salesperson into a pleased telephone conspirator, and often, if not available yet, you will learn if and when the juniper candleholders will arrive, and if you play your role well, a back order will be taken. The power of persuasive, well-planned helplessness!

Even though Internet auction houses are discussed below, a comment must be made at this point. Some Internet auction dealers have succumbed to both greed and falsehood: they must be exposed! An infamous example of this double negative (overpricing and lying) took place when the large and impressive Post86 pizza tray was first introduced. A certain dealer (with whom I have had words) touted this tray as "new" (true) and "hard to find" (untrue), and placed an opening bid of $49.99. And several bids already were placed. At this time, a simple telephone call to Bloomingdale's-By-Mail would have allowed anyone to purchase this same tray for $19.99!

The adage is to be informed, aware, and cautiously suspicious!

For those who have the desire and the stamina for actual shopping and enjoy the ambiance of the actual store aisle, a marvelous manner of discovering Post86 is just to visit Dillard's, Burdine's, J.C. Penney, or even Linen 'n Things. Here too if the shopper is clever, non-aggressive, or even slightly submissive and somewhat helplessly vague, a relationship can be formed with the powerful saleslady. One woman I know gets telephone calls from the local Burdine's whenever any interesting Post86 arrives.

Finessing works as well in the department store as it does at the bridge table!

POST86 FIESTA ON THE "NET!"

A startling buying and selling phenomenon is now striding through the world's computers: striding like a giant colossus while we, small computer users, peek around and about its ankles trying to understand the rules of bidding and selling.

But this phenomenon is so young it, like any youth, is still feeling its way and proving inconclusive on some points, contradictory in other situations, and combative in a general way. There are a number of these electronic auction houses, but we all know the name of the largest! eBay!

No matter the object of your personal interest, these auctions are excellent as a research tool. The screen can be monitored as a source for Fiesta prices or identification, but, as to prices, it is wise to remember under the excitement and pressure these prices tend to be higher than normal — "Should I?" becomes "I must," and the prices reflect the result of this adrenaline rush!

A vital positive result of the auction is suddenly you, as a buyer, are confronted with Fiesta pieces, both vintage and Post86, that normally would never be seen in person. Even if no bid is dared, to view and copy a photograph gives the Internet auction devotee vast advantages over other collectors. While a photograph is not as exciting as owning a rarity, it is much better than nothing at all! Who among average collectors would ever see the footed French casserole in ivory, the one-piece vintage Fiesta relish in red, or the Post86 carafe in roguish lilac? (See section on the carafe.) Ordinary mortals snuggle safe on the sidelines and view the rich and the famous in "Fiesta Collector-Land" vie with astronomical bids.

Buying and selling Fiesta via an Internet auction does have inherent problems. The majority of these have to do with the fact that you never really know with whom you are dealing — and there is a tendency to treat anonymity as a friend. Written confidences are too easily exchanged. If something is sold at a marvelous profit, will the money really be received? What about those fantastic Post86 rogue pieces? If one appears for sale — say, a pair of pyramid candleholders in sapphire — the Homer Laughlin Company might send the police to the dealer's door because those pieces are considered illegal and stolen property. This has happened!

Also prepare for less than adequate auction house intervention if there is a dispute between the buyer of say, a lilac teapot and its seller. There are so many sensitive, appreciative, honest and understanding dealers, but these are counterbalanced by a few who are vicious, rude, and even obscene.

A personal experience reflecting the powerless ambiguity of electronic auction house administrators: a seller of a piece of Post86 damaged it before the money could be sent. She offered to sell it for one-third less. Since it was a desirable piece for research, there ensued considerable back and forth banter. However, it was learned by one of the eBay administrators that damage

releases the buyer from any obligation, the lower price was declined and the situation forgotten. Weeks later, the woman e-mailed a furious message, followed by another using obscene language. She posted a vitriolic negative feedback.

But even though the advice of the auction house had been followed, they would, could, do nothing. The negative feedback stood! And, also, even though there is a very strict rule against the use of obscenity, nothing would be done. The administrators had no jurisdiction. So beware! Who can know! You, dealer or buyer, might be dealing with an ex-mother-in-law seeking exquisite revenge, a weirdo woman with a questionable agenda, or even a truthful person with honesty in his heart! You make your bid and live with the result!

Thus, all these electronic auction houses are an excellent source of both knowledge and items for actual collecting. But while most negotiations are completed positively, be prepared for an occasional negative experience. Or perhaps be ultra-wise and just look and learn!

TELEPHONE SOURCES FOR POST86 FIESTA

Macy's-By-Mail catalog 1-800-431-9644	J.C. Penney 1-800-345-5273
Bloomingdale's-By- Mail catalog 1-800-777-0000	Dillard's 1-800-345-5373
Warner Bros. NY Store 1-212-754-0300 ext. 212	Homer Laughlin Retail Outlet 1-800-452-4462
Betty Crocker catalog 1-800-233-5780	Table-Top Direct 1-330-225-3684

INTERNET SOURCES

Information:

<http://www.fiestafanatic.com> One of the best places to keep current with all that is happening in the world of Fiesta. Candy Fagerlin has very close connections with the Homer Laughlin Company, and she gladly shares all information.

<http://www.ohiorivervalley.com> This is a general American dinnerware site, but there is some excellent information on Post86. Mark Gonzalez also maintains a message board.

<http://www.hlchina.com> The website site of the Homer Laughlin Company. There is a great deal of information posted, but the site is not very user friendly. Be persistent: it is well worth the effort.

Purchasing:

<http://www.megachina.com>Site to purchase those beautiful MegaChina designs on Post86 Fiesta.

<http://www.fiestaontheweb.com>

<http://www.fiestawarefiesta.com>

A collector can research Post86 on the Internet by clicking on Net Search and typing in "new Fiesta."

Price Guide

What, a price guide? Some readers will comment, after all, you can buy new Fiesta in department and specialty stores from coast to coast. At this junction, the Post86 purchaser is again running into mild opposition from the vintage collectors. But now, even these people must realize that the new line — for some items and in some glazes — has left the store prices behind.

This list is only representational and limits itself to only those colors no longer in full production. The prices are merely suggestions and are for pieces in excellent condition. No prices are given for decorated/decaled Post86 Fiesta or for unofficial rogue items.

Piece	Lilac	Sapphire	Chartreuse	Black	Apricot
Medium Vase	$400(*)	$200	$100	$50	$60
Bud Vase	$125	N/A	$35	$20	$30
5-piece Setting	$150	$100	$50	$35	$35
10" Plate	$60	$35	$20	$15	$20
7" Plate	$30	$15	$12	$10	$10
Chop Plate	$70	N/A	$35	$20	$30
Platter 13"	$50	$35	$35	$15	$20
Teacup/Saucer	$35	$25	$20	$10	$15
AD Cup/Saucer	$80	N/A	$45	$20	$30
Jumbo Cup	$50	$30	$20	$10	$15
Jumbo Saucer	$15	$12	$10	$8	$8
Mug	$45	N/A	$25	$15	$18
Tumbler	$30	$25	$20	$10	$15
Carafe	N/A	$45	$25	$18	$20
Coffee Server	$200	N/A	$850(**)	$30	$40
Teapot	$100	N/A	$50	$30	$40
Butterdish	$45	N/A	$20	CRP	CRP
Rd. Candleholders	$100	N/A	$40	CRP	$25
Pyr. Candleholders(***)	—	—	—	—	—
Sauceboat	$40	N/A	$25	CRP	CRP
Sugar	$25	N/A	$19	CRP	CRP
Creamer	$20	N/A	$12	CRP	CRP
S/C/Tray	$85	N/A	$30	$20	$25
Beverage Set	$125	$75	$40	$25	$30
Disc Pitcher	$60	$40	$25	$18	$20

CRP: Current Retail Price; N/A: not available in the designated color.

(*) Has been advertised as high as $600.
(**) Only 24 were officially produced.
(***) With the May 2000 discontinuation of the pyramid candleholder, prices for these pieces in all colors entered a state of agitation fluxion. Dealers had begun to quietly hoard this candleholder as soon as rumors were whispered. Rising prices are in order.

Juniper prices are — because of its limited edition status — slightly higher than the other available glazes. This tends to be true even of commercial dealers. On the secondary market (eBay, for example) opening prices for juniper can be quite high. However, most potential customers are wary of auctions because most of these pieces were obtained in the Retail Outlet's seconds room and could be flawed — badly or to a lesser degree. Certain pieces — those most popular — such as the napkin rings, sugar caddies, round candleholders, medium and bud vases, AD cups and saucers — are in great demand. Prices reflect this desire. The pyramid candleholder in juniper will be one of the more valuable items; it will be touted as the last of its kind.

Generally, I believe, when juniper is discontinued, prices will float higher than limited edition chartreuse. Two reasons are possible: juniper is a more spectacular glaze and more popular; and collectors hoarded chartreuse and then were informed — by the wizardly gurus — that because of immense hoarding, chartreuse prices would never reach the heights of lilac! Thus collectors, dealers, and hoarders tend to be more cautious about acquiring juniper for future resales.

Decorated Post86 has many problems regarding pricing. There are so many decorated pieces available; the market has been swamped and collectors are drowning in a sea of decaled Post86 Fiesta. The wisest advice seems to be to purchase items or sets that possess personal appeal, and pass by all the others — no matter the amount of advertising hoopla!

The limited edition millennium vases, beverage sets, and the presentation bowl ceased production in December 1999. Millennium Vase I (10 colors of 1,000) very desirable in chartreuse: these two colors will escalate. The remaining colors (remember they were not made in apricot, lilac or sapphire) will rise more slowly. In October 2000, a white Millie I vase was auctioned on eBay: the opening bid was set at $800.00.

Millennium Vases II and III were not limited to number. They were widely collected, and while prices will rise, no estimation can yet be given. In early 2000, the price tendency for these two vases was in an obvious slump. No black, apricot, lilac or sapphire vases were made. The presentation bowl in black was an exclusive item at the outlet and was not available until after the other glazes had been selling for a few months. Black and chartreuse will probably be deemed more collectible. There are no apricot, lilac or sapphire presentation bowls.

Epilogue

As an author, I am very pleased readers have spent some time with me — reading my words, absorbing my ideas, agreeing or disagreeing with my personal pronouncements. As I promised, or warned, in the Introduction, my feelings are strong, my approach direct, my opinions subjective: subjective, indeed yet never offered without careful deliberation.

If this book has pleased, vexed, or stimulated, I would love to know what my readers feel. Please contact me through Collector Books.

If I have offended or displeased anyone, or treaded upon a long-held belief, perhaps this too requires communication. An exchange of conflicting ideas can bring bright growth to me, the author, and you, the reader.

I domatise and am contradicted,
and in this conflict of opinions and sentiments
this I find delight!
Samuel Johnson, 1709 – 1784

Index

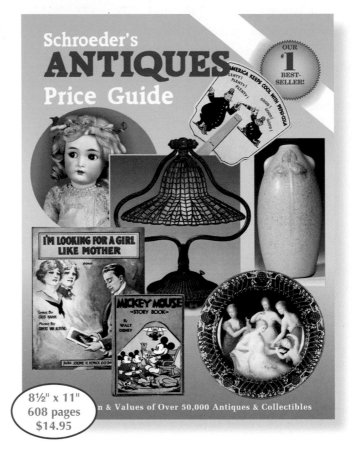